The Impressionists' Corner at Café Guerbois

Karen B. Owens

I have dedicated this book to my namesake and one of the Best Granddaughters – Ever.

Karen Parker Owens

The Impressionists' Corner at Café Guerbois Preface

Writing a book on The Impressionists is something like writing about George Washington, Napoleon I or Abraham Lincoln. Although the number of Impressionist books may not compare to these biographic giants, I suspect that enough has been written about this movement and these avant-garde artists to bring up the question as to why this book is being written. Therefore, if a writer has reasons for adding to the stream of literature about the Impressionists, I offer these:

In doing a rather extensive search of books written on the Impressionist Movement and its founders several of them are behemoth affairs - many approach a bench-pressing number of pages. Can any biographer profess to give a detailed and complete history of the Impressionist Movement and its artists – or on any topic or person? Robert Caro comes to mind; he has written several, quite lengthy biographic volumes on Lyndon Johnson, but they may take more time to read than it took the former president to live them. Some books are merely picture books, displaying the Impressionist art accompanied by a brief biographical sketch of the artist. I like to think that the coverage of this book is "satisfactorily concise." It is for those readers who have an in-depth interest in these wonderful artists and their work but are not planning to research this topic for an academic thesis.

Many of the books I have perused are written by art-scholars who hold stronger art pedigrees than I. They can analyze the painting technique and point with their authorial fingers to the artist's subject, composition, buildup of the paint surface, brushwork, color delicacy, juxtaposition of touches, pentimento … The book certainly consults and shares the expertise of these scholars but rather than giving a detailed presentation and technical analysis of the Impressionists' oeuvre, I shall concentrate on the lives of the artists. But even here I will take a new tack that may lead to less traveled waters.

Some of the books begin in the 1860s or even later taking an "Athenian approach" that the artists, like she, sprang forth fully-grown. The early lives of the Impressionists represent germinating decades that tell us so much about how their personal histories impacted their lives and art. Then, too, many of the books discuss the artists individually – isolating rather than interweaving the lives of the Impressionists - "Monet – A Life." Discussing the lives of the avant-garde personalities as compartmentalized entities misses the nuances of how each of their lives was influenced by each other. In order to create fully three-dimensional figures, the lives of the "founders" of Impressionism - Manet, Degas, Monet, Renoir, and Cezanne – will be followed simultaneously as their lives and works mature and the movement unfolds and grows from steady rising wave into an unstoppable tsunami.

Many books on Impressionism are "history-less" and much is lost when history is not given inclusive coverage. The cultural and historical times in which the Impressionists lived certainly impacted their lives and art. The Impressionists were shaped by their age, and in art, they became the supreme shapers of the age. It was a volatile time in France – a time of revolutions against the status quo and of monarchs who claimed the status of deities. Anti-establishment thinking by the working classes was spreading, which certainly generated fuel for revolutionary thinking in political, social, and literary spheres. It was a time of and for change. The paintings of the Impressionists reflect not only the anti-establishment atmosphere, but their lighter pallets also focus on the carefree life so in contrast to the revolutionary times in which these artists lived – something like the glittery Hollywood musicals that dominated the screen during the Great Depression in America.

Impressionism is often attributed to Manet and to Monet but a movement is never the result of one or perhaps two people but is a composite of so many more who are often forgotten or mentioned with footnote-type coverage in other Impressionist books: Caillebotte, Zola, Durand-Ruel, Morisot and Cassatt and the many supporters of this movement while it was in its initial stages. Moreover, readers of this movement may be fully aware of the artists' trials and tribulations and the cruel criticisms their art suffered "Wallpaper in its embryonic state is more finished," along with personal abuse "Manet is the Apostle of Ugliness." Often overlooked is the other side of that abusive-receiving coin - the friendships and resolutions of this group of men as they met each night at the Café Guerbois. The definitive foundations of Impressionism were formed at this Café. It was their place where they brought forth their ideas, views, and talents toward a new approach to art. The camaraderie formed at the Café Guerbois was a strong shield against their being the brunt of criticisms by the Salon, critics, and the French art-viewing public. It was a long and precipitous climb to success; France herself would take years before she became aware of her greatest artists.

Cover Art:

So delighted to have procured the cover artwork by Randy Blasquez - a wonderful Impressionist artist whose work can be found at blasquezfineart.blogspot.com. It's well worth your checking out her website.

Acknowledgements:

Greg Pearcey and I have been working together for two years; he has the patience of Job and technological expertise extraordinaire, feel free to contact him through his website gregorypearcey.com. To an old friend, Nada Ciriello, who listened (and often added words of wisdom) to countless readings from various passages from the book. And, to a new friend, Marlee Elkins, whose contributions have been so valuable. Her fastidious workmanship enabled her to find errors that were frustratingly missed by the author's "mind's eye" reading of the manuscript.

By the same author

They Changed The World

Franz Joseph and Elisabeth: The Last Great Monarchs of Austria-Hungary

In Pursuit of Dreams: Women of Extraordinary Achievement

The Impressionists' Corner at Cafe Guerbois

The Age of Perfection: Leonardo, Michelangelo, Raphael

Table of Contents: Café Guerbois: Manet & Monet and Their Contemporaries

Chapter One: Meissonier: Le Grande Art

Chapter Two: Café Guerbois

Chapter Three: The Spirit of Revolt

Chapter Four: Scolarité

Chapter Five: Liberté from Family Ties

Chapter Six: The Salon des Refusés

Chapter Seven: A Dozen Men and Two Women – Morisot and Cassatt

Chapter Eight: The Exposition Universelle

Chapter Nine: Bismarck Strikes

Chapter Ten: Is Paris Burning?

Chapter Eleven: Fleeting Impressions of Contemporary Life

Chapter Twelve: Independent Exhibitions

Chapter Thirteen: Public Sales

Chapter Fourteen: Hors Concours

Chapter Fifteen: Impressionism de la tour Eiffel à La statue de la Liberté

Chapter Seventeen: Into History

Chapter Eighteen: Legacies

Chapter One: Meissonier: Le Grande Art

In the mid-1800s a movement known eventually as "Impressionism" was in its embryonic state and as fledgling affairs go - a state of revolt as well. Its young artists – Monet, Renoir, Degas, Sisley, Cézanne - were boldly seeking new inspiration from Salon-sanctioned paintings with their deftly effaced brush strokes capturing the historic past with dark somber tones.   The avant-guarde minds of this handful of artists were overflowing with enthusiastic, albeit rather unorthodox artistic thoughts about subject matter, color, and light. They met nightly at a small café on Avenue de Clichy in Paris - the Café Guerbois. It was their Café or at least a small corner of it. Manet presided at the head of a collection of small marble tables around which they all sat – Manet their unspoken counselor and leader …

On a fashionable street far from the bohemian miasma of the Café Guebois was another most dashing artist whose atelier was within steps of both the Jardin des Tuileries and the Louvre. The artist's name - Jean-Louis-Ernest Meissonier – who was unquestionably the most popular, wealthiest and celebrated artist not in France alone but throughout Europe. His art captured the essence of what art should be according to the Salon's experts who, in turn, influenced the minds of art-loving Parisians. To overstate his fame, his fortune or his influence would be difficult…

NEW ART CANNOT BE IMMEDIATELY UNDERSTOOD BECAUSE IT HAS TO PROCEED THROUGH A PERIOD OF REORGANIZATION OF THE VIEWER'S EXPECTATIONS …

Outside on his balcony, he swung into a saddle cinched to a horse and in imitation of the famous gesture, tucked one hand inside the gray riding coat. Then, examining his reflection in a mirror, he took up his paint brush and as the snow drifted down from the winter sky, began painting his own somber image on the wooden panel placed on the easel before him – a study for a historical work, then well under way, called *1814: The Campaign of France (*1864 Musée d'Orsay): Jean-Louis-Ernest Meissonier. [1]

Meissonier's artistic meticulousness also applied to the historical accuracy and preparatory research so evident in all his works. He would collect an inordinate amount of documentation and question, when possible, eye witnesses. *The Campaign* would depict the Emperor Napoleon astride his white steed leading his Grande Armée across a snowy, desolate plain. Charles Blanc was the Directeur of the École des Beaux-Arts, the most prestigious École and the apex of achievement in art, founded in Paris in 1671 by Jean-Baptiste Colbert, minister of Louis XIV. Blanc recalled the minutest details of Napoleon's "sprouting beard, the veins on the horse's legs, and snow dirtied by the marching troops."

All of Meissonier's works were created with similar methods of conscientious labor and minute study of detail, as was the case with his splendid rendering of Napoleon I. Meissonier, who could not paint anything without first having the correct specimen before his eyes, prepared a three-dimensional model, with infinite pains, to depict *The Campaign*. He created a miniature landscape, strewn with white powder, adding a pinch of salt to give it glitter. He created models

Napoleon (1769-1821) on Campaign in 1814, 1864 (oil on canvas), Meissonier, Jean-Louis Ernest (1815-91) / Musee d'Orsay, Paris, France / Giraudon / The Bridgeman Art Library

from which he would copy his grand masterpiece. There were small wagons on heavy wheels, which he drew through the powdered landscape, so that he might study the furrows and deposit of the scattered snow at his leisure. Before commencing the drawing, Meissonier modeled all the horses in wax. The powdered landscape, however, caused the arrival of insects and rodents, at which point Meissonier staged his drawing on a much larger scale – on the grounds of his house at Poissy.[2]

Each and every figure was drawn from the live models Meissonier hired. A white horse, a double for Napoleon's charger, was brought to his home from the stables of Napoleon III. On the balcony of his home, from a mirror before him, he painted in the gray tints of the winter sky and the flakes of snow on his coat-sleeves. Meissonier had selected himself as the model for he, too, had a short, powerful physique and proudly proclaimed, "I have exactly his thighs!"

The reflection that gazed back at Meissonier, as he painted his *Campaign*, was also painted with remarkably authentic Napoleonic artifacts. The saddle on which Meissonier posed with his Napoleonic thighs was lent to him by one of Napoleon's nephews, Prince Napoleon-Jerome. He tried to borrow the Emperor's gray riding coat from the Musée des Souverains, which housed many of Napoleon's relics, but they refused. They did, however, allow Meissonier's tailor to copy the coat and he did so with *une exactitude Chinoise*, stitch by meticulous stitch, button for button, creating a coat replete with its frayed areas and tattered creases. Meissonier's paintings were executed with an almost unbelievable "punctilious craftsmanship." It is said that he worked on this picture for fifteen years.

The Campaign was unusual because of its rather small format. But, pecuniary Meissonier was well aware that these smaller paintings sold well. The Parisian newly affluent middle-class was always eager to fill their fashionable pied-à-terres with renderings by this most sought-after artist. While this painting may not be indicative of the size of Meissonier's paintings, it was reminiscent of his taste for military, historic paintings. He was also drawn to seventeenth-century Flemish and Dutch works portraying his *bonshommes* (good fellows) as they were "reading books, smoking pipes, and playing chess." Meissonier was famous for his complete resurrection of a lifelong gone - of chivalry … of eighteenth century idyll … of periwigs and cavaliers … relived through Dumas' novels and of men in Meissonier's paintings posing in uniforms of the musketeers. During the Second Republic of France with Napoleon's nephew, Charles-Louis-Napoleon III, as the reigning Monarch, paintings of well-known characters from the Bible, national history or classical mythology performing heroic deeds (thus providing moral inspiration for the viewers) were the ideal.

Another of Meissonier's paintings, *La Rixe* (The Brawl), depicts a fight over a game of cards that takes place in a tavern. The two ruffians are picturesquely attired in eighteen-century opulence. The sense of drama is heightened through the twisting and straining poses of the figures. *La Rixe* evokes a nostalgic vision of the early part of the seventeenth century - the age of the musketeers. Being awarded the Grand Medal of Honor of 1855, *La Rixe* was the star of the Salon exhibition. Napoleon III purchased the work from Meissonier for twenty-five thousand francs – "eight times the annual salary of an average worker - and presented it as a gift to Queen Victoria whose husband and consort, Prince Albert, had prized Meissonier above all other artists." [3]

Meissonier's "tremendous success bought him a stable housing eight horses and a coach house with his fleet of carriages, a greenhouse, an English garden, a photographic workshop, a duck pond, lodgings for his coachman and groom, and a meadow planted with cherry trees all ranged across a patch of land sloping down to the embankments of the Seine, where his two yachts were moored." [4] He had another mansion at Poissy, located in the western suburbs about fifteen miles from Paris, where he lived in the summertime. Each place had cost him something in the millions.

The prime wonder of the Italian Renaissance house was Meissonier's atelier: "You pass from the courtyard to the studio, through a pillared hall, and up a staircase rich in carved paneling, for in the interior the style admits of somewhat greater luxuriance. Then you come to its immense studio. There are two ateliers; the larger one, for some reason best known to the painter, serves as a kind of antechamber to the smaller. The latter is a retreat to which Meissonier, who is one of the shyest of men, escapes from the world. It is difficult to give an idea of the amplitude of the great room without going into measurements; but certainly it would hold the deliberative assembly of a small State. Here again, a rich paneling runs round the walls, and the place looks too fine for daily work. From the smaller studio we may pass out into the open air by a gallery which forms the roof of the arcade, and make the round of the premises to the coach-house and stables, all in perfect keeping of style. Even the back stairs are, in their way, exquisite specimens of early Italian work." [5]

To overstate his reputation would be difficult as well. "At no period, can we point to a French painter to whom such high distinctions were awarded, whose works were so eagerly sought after, whose material interests were so guaranteed by high prices offered for every production of his brush." [6] The critics equally praised Meissonier; from the pen of an art critic who wrote about Meissonier's 1860 "very remarkable exhibition" held on the Boulevard des Italiens, that there did not contain *one* bad or mediocre picture. A chorus of critical praise as "the painter of France" accompanied his success. He was simply, "the most renowned artist of the time."

On Sundays, when museums would open their doors gratis to the viewing public, the art-loving Parisians would often spend their afternoons gazing at the paintings in the Louvre. As they entered the galleries, they were accustomed to standing close to the paintings, studying them minutely and marveling over the delicacy of the handiwork. The work of a master like Meissonier would even stand up to the scrutiny of those viewers with their magnifying glasses. An awestruck art critic, Théophile Gautier remarked, "It is impossible to comprehend that our clumsy hands could achieve such a degree of delicacy." [7]

In the mid-1800s paintings – almost all paintings – fell under the yoke of the classical, historical, and religious tradition. These were *the* subjects considered worthy of art. Similarly, devotion to certain fixed principles of execution was routinely transmitted on canvases saturated with dark colors, accompanied by black shadows. The result was the production of pictures of a laborious kind. *Le Grande Art* portrayed Greeks and Romans in classical antiquity and the female nude – whose proper function, as it was then conceived, was "to assist in the rendering of fable, mythology, and ancient history." The number of Venuses, nymphs, Greek and Roman nude divinities painted in France during the first two-thirds of the nineteenth century, noted art critic Théodore Duret, is beyond calculation. Duret, the first art historian of Impressionism, was raised in a privileged Charente family whose fortune derived from the cognac firm *Duret et De Brie*; monies from the family business allowed him to pursue interests without concern of support.[8]

The viewing public, as well as connoisseurs of art, were used to Romanticism, which is a multilayered movement conjuring up nostalgic views of the legendary past, generally set between the fall of Rome and the Renaissance, known as the Middle Ages. Within this tradition, the artists Jean-Auguste-Dominique Ingres and Ferdinand-Victor-Eugène Delacroix, rendered paintings of sound draftsmanship with a highly detailed, enamel-like finish of smooth surfaces void of any indication of the artist's hand (or personality) as the most important aspects of art. Romanticism of the 1800s gave rise to Realism, the precursor of Impressionism.

While Paris and art were synonymous, the Paris *vie insouciante,* however, did not apply to the world of art. The École, with its strict rules and proper means of construction for all artists to follow, dominated art. The École existed to preserve traditions, not to create new ones. The original purpose of the École des Beaux-Arts was to guarantee a pool of artists available to decorate the palaces and paint the Royalty. The academy offered instruction in drawing, painting, sculpture, architecture, and engraving to students selected by competitive examination. Simply stated, the École set the standards for French art and artists rarely went against these expectations. The École keyed on studying and imitating the Great Masters. In painting, accurate copies came to be regarded as proof of an artist's ability; a copyist's skill was admired enough to be marketable and was held in high esteem.

The highest honor bestowed by the École, was the *Prix de Rome*, a five-year scholarship at the French Academy in Rome. The *Prix de Rome* laureates studied at the Villa Medici and on their return were assured of a career facilitated by commissions from the French government or from private clients who leaned toward prizewinning artists out of sheer conformity. But before they were eligible for this grand honor, students had to go through a rigorous progression of advancement with an emphasis placed on drawing before being allowed to advance to painting of live nude models – models always illuminated by the same light, in the same spot, and always assuming catatonic-like poses.

A description of the official studio was given by Jules and Edmond de Goncourt in *Goncourt Journals*, 1866, "Some thirty or forty art students drew and painted from the nude model every day but Sunday from 8 till 12, and for two hours in the afternoon, except on Saturdays. … One week the model was male, the next female. … The bare walls were adorned with endless caricatures in charcoal and white chalk; and also the scrapings of many palettes … A stove, a model-throne, stools, boxes, some fifty strongly-built low chairs with backs, scores of easels and many drawing-boards, completed the *mobilier*" [9] - a rather regimented and Spartan atmosphere.

Students who were not accepted at the École would seek out independent ateliers where they learned from established "masters" who were affiliated with the École and were most likely graduates of the École. These students trained with these masters while continuing to entertain the hope of one day passing the École's entrance exam. For only the most compelling works (those generated by the students of the École des Beaux-Arts and students of the École's affiliated studios) would be permitted to be shown in the Salon's artistic sanctum sanctorum. Since its inception, exhibition at the Salon de Paris was essential for any artist to achieve success in France and that would be so for at least the next 200 years. As late as 1897 females were not allowed to enter the most prestigious and principal Parisian art academy.

It was known as the "Salon" because for many years from its inception in 1673 it had been housed in the Salon Carre, or Square Room of the Louvre. By 1855 it had moved to more spacious surroundings but certainly less regal at the Palais des Champs- Élysées. The new surrounds were "a cast-iron exhibition hall whose floral arrangements and indoor waterfall could not disguise that fact that when it was not showing paintings from the Salon, it accommodated equestrian competitions and agricultural trade fairs." [10]

Throughout the eighteenth century, and well into the nineteenth, the École des Beaux-Arts dominated art instruction and taste. Predictably, the works of the established artists - notably Meissonier, Delacroix and Ingres, with their preponderance of historical, military, and mythological scenes - were selected. The second focus of the Salon was to display the work of recent graduates of the École des Beaux-Art. Parisians knew what they liked and expected to see what they knew. And what they knew was what the Salon exhibited.

One of the high-level civil servants during the Second French Empire was Alfred-Emilien O'Hara, the Comte de Nieuwerkerke, who, in 1849, had been appointed Directeur-General des Musées. In this capacity he was given charge of a number of museums, including the Louvre and the Luxembourg. It was most important to Nieuwerkerke to "preserve" art and nurture the highest artistic and moral standards. To this end, he, along with his jury of forty or so men, encouraged historical paintings and turned away from a relatively new movement, led by Jean Désiré Gustave Courbet along with works by Honoré Daumier and Jean-Francois Millet, known as Realism. Realism abandoned noble and elevated subjects and chose to paint unembellished depictions of life without any artificiality and often featured gritty portrayals of peasants and prostitutes. *Le Réalisme* was a radical departure from the past. "Its subjects were peasants, provincial townspeople, the activities of ordinary people in ordinary life. Its purpose was not to tell a story, refer to Scripture or to some historic event, or preach a homily, but to portray the immediate, the momentary." [11] The movement is nicely summarized by artist Honoré Daumier's slogan: *"Il faut être de son temps"* – one has to be of one's own time. Realism was a late flowering of Romanticism, and of Impressionism in its concern with the matter-of-fact and the ordinary.

Besides the Realists, there were others who did not fit the Salon's mold and challenged its strict stylistic standards. They did not constitute a school of painting but were merely known as naturalists or the "Batignolles group," a neighborhood of Paris in the seventeenth arrondissement where most of the artists like Manet, Monet, Pissarro, Renoir, and Degas lived. Each believed that the École des Beaux-Arts was not the final authority. They grudgingly knew, however, that in order to attain success as an artist, it was necessary to first succeed at the state-owned and tuition-free École.

The dignified École was steeped in the classical ideals of order and symmetry in art and was hopelessly stiff – edges were hard and lines were straight - as it produced a plethora of classical painters dedicated to perfection of line and form. Delacroix disdainfully remarked, "They are taught the beautiful as one teaches algebra." The colors would be dark and unadventurous creating rather dismal scenes. Paintings were expected to be microscopically accurate, properly 'finished' and formally framed with proper perspective and all the familiar artistic conventions. The scenes portrayed should not only be 'accurate,' but should also set a morally acceptable tone." [12]

Because of its monopolistic power, the Salon's jury members' preferences remained frozen in an antiquity mindset and their instructor's teaching techniques followed suit. "The Salon stifles and corrupts the feeling for the great, the beautiful; artists are driven to exhibit there by the attractions of profit, the desire to get themselves noticed at any price, by the supposed good fortune of an eccentric subject that is capable of producing an effect and leading to an advantageous sale. Thus the salon is literally no more than a picture shop, a bazaar in which the tremendous number of objects is overwhelming and business rules instead of art." [13] But, these rumblings of discontent were now just a steady rising wave - not yet an unstoppable tsunami that they would later become. For now an artist ambitious for a successful career had no choice but to digest the teachings of the École and hope his paintings would be deemed worthy by the Salon jury.

Directeur Niewerkerke's busiest time of the year was in May when the Salon held its exhibit in the Palais de l'Industrie, a huge exhibition center in the Champs-Élysées. For artists it was the only real public venue for their works. In preparation for the event the Parisian streets were bustling with artists eager to get their works to the exhibition center.

The Salon's exhibition was the social event of the year for Parisians, visitors, and artists: "During the first two weeks of May some three thousand visitors queued to see the show. Up until the last minute horses and carts arrived bearing vast canvases and colossal sculptures; the top decks of the omnibuses were crowded with artists and weighted down by pictures. Celebrated artists sent canvases measuring ten or twelve by twenty feet; the larger the canvas, the greater the opportunity for attention from critics and patrons. The vast exhibition filled more than two dozen rooms, and the exhibits took up the equivalent of some eight miles of space. The walls were crammed four deep with paintings, hung by the jury in spaces selected according to perceived importance; to be 'skied' (hung near the ceiling) was regarded as the ultimate slight, since work hung there could barely be seen." [14] So in addition to being accepted by Salon, there was another issue of importance, the problem of obtaining an auspicious place.

When their upturned-faces were not viewing skied art, the leisure- and entertainment-oriented Parisians could be found enjoying the *joie de vivre* so characteristic of the "Belle Époque." If one were to judge by reading *Galignani's Illustrated Guidebook of Paris* (1860): "its streets were dominated by parks, gardens, theaters, opera houses, music halls, and the ubiquitous cafés. Tourists came to enjoy what the Parisians already prized – an elegant way of life. But, as always, there were smudges of black that filtered through; the belle era was not without its downsides. The immigrants were poor and settled in shabby areas of the city. Their lives were difficult, often void of joy and hope." [15] These images were reflected in Hugo's *Les Misérables* and the novels of Balzac, among other works of the day. The themes of these works involved a "pathological fear of the slums, the inner suburbs, a misunderstanding of the causes of impoverishment, and an overall moral decline."

There were also a high percentage of single men and women. Paris and its immediate suburbs had the highest divorce rate in France – perhaps, showing that the traditional family and the domestic hearth, so vital to middle-class mores and to traditions of painting earlier in the century, were no longer as central to Parisian life. Montmartre often reflected this lack of middle-class mores. According to one Montmartre resident, it was home to "rag pickers and other less desirable characters."

Perched atop a hill to the north of Paris's city center, Montmartre was initially a rural village dotted with vineyards and windmills. The area's picturesque appearance and its views of the Paris below had long been popular with artists. Life on the Montmartre hillside, or *Butte*, was essentially rural with sycamore trees shading the cheap taverns. The word Montmartre is translated to mean "mountain of the martyr" and was derived from the martyrdom of Saint Denis - the Bishop of Paris - who was decapitated atop the hill in 250 AD. But its streets did not reflect a saintly picture; much of the town was dotted with ramshackle shanties and hovels encircling the great windmill; alleys were crumbling and were dirty and dilapidated.

At the top of the hill stood the Moulin de la Galette a long-established center of local amusement with its iconic double windmills, owned by the Debray family. The Moulin was a friendly place; in mid 1800s, people used to come there on Sundays for a bit of "galette" a small round cake often accompanied by a glass of wine. In 1833 Père Debray converted the grounds into an open-air dance venue and it became popular with the lively crowd of Montmartre. The Moulin de la

Galette became the first architectural symbol of Montmartre's bohemian culture and a popular subject to paint, as did Renoir, at the *fin-de-siècle*.

Montmartre also offered a sense of peace and calm; a quiet hung between the noisy bustle of the Boulevards of Paris and the silence that reigned on the hilltop of Montmartre. "It is possible to take your luncheon on the Boulevards and visit Montmartre afterwards without imagining that you are the victim of some hallucination. One minute the roar and rattle of the traffic – the clanging of the bells on the steam-cars, and the hooting of the automobiles –and then an old world quiet. The impression grows upon you that it is a village that has strayed, and once locked up within the fortifications could not get out again." [16] In 1870 Montmartre was incorporated into the ninth arrondissment, but it still was able to keep its village-like feel.

All sorts of people were drawn to Montmartre. Writer Félicien Champsaur, in 1882 captured its cosmopolitan demographics: "In this bizarre land swarmed a host of colorful artists, writers, painters, musicians, sculptors, architects, a few with their own places but most in furnished lodgings, surrounded by the workers of Montmartre, the starchy ladies of the rue Bréda, the retired folk of Batignolles, sprouting up all over the place, like weeds. Montmartre was also home to every kind of artist." [17] It was during the mid- to late-1800s that artists also began calling Montmartre home. Pissarro was one of the first to live there, followed by Degas and Renoir. "Manet took up residence on the rue des Batignolles, located just southwest of the center of the Montmartre district. It was in the district that he encountered many of the subjects seen in some of his earlier works: rag pickers, street musicians and those living on the outer edges of polite society. Interestingly enough, some of Manet's neighbors were the antithesis of these marginal citizens and represented well-respected members of the Academy - Alexandre Cabanal, Jean-Léon Gérôme and Thomas Couture all lived in the area." [18]

This new generation of artists and writers gravitated to Montmartre for a number of reasons. Certainly the cheap rents were a factor; the rents dropped precipitously as one mounted the precarious steps to the top of the hill. Montmartre retained a certain rural quality, especially near the top of the Butte and that quality drew those artists whose greatest interests lay in the study of nature and drawing landscapes. It provided an oasis of freedom thanks to the recent invention of paint tubes and portable easels. Painters could now forsake their studios as they set out to paint with broad luminous brushstrokes, the unspoiled natural landscapes of Montmartre. More important was the free-and-easy atmosphere of the area. It was a place of free thinkers, writers and artists. Montmartre must have been irresistible to any young artist who craved an environment of modern thinking. For these young artists, Montmartre seemed to be a symbol of everything that was modern and forward thinking in art. It was everything that the École was not.

Together the artists gathering at the Café Guerbois constituted a movement and in the end success could not be denied them. But for now the viewing public was solely enamored with Monsieur Meissonier who employed in his genre painting all the serious qualities of *Le Grande Art*. He was the master of his style; whatever he essayed to do he did thoroughly. Parisians were accustomed to paintings featuring models in historical dress – the Roman togas and plumed helmets, the Louis XV costumes so authentically rendered by Meissonier. The artistic Parisians loved his attention to detail, the delicacy of his touch, his somber tones of burnt sienna and ochre, his completeness of treatment where even the smallest trifle acquired importance under his brush. All of his fellow countryman regarded him as *the* master ...

Chapter Two: Café Guerbois

Cafe Guerbois by Édouard Manet

Scattered throughout Montmartre and Paris were numerous cafés, which held a place of social prominence in Parisian society. What is more quintessentially Parisian than a small café where guests could sip on an espresso while nibbling on a croissant? "Cafes offered to painters and writers a bohemian atmosphere of pipe smoke, bonhomie, and drinks that tasted, in the worlds of one habitué, like a mixture of cheap mouthwash and soot." [1] Many began their day for a quick gulp of cheap soot before going to work and others ended their day often staying until the wee hours of the morning. "The huge Paris world centres twice, thrice daily; it is at the café; it gossips at the cafe; it intrigues at the café; it plots, it dreams, it suffers, it hopes at the cafe." [2] During the course of the day, a laborer could visit the café before work, at noon for an *aperitif*, after lunch for a *digestif*, and after work during the "hour of absinthe."

Although many of the artists' new studios were equipped with novel gas lighting, nightfall still signaled the end of the painter's working day. How else to spend their evenings, if not in the cafés, which became the artistic salons during the latter half of the 19th century? The bourgeois preferred to receive guests in the privacy of their own manicured homes, rarely going out in the evening. The cafés were left to the intellectuals and artists. At the "green hour" over a glass of absinthe, white wine, or beer, they would gather in these informal surroundings. The café was "one of the great elements of Parisian life."

One café, the Café Guerbois was, during the day, just another Paris street café serving *déjeuners a la fourchette*, lemonade, coffee, tea, and wines. But at five o'clock, Édouard Manet held court and the Café would become *exceptionnel* as the birthplace of a movement later to be known as Impressionism. The first principles of the Impressionist movement were laid down there - inspired by the lengthy brainstorming of ideas that led to artists challenging the perception of art and how it should be viewed - ideas that would revolutionize art - ideas that would turn them away from the inflexible stance of the Salon. Through their camaraderie at the Café Guerbois, the group formed the basis of a movement that challenged all existing notions of art and the art market.

Émile François Zola – a regular at Manet's table – also immortalized the Café Guerbois in his 1886, *L'Œuvre* (*The Masterpiece*) although the café was renamed: "The Café Baudequin was situated on the Boulevard des Batignolles, at the corner of the rue Darcet. Without the least why or wherefore, it had been selected by the band as their meeting place, though Gagnière alone lived in the neighborhood. They met there regularly on Sunday nights; and on Thursday afternoons, at about five o'clock, those who were then at liberty had made it a habit to look in for a moment." [3] The Café was also described in a short story by Louis Edmond Duranty, *La Double vue de Louis Seguin*, where it is called the Café Barbois. The only images of it that survive are a drawing and a print by Manet.

Duranty, who was called "an unknown Stendhal," was a habitué of the Café Guerbois. He attempted to write novels but failed, at least in the public eye. He was now earning his living, such as it was, by journalism; he was the art critic for the *Gazette des Beaux-Arts*. "Every Friday evening in the back room of the Café Guerbois at 11, grand-rue des Batignolles, near where the Avenue de Clichy begins, just on the left as one entered, two tables were reserved for the *Interieur de café* - tables reserved for the Batignolles group. Manet wrote to his friend Émile Zola to join the group of artists and in his letter said, "Do come to the Café Guerbois on Friday evening, but not too late." [4]

One can feel the inviting atmosphere of the Café Guerbois as captured in the writings of one foreign visitor, the engaging Irish writer, George Moore: "I can hear the glass door of the café grate on the sand as I open it. I can recall the smell of every hour. In the morning that of eggs frizzling in butter, the pungent cigarette, coffee and bad cognac; at five o'clock the fragrant odor of absinthe; and soon after the steaming soup ascends from the kitchen; and as the evening advances, the mingled smells of cigarettes, coffee and weak beer. A partition, rising a few feet or more over the hats, separates the glass front from the main body of the Café. The usual marble tables are there, and it is there we sat and aestheticised till two o'clock in the morning." [5]

The first room at the Café was white and gilded, full of mirrors and ablaze with light. But on entering the second room you immediately found yourself in astonishing surroundings, a vast, low-ceilinged crypt. The room was filled with smoke densely swirling over the tiny cramped marble-topped tables. There were lace curtains and along the dark paneled wall there were a line of pegs hung with shiny top hats. The bar was across one end of the room and a friendly plump proprietress in a black dress and white apron took orders and delivered drinks. "The outer room looked like most cafes on the streets of Paris -- white and gilt, with mirrors -- but the inner room was more than a cafe. There were five billiard tables, and their green baize tops created an indoor lawn that merged with the garden beyond the windows at the back. The Café was dark, smoky, masculine, and intimate; the walls were painted brown from the wainscoting down." [6]

Manet lived only a few minutes away on the Boulevard des Batignolles and his studio was in the rue Guyot. In 1866 those in revolt against the official art world were boldly seeking a new inspiration and they became regulars at the Café Guerbois. Soon their meeting place at the Café would be known by the locals as the "artist's corner at Café Guerbois." As his friends used to meet him in this obscure Batignolles café, Café Guerbois, the art critics baptized their meetings with the name of "L'Ecole des Batignolles." At the table were the regulars - Manet, Bazille,

Degas, Monet, Pissarro, Renoir, and Cézanne when he was in Paris. Renoir, Manet and Degas were the most regular visitors from the original Batignolles group.

Although Manet painted few if any Impressionist pictures in the strict sense, he was the leader of the second generation of Realists, following Courbet, and a crucial inspiration to the Impressionists. He was their leader so to speak, perhaps because of his greater fame or because, as an artist, he suffered from constant persecution or maybe because he was rejected, time after time, by the Salon. In any event, they looked to him for guidance and affirmation. For whatever reason, Manet was the presiding genius of the Batignolles circle that met in the Café Guerbois to thrash out artistic matters. Camille Mauclair was a French novelist, biographer, and art critic who noted that "Without Manet all these artists may have remained unknown, or at least without influence; they all were bold characters in art, but timid or disdainful in life. Degas, Monet and Renoir were fine natures with a horror of polemics, who wished to hold aloof from the Salons, and were resigned from the outset to be misunderstood." [7]

Antonin Proust, Manet's faithful friend since childhood, described him as being of medium height (at that time, little more than five foot seven) with a muscular build. He had a lithe charm. No matter how much he exaggerated his gait or affects the drawl of the Parisian urchin, he was never in the least vulgar. One was conscious of his breeding. He walked with a brisk step that had a character all its own – a rolling gait he may have acquired walking barefoot on the deck of a sea-tossed schooner. Manet was a fine dresser and according to Zola, had "an expressive face, light hair, a somewhat pink complexion, a quick intelligent eye, a mobile mouth, at moments a little mocking; the whole face irregular and expressive, with I-don't-know-what expression of sensitiveness and energy." [8] Another described Manet as "elegant and seductive, with golden hair receding since he was seventeen, a fashionable silky beard penetrating, deep-set eyes and an alert, nervous step. He was broad-shouldered with a slim waist, impeccably dressed in the latest tight-fitting trousers, lemon suede gloves, top hat and chic, slip-on shoes; he walked with a cane and a suggestive swagger." [9]

Manet was not only the leader, he was, next to Pissarro, the oldest. Manet was "overflowing with vivacity, always bringing himself forward, but with a gaiety, and enthusiasm, a hope, a desire to throw light on what was new, which made him very attractive." [10] According to French poet Armand Silvestre, one of the regulars of the Café Guerbois, Manet was described as being very generous and kind. When a collector bought his *Bunch of Asparagus* and was so pleased with the painting that he paid an additional 200 francs, Manet painted another still life of a single asparagus spear, and sent it along with a note that read: "There was one missing from your bunch." [11]

Manet "was naturally ironical in his conversation and frequently cruel. He had an inclination for punches, cutting and slashing with a single blow. … He was the strangest sight in the world, his elbows on a table, throwing about his jeers with a voice dominated by the accent of Montmartre, close to that of Belleville – an area even less refined popular quarter. Yes, strange and unforgettable with his irreproachable gloves and his hat pushed back to his neck." [12] He delivered his insults in an affect working-class accent.

"Manet," recalled Monet of his first encounter at Café Guerbois, "invited me to accompany him to a café where he and his friends met and talked every evening after leaving their studios. At Café Guerbois I met Fantin-Latour, Cézanne, Duranty … I myself took along Bazille and Renoir. Nothing could have been more stimulating than these debates with constant clashes of opinion." [13] In a letter to a friend, Monet wrote, "I am surrounded by a small group of young landscape painters who will be very happy to get to know you. Besides, they are real painters … I find myself very well fixed here: I am drawing figures hard; that's a fine thing. Although his work, like Monet's came to diverge widely from Manet's, during the Café Guerbois years both were convinced of Manet's supreme importance as a pathfinder for the new painting." [14]

Monet was the real Michelangelo of the Impressionist era. He was a reassuring figure, a refined, polite, distinguished man, a lover of elegance, a hard worker and a person whose home life embodied "the calm joys of the modern bourgeoisie." His pictures had the same qualities of solidity and elegance. Monet's face was open and expressive; he could never mask his feelings. He was all exuberance and impetuosity. He had a brilliant wit; his sayings, however, could be very bitter. At the same time, however, he was extremely sensitive to the respect or disrespect shown to him and could never treat the insults which were heaped upon him as an artist with indifference. He felt them acutely both psychologically and financially, at the end of his career as well as at its beginning.

Manet differentiated his style before the Impressionist dawn – and Degas and Renoir's interests led them to search even beyond Impressionism. As such, Degas was not a pure Impressionist; the origins and the nature of his art differentiate him from them. To regard him as one of them is also contrary to his own wishes; he always personally repudiated the title of Impressionist. Degas had only his color in common with the Impressionists, and, in part, he owed that to them. For the rest he did not, like them, practice painting in the open air systematically; his technique was of a different order. His starting point was classical tradition. He was before all things a draughtsman.

Manet and Degas were educated and articulate upper bourgeois and cultivated refinement and elegance. Degas was "rather small, very slim, with an elongated head, a high, broad, and domed forehead crowned with silky chestnut hair, with quick, shrewd, questioning eyes, deep-set under high arched eyebrows shaped like a circumflex, a slightly turned-up nose with wide nostrils, a delicate mouth half hidden under a small mustache. Degas had a somewhat mocking expression. When working he wore a crushed felt hat and a housepainter's smock. He must have appeared almost frail compared with the others, especially as there was in his features as well as in his manners and his speech an aristocratic, even old-fashioned refinement that contrasted sharply with the surroundings at the Café Guerbois." [15]

His mannerisms were more studied, his delivery more archly. He developed a reputation as a great wit, and his sayings were remembered and repeated. Though he loved the life of the streets, he was shy and essentially a loner. His studio was sacrosanct and he worked entirely in private. No one was allowed to enter, let alone to watch him as he worked. Degas was also the consummate perfectionist: "No art is less spontaneous than mine. What I do is the result of reflection and study of the Old Masters. I know nothing about inspiration, spontaneity, and temperament." [16]

Degas's love for reading is underlined in his *Notebooks (Notebook 21)* along with his liking for the romantic poets. He also read the venerable poet of democracy Baudelaire's works along with Balzac whose books on the theme of *la comedie humaine* deal with the interplay of emotions and interests often set against a Parisian background. Balzac's works represent a number of characters coming from different social classes and his books meant a great deal to many of Degas' generation. Degas also read the works of Charles Dickens who visited France quite frequently and had many friends in artistic and literary circles, although Degas and Dickens' paths never crossed. [17]

Paul Cézanne, though being generally considered as representative member of this movement, cannot be called a "pure impressionist," but his relation with that art movement is more than evident. His artistic affiliation with its members, his equally intense admiration for Manet, and his close ties with Zola, Bazille, Renoir, and Pissarro granted him auxiliary acceptance. Cézanne was not as frequent of a guest at Café Guerbois for he divided his time between Paris and Aix-en-Provence. While Manet and Degas represented a cultivated, wealthy bourgeois façade, Cézanne, in spite of his upper middle-class status, exhibited rather rough manners and often exaggerated his southern Provencal accent. While coming from a wealthy background, he was distinguished from the rest by his sometimes-ragged exterior - friends and biographers alike have commented on his charmless personality and uncouth appearance.

Cézanne often deliberately and willfully neglected his appearance and seemed to take pleasure in shocking. He most certainly did not even look like a son of a wealthy banker – he wore a "bandito mustache, dressed sloppily, bathed infrequently, and swore incessantly." His studio near the Place de la Bastille was "inches deep in dust, ashes and carelessly strewn piles of meager possessions." In his initial stages of career, Cézanne was obsessed with transferring onto canvas his own morbid and tormented inner world.

"Cézanne was quite tall and thin, bearded, with knotty joints, and a strong head. A very delicate nose hidden in the bristly mustache, eyes narrow and clear … deep in his eyes great tenderness. His voice was loud. … He had a nervous shudder, which was to become habitual. He didn't talk as much as the others, but if something interested him he spoke up with the 'vehemence of deep conviction.' " [18] His shoulders stooped forward in a way suggesting a cheerless energy. Cézanne came to the Café Guerbois erratically, sometimes joining the table, then suddenly taking umbrage and storming out not to reappear for weeks on end.

Pissarro, whose entire family had cut its ties with their original home in St Thomas, returned or relocated to France. Pissarro was by far the best educated and the wealthiest. He dressed with great care, spoke with modesty and kindness, but by nature was ambitions and impetuous. He was often argumentative, witty; at times he could be ironic, and occasionally even cruel. Jean Frédéric Bazille, along with Renoir, was the youngest of the Guerbois regulars. Bazille was a gifted painter whose career was cut short by the Franco-Prussian War; he was barely thirty years old when he was killed in action.

Renoir, having left school at an early age, may have felt a certain lack of education among the regulars at Café Guerbois. Monet was the one who gave Renoir moral and artistic support. "I would have given up, if not for him," Renoir admitted several years later. Renoir was thin, nervous, and quite poor but his personality was imbued with an infectious gaiety. He loved to laugh at jokes and appeared unimpressed with Degas' *bons mots*. Life was enjoyable and painting should, thought Renoir, be part-and-parcel of life's joyfulness. Renoir was not as contentious as some of the others and he often confessed that he did not have "a fighter's spirit."

He often made himself something of an outsider in the studio in spite of his genuine application. "While the others shouted, broke the window panes, martyrized the model, he once told a friend, " I was always quiet in my corner, very attentive, very docile, studying the model, listening to the teacher .. and it was I whom they called revolutionary." [19]

Despite their varied personalities, all seemed to feel a general intellectual excitement that intoxicated these forward thinking minds. Pissarro's chief conversational rival was Edgar Degas. Few in the group could match Manet's intellectual prowess. Of the others, only Jean Frédéric Bazille had the education and taste for verbal sparring to tangle with minds as sharp as Degas' or Manet's. Shy, but firm in his beliefs, Bazille stood up for them with undeniable logic and passion.

Together, these artists made up the main event and the only source of entertainment at the Café Guerbois. George Moore was an eager participant in the discussions that took place at the Café Guerbois. He remembered Manet as being "loud and declamatory," while Degas was "sharp, more profound, and scornfully sarcastic." Duranty was "clearheaded, dry and full of repressed disappointment. Pissarro "sat listening, approving of their ideas, joining in the conversation quietly."

On certain evenings the Café Guerbois was filled with a whole world of artists, writers, critics, and literary men. Edmond Bazire, close friend and first biographer of Manet, (published in 1884) recounted the members of the group: "There were about twelve of them ... A. Legros, Whistler, Fantin-Latour would be joined by the writers Babou, Baudelaire, Gignaux, Duranty, Zola; the engraver Belloc who was to be immortalized in Manet's *Le Bon Bock*; another engraver, Desboutin, who was equally well known at the time as a painter though less so as an artist's model; a painter, Guillemet; an orientalist, Tobar; a universalist." [20] Also present was Zacharie Astruc, a poet and sculptor, one of those whose pens was to serve the new art movement; he wielded the paintbrush, the chisel and the pen with equal passion. Gustave Caillebotte was a friend of the Impressionists from the very first hour. He was rich, fond of art, and himself a painter of great merit who modestly kept hidden behind his comrades.

The café in Parisian society not only served as places of meeting and escape from the struggles of daily life but for the artists who often work in isolation from others, the Café granted them a sense of camaraderie and formed a substitute society. Pettiness, jealousy, envious faultfinding played no part in their conversations. Monet needed the Café Guerbois in order to overcome the feelings of complete isolation, which may have oppressed him occasionally during his retreats to the country. "It was good for him, no doubt, to find there kindred spirits, cordial companions, and the assurance that ridicule or rejection were powerless against the determination to carry on." [21] The evening talks gave the artists a shared confidence in the rightness of what its members were undertaking as an important source of reassurance and confidence, at a time when most outside reactions were still hostile. Café Guerbois replaced the Academy studio as a meeting place for artists.

These were the good old days of social gatherings that brought together artists of the future Impressionist movement – the regulars that made up the Artists' Corner. "In the beginning the café was a place where young people could meet, mix freely, speak openly of politics and literature. Often the proprietor of the establishment participated in these informal meetings, sometimes even presiding, not particularly concerned about making money. He was happy to provide his small clientele with an ordinary room and good drinks at a low price." [22]

The Parisian café was also a place for "intellectual discussion and debate and was by no means a nineteenth century invention. Parisian intellects were gathering together in public establishments as early as the 1680's. The first coffeehouses attracted a more elite crowd whose political discussions caused a great deal of anxiety for King Louis XIV (1638-1715). King Louis XIV was so anxious about the political discussions that he ordered them monitored by his police prefect." [23]

There are several literary references to the discussions that took place between the artists at the Café. A letter from Paul Alexis to Émile Zola written in 1879 recounts one such discussion, "The other day, there was a big discussion about a congress on the arts that had been announced. Manet said he wanted to go there, get up and make a speech and overthrow the École des Beaux-Arts. Pissarro, who was listening, was vaguely worried; Duranty, like a wise nestor, brought him back down to earth." [24]

Most often they discussed issues pertaining to theoretical or technical problems of painting, including exhibitions and dealers, politics, and art-politics. The subject of shadows may well have been a topic frequently discussed at the Café Guerbois. What constituted a shadow was one of the painter's main problems. They discussed colors – nature was now represented in conventional colors blue skies and green grass … Does not color depend upon the environment that surrounds it? As a result of these observations any discussion of shadows at the Café Guerbois actually became a debate for or against painting in *plein air*. Manet and Degas, for example were mainly opposed to working out-of-doors – perhaps because the Old Masters never did so. In all likelihood discussions may have touched on practical matters such as whether art should be made available to the lower classes and whether they should allow the production of pictures to be sold for 13 sous.

At times, they discussed political issues, particularly so when Pissarro and Zola were present. Talks often turned to the immense power the government held over its subjects and the inevitable hardships the struggling working class encountered. The Café atmosphere was an arena where the patrons could witness many of the social issues of the time. And those social issues often centered around new awakenings as the working class developed a more "modern consciousness." For the art world it meant the veritable dictatorship of the academies and juries; a topic often debated by the artists who frequented the Café Guerbois. Thus, the café was a perfect venue for artists to meet, eat, talk, drink, argue, and expound.

The artists did not always agree; in actuality they seldom agreed fully with all that was said. Cézanne observed that they argued and drank so late they couldn't get up to paint the next morning. Even their opinions concerning the Salon were rather divided. To Renoir, submitting paintings to the Salon seemed like the natural thing to do. Manet, in agreement, used to proclaim that the Salon was the real field of battle. It's there one must take one's measure. Manet argued that they should accept the challenge of the jury. Cézanne advocated that the painters should always send their most contentious paintings – the most "offensive" - to the Salon.

Conversations were often heated. Degas and Manet did not see things the same way. Whereas Degas was acerbic and short-tempered, ironic and cynical, Manet, though not without a cutting edge, was generally considered loyal, encouraging, and generous. On one evening in February 1870, things became so heated that Manet, insulted by a review that Duranty wrote about the Impressionists, wounded Duranty in a duel. The injury was not fatal, and the two remained friends. At another time Manet and Degas had a vehement run-in and subsequently returned the paintings each had given the other.

"When Degas thus received back the portrait he had done of Manet listening to his wife playing the piano, from which Manet had cut off the likeness of Mme. Manet, the mutilation did anything but assuage his anger. He immediately added to the painting a piece of white canvas, apparently with the intention of redoing the part cut off, but never did so. Even when they were actually quarreling, Degas and Manet retained few 'grudges.'" [25]

Nevertheless, of all the painters at Café Guerbois, Degas unquestionably was closest to Manet, both in taste and in the *esprit* with which he was so richly endowed. But disagreements and quarrels aside, all put forth new ideas, enriching their minds, drinking their limit, and depleting their purses.

Monet remembered fondly his days at the Café Guerbois: "Nothing could be more interesting than these causeries with their perpetual clash of opinions. They kept our wits sharpened; they encouraged us with stores of enthusiasm that for weeks and weeks kept us up until the final shaping if the idea was accomplished. From them we emerged tempered more highly, with a firmer will, with our thoughts clearer and more distinct." [26] Despite all the personal contrasts and differences, a strong sense of unity drew the group together around a shared desire to evolve a new art form. Yet at this time, they were still finding their style.

Their place was the Café Guerbois at 11 Grande Rue des Batignolles. Disparate and remarkable painters now began to cohere as a group. Their range of circumstances, backgrounds, talents and tastes could hardly have been more different. But they had one thing in common: the determination to paint and to succeed. They shared a common disdain for the Academy and the juried Salon. They had all felt the sting of rejection and the frustration of depending on the system they despised to gain any attention in the art world. For these artists the Café was a safe house. In this refuge, the Batignolles group could discuss how to get their work noticed by the public.

To that end the Café Guerbois played an invaluable role in the eventual success of the Impressionists and the creation of an art system independent of the École des Beaux-Arts and the Salon. But they had to wait until the public was able to accept canvases without a single definite line, and surfaces rendered with small comma-like brush strokes, and colors composed of various pigments of colors. It took many years before the Impressionists' works would be seen with a vision that had not yet developed. Indeed, France herself would take years before she became aware of her greatest artists.

Chapter Three: The Spirit of Revolt

The political and economic situation in France during the years when Manet, Degas, and Cézanne were growing up was far from tranquil. One event that shortly preceded the birth of Manet was an anti-monarchist insurrection on the streets of Paris, known as the Revolution of 1830. That event would most likely have been a buried footnote in history, if it hadn't been for a somewhat unknown writer and his novel, *Les Misérables*. Victor Hugo, who would become one of the greatest sons of France, ensured that this story would hold a pronounced place in history. The Revolution began with a number of students and workers who sacrificed their lives for a cause that was both tragic and heroic. On 29 July a revolutionary surge of several hundred men forced their way into the Royal Printing Workshop in Paris and with any implement at hand they smashed and damaged the printing presses. Destruction of these machines, they thought, would restore their lives. They soon realized, however, that it was not the machines, but the Imperial owners of those machines that were their greatest threat.

A major thread woven within the cultural fabric of the 1830s was the imperialistic belief that monarchs, kings, and emperors were superior to the masses. They gave themselves deity-like statuses seeing themselves as rulers "by divine right." For centuries the masses believed in the inherent sacredness of sovereign power. Their rule was absolute over their subjects who were deemed incapable of ruling themselves. Subsequently the history of the mid-1800s and even into the early 1900s is a history of the upheavals that occurred throughout all of Central Europe as the laboring classes fought against their Imperial occupiers. When liberal ideas emerge, revolution, or at least an attempt at revolution, is inevitable. The middle classes wanted more voice in government and more control over their lives.

The July Revolution of 1830 was against the rule of King Charles X who rose to power after his brother Louis XVIII died. Charles X was a staunch believer in an absolute monarchy and in the divine right of kings. To this end, he established a French Constitution that was opposed by nearly all proletariat citizens of France. An equally unpopular event was Charles' appointing Jules Armand de Polignac to form a new ministry. The two concocted the July Ordinances, which abolished the freedom of the press and reduced the number of French citizens who would be eligible to vote. The king and other royals simply were incapable of realizing that the working class had an agenda all of their own, and they myopically underestimated the power that the working classes would eventually seize.

The volatile flame was lit and pockets of Parisians built barricades throughout the streets of Paris. Fighting between angered citizens and royal troops followed. The citizens were victorious and Charles X abdicated – fleeing to London. A constitutional monarchy, limiting the king's power was established, and the duc d'Orléans, Louis-Philippe, was crowned King of France. Initially, Louis-Philippe, a more progressive member of France's Bourbon family, was sensitive to the workers' plights but he, too, would eventually lose his "Citizen King" title as he increasingly became more monarchical.

The economic situation in France was deplorable. People were burdened by lack of food supplies and soaring prices for food that was available. "In Paris there was once again soaring bread prices, wage cuts and unemployment; some 64,000 Parisians had no stable employment, signifying that they were dependent either on charity or crime." [1]

These were the environs to which the founders of Impressionism were exposed. For Manet, Degas, and Cézanne who were born in the 1830s, it was an incredibly messy time with almost continuous uprisings over the absolutism of the monarchy. But these revolutions did bring an unprecedented voice to the people; they brought the working classes to another level within society – not an elevated one, but one in which their voices would be heard and noticed.

The Impressionist movement was inspired by a variety of factors, but certainly the spreading of anti-establishment thinking by the working classes was an important factor. These winds of change not only marked a new beginning in the social, political, economic world, they also signaled a change in the literary world of art as well. Perhaps the first to passionately breathe in these revolutionary winds against dominance by "the controlling members of society" was Manet. But all the founders were affected by the innovations brought about by 1830 and the 1848 Revolutions. Their impact found their way into the ateliers of Manet and Monet and their contemporaries. All these artists actively experimented with subject matter and technique in order to bring out their new revolutionary way of art. At the forefront of these progressive thoughts was Édouard Manet who began his life in a rather imposing building, still standing, on 5, rue Bonaparte on the Left bank of the Seine.

The small-sized baby did have a rather passionately loud cry that seemed to please his distinguished father and perhaps all the other preceding eight Manet generations of Parisian countryside landowners. For all the Manet "ancestors had made money, bought land, and established solid positions in the learned professions and in upper class society." [2] Along with his many forbearers, Auguste Manet, like his father before him, graduated, in 1821, from the University of Paris and began his career in law. Auguste became quite prosperous under the reign of Louis-Philippe - earning in excess of 12,000 francs a year - a skilled worker made less than fifteen hundred francs a year; a museum curator made up to five thousand; ten thousand was a solid middle-class salary. With due diligence and the right connections, he became a *Chevalier de l'Ordre de la Legion d'honneur*, Judge of the First Instance of the Seine.

As Auguste walked to his court office at the Palais de Justice to hear cases that included "contested wills, paternity suits, legal separations, negligence charges and copyright violations," he seemed to exude centuries-old respectability from his highly shined shoes to his impeccably somber suit crafted by his fine tailor. By all biographical accounts, Auguste was self-righteous, and a sternly honest man of duty with unflagging virtuosity.

Upholding other proper family traditions, at the age of thirty-four, Auguste decided it was time to marry and produce progeny in his likeness and, thus, married Eugénie-Désirée Fournier who belonged to the same venerable social class. The information surrounding her life is quite sparse. We do know that her maternal grandfather, Joseph Fournier, a successful merchant in Sweden, helped Napoleon's Marshal Jean Berndotte become crown prince and then King Charles XIV of

Sweden and that because of these efforts Eugénie became the king's goddaughter. We also know that Eugénie was a cultured and artistic woman who ran an impeccable home ranging from overseeing exquisite dinners to making sure that Édouard and his two brothers gathered some musical culture by taking piano lessons.

The young Manet couple lived with all the bourgeois comforts due to their gentry class. Each of their three sons was expected to emulate the same austere, high-minded and pious paths followed by generations of Manets, with the major responsibility falling to first-born Édouard. Édouard's maternal uncle, Colonel Fournier, used to spend his leisure time in drawing, and it was from him that Manet, while still quite young, acquired that taste for drawing and painting, which circumstances would develop into a life-encompassing passion. "There appears to be little doubt that Édouard's artistic temperament and charm came from Fournier genes. But the Manet side gave him a sense of his own worth, a capacity for 'digging in his heels when it muttered, and a dedication achievement even in adversity.'"[3]

By all accounts, it was an idyllic childhood with the three boys taking full advantage of their parents' wealthy and prosperous lifestyle within and outside the confines of Paris. The Manets owned large areas of land in Gennevilliers, a wealthy suburb of Paris near Argenteuil, where as children, the little Manet brothers spent their summers in the countryside. But soon the frivolous side of Édouard's life would come to an abrupt halt; he was sent to school – the first step in his father's planned journey for his son's career at the bar or bench.

The seven-year-old - and most reluctant Manet - was enrolled at a Catholic school in Vaugirard, then a municipality outside Paris, headed by Priest Abbe Poiloup. Even at this young age, Édouard showed little academic talent so prized by his father. But Manet continued to follow in the steps of his familial ancestors and from the age of twelve to sixteen Manet entered the College Rollin. While he lived within walking distance of the school, Manet became a boarder along with four hundred other boys from equally prominent social classes. During the first year at Rollin he met another new boy, Antonin Proust, who would later become a French journalist and politician. The boys remained close friends all their lives. The College Rollin had impressive academic credentials coupled with an equally oppressively grim school atmosphere.

Relying on his own memories, Proust declared that the austere school was "an ill-lit prison … the classrooms, stinking of smoky lamps in the evening, furnished in the most primitive manner with narrow, rough benches, screwed so close to desks that they crushed your chest. We were packed in their like sardines. There was nothing on the walls, not even a map." [4]

The only lessons that interested Manet at Rollin's, apart from gymnastics and drawing lessons, was history. Drawing class, however, was not an inspiration for the future artist. In all traditional art classes, even at the level of secondary schools, students were obliged to make drawings of ancient statues after plaster models or engravings in specially-prepared manuals. Édouard, despite the way in which he was taught, quickly displayed his gift for drawing – a talent that was barely recognized by his rule-oriented, linear-thinking teachers.

School was not a motivating place for Édouard, and at the end of his first academic year, the headmaster noted on his report card, "This child is feeble, but he shows zeal, and we hope he will do well." [5] But Édouard did not do well and had to repeat fifth grade. He then, for reasons unknown, skipped the next grade. There does seem to be a slight academic improvement, if one notes that his reports improved from "feeble" to "distracted," to "slightly frivolous and not very studious." But, perhaps, we're reaching for stars; his overall academic work was described as "entirely inadequate." He showed no interest in classical studies, worked little, and was often distracted. He had a Gentlemen's "C" ranking in Latin - forty-second out of sixty-six. However, one must also consider that poor reports at Rollin were also assigned to other gifted boys such as the literary giant Baudelaire: "much frivolity, not very conversant with ancient languages, too lax to correct his faults."

Édouard's only consistently respectable grades were in English "fairly good," drawing "very good," and conduct "fairly good." One can imagine how upsetting these grades were to his father for up until Édouard, no Manet had ever been found with such a black-sheep academic record. His teachers related to Auguste that his son's rhetoric on his compositions was weak; he was insufficiently prepared, and his handwriting "will do him a disservice." The future lawyer did not even have a legible hand. With this dismal performance at school, one can imagine his home life and the strained relationship between father and son. It appears quite probable that Auguste's disappointment in his son caused considerable friction.

High points were few and far between in Édouard's academic life. One of the few pleasures was simply hanging around with Proust, whose background was even more impressive than Manet's. Both boys eagerly awaited Thursdays and Sundays when they could spend their free time with Proust's Uncle Edmond. Most often, since both the boys were interested in art, they would visit the museums in Paris. They would often seek out the gallery in the Louvre that held an impressive number of Spanish paintings. Manet seemed to have been drawn to Velázquez, who was an individualistic artist of the contemporary Baroque period. He painted scores of portraits of the Spanish royals with many art scholars calling *Las Meninas or The Family of Felipe IV* (1656) his masterpiece. Manet's exuberant and youthful attraction to Velázquez was apparent "He's the greatest painter there ever was." It is no wonder that later, Velázquez's work would become a model for Manet's early drawings.

Manet spent his adolescence and young adulthood living at home in the shadow of his parents' unhappy marriage. At the age of sixteen, he announced to his father that he wanted to become an artist – a most catastrophic decision driving Auguste to a state of despair. The eldest son from such an illustrious family did not become an artist - the family of old traditions would not allow this. In the heat of the battle between father and son with Manet refusing to study law, a compromised-proposal seemed to appease both parties - Édouard would become an officer in the navy. Manet was thinking about high-seas adventures and his parents preferred that their son was going to sea rather than to an atelier. Judge Manet persuaded Édouard to enter the École Navale. Unfortunately, Manet failed the entrance exams. However, the École Navale permitted potential cadets who failed their initial tests with an option. They would be allowed to retake the exams after they had made an equatorial voyage.

At age seventeen, Manet joined the crew of *Le Havre et Guadeloupe*, a cargo ship bound for Rio de Janeiro. It took over two months to reach Brazil – two months of severe discipline, arduous work, bullying, horrible food, sickness, ennui, and dreadful weather. Possessing no appetite for the high seas, Manet wrote a series of letters to his parents and, of course, most were laments about his arduous journey: "It's no fun taking in a reef perched on a yard that is sometimes underwater, working day and night in all kinds of weather. The second-in-command, he's a real brute, an old seadog who keeps you on your toes and pushes you around like anything." … "The weather is dreadful; it's impossible to form an idea of the sea if you haven't seen it as wild as we did, you can't imagine the mountains of water that surround you and suddenly engulf the whole ship." … "A sailor's life is so boring! Nothing but sea and sky, always the same thing, it's stupid; we can't do a thing, our teachers are sick and the ship is rolling so bad that you have to stay below deck." [6] The time on terra firma was just as miserable; he even considered deserting. "On an excursion to the country with people from the town, I was bitten on the foot by some snake; my foot got terribly swollen; it was agony, but now I'm over it. In the end I haven't really enjoyed my stay in the roadstead; I've been harassed, a bit roughed up; and have been more than once attempted to jump ship."

There were more aesthetically pleasing times when Manet was able to view his surroundings with his artistic eye. On board ship, he lay on deck and would watch the extraordinary skies with "great, changing swathes of vivid color." His discovery of tropical light and his physical experience of the sea were retained with such vividness that, long after, they would determine the way he painted light and water. Always observant: "This evening the sea was more phosphorescent than usual, the ship seemed to slice through blades of fire; it was very beautiful."

After his return from Rio, upon his father's insistence, Manet took the naval entrance exams and, once again, he failed. He persuaded his exasperated father to allow him to pursue an artistic career and his father finally relented. Judge Manet wanted him to enter the École des Beaux-Arts, but this was too conservative a route for Manet. He did not wish to enter this school where "originality and individuality were discouraged, and where students learned anatomy and geometry but not how to paint." He thus began his training as an artist in the studio near Place Pigalle with a young painter named Thomas Couture. Couture was an historical and genre painter and was the notorious creator of sexually daring paintings. Couture was beloved by his friends and despised by the critics and the public. Manet soon outgrew the teachings of Couture and often turned to the Louvre to copy the Old Masters. One afternoon, he met Edgar Degas.

Like Manet, Degas experienced the same revolutionary spirit of the 1830s. Like Manet, Degas was born and raised in comfort and attended the most elite schools that Paris had to offer. "Manet was charming, with a richer, warmer, more responsive personality; the unsociable, caustic Degas was guarded and hostile. Manet was naively optimistic and resilient; Manet sought honors in the Salons; Degas was cynically indifferent to public acclaim. The more self-assured Degas despised and distrusted all medals and honors. He hated anything controlled by the state, the salons, the Academie des Beaux-Arts and the *Legion d'honneur*. Degas' relationship with models was conflictual; he could be both severe and affectionate. One of his models commented, 'Is that my nose, Monsieur Degas? My nose was never like that.' She was put out of the room, and her clothes thrown out after her. And she was left to dress on the landing at the head of the stairs.'[7]

His feelings about women may have been captured in his female nudes, which were utterly without grace or allure. He particularly liked to paint them bathing or toweling dry. Degas tried to "show them deprived of their airs and affectations, reduced to the level of animals cleaning themselves."[8] He was asked why his painted nudes were always so ugly. "Because," Degas explained, "Women *are* ugly." "Women can never forgive me; they hate me; they feel that I am disarming them." "You think they don't like you?" asked a M. Georges Jeanniot a Swiss-French painter, who recorded the conversation. "I am sure of it," Degas answered; "fortunately, for if they did like me, that would be the end of me!"[9] As he got older, he often felt sad about missed opportunities.

Degas was a man of intelligence and ready wit – a rather caustic wit. From his early years, he was known as "the bear," – "the Degas who grumbles and the Edgar who growls." A way, perhaps, to keep people at a distance and ensure his privacy, Degas practiced a kind of tender cruelty. He liked to tease friends and deflate them with cutting remarks, and few risked deeper wounds by daring to reply. Pissarro called him a "terrible man, but frank, up-right, and loyal."[10] Despite his "bear-like" qualities, Degas was a modest character, fond of silence and solitude with a horror of the crowd and of controversies.

Manet and Degas were temperamental opposites, which was even apparent at birth. Hilaire-Germain-Edgar de Gas, born on 19 July 1834, was named after his paternal grandfather. He looked "pensive" as a newborn; his eyes were silent and soulful and unlike Manet's beginning lustful cry, Edgar was quiet; his temperament reflected an easy complacency. While Edgar was named after his paternal grandfather, Edgar's genetic constitution reflected neither his paternal nor his maternal grandfathers'. Both grandfathers led very adventurous lives; each escaped from bloody revolutions, ventured abroad, and earned fortunes in foreign cities.

Rene-Hilaire de Gas came to manhood during the dangerous days of the French Revolution. As a young man, when food was scarce and currency unstable, he built his fortune by speculating in grain and changing money. As a result of the volatile revolutionary situation in Paris, he escaped to Naples. Here he also proved to be a resourceful businessman and opened a bank. He married, Jeanne-Aurora Freppa, and in quick succession produced ten off-spring – Auguste de Gas, Edgar's father, was the eldest of the five surviving children. Hilaire became wealthy enough to buy a rather grand palazzo in Italy and it was he who gave the de Gas family its affluence.

His maternal grandfather, Germain Musson, fled the Caribbean uprisings in Haiti, led by the black Haitian leader Toussaint L'Ouverture and settled among the French-Creole families in New Orleans in 1809. In New Orleans, he made a fortune in cotton. Edgar's mother, Celestine Musson, was born there in 1815. When Germain's wife died, he moved to Paris but maintained his business in Louisiana.

Auguste de Gas married Celestine Musson in the Church of Notre-Dame-de-Lorette when she was just nineteen. She was described as "gorgeous, impulsive, exotic – a real Creole bell." In fourteen years, she had seven children. While the family was middle class, they sought nobler pretensions. For many years the Degas family spelled their name "de Gas;" the preposition "de" divided his last name in two to give it cachet suggesting a landowning aristocratic background, which they did not actually have. As an adult, Edgar Degas reverted back to the original spelling.

Degas' father, Auguste, took over the family bank. He appeared to be a model of "apathy and egotism." Edgar, however, remembered him as "a very gentle very distinguished, very kind man, witty, and above all devoted to music and painting." His mother died in 1847 at the age of thirty-two; Degas was just thirteen. She died "evidently worn out by childbearing, perhaps fatigued by an almost nomadic existence, quite certainly unhappy, and probably still dreaming of [youthful] winter nights of dancing and flirting…" [11] In spite of his parents' unhappy marriage, Edgar was deeply attached to his father and devoted to the memory of his mother.

His mother's death and his permanent sense of loss filled him with bitterness and feelings of guilt. His anger and sense of abandonment would later contribute to his suspicion of and hostility to women. He seldom mentioned her in later years; whereas he often reminisced about the man he referred to as his "dear papa." Unfortunately, through Auguste's neglect and mismanagement, the family business languished and after his death in 1862, collapsed. Auguste's real passions were painting and music. Auguste never remarried and settled into a quiet life with his children.

During his mother's lifetime, in October 1845, Edgar entered the Parisian Lycée Louis-le-Grand, a prestigious and rigorous boys' secondary school where he received a classical education. He received all of his formal education – eight years of study – at this institution. School records inform us that he was a lackluster pupil, uncommunicative, and often "in the clouds." He was often reprimanded for carelessness. The only bright spot of his day occurred when school let out and Edgar and his father would regularly call on noted art collectors of the day. No doubt, these visits had more influence on Degas' education than the lessons parceled out at his school.

It would appear that his Don Quixote "in the clouds" persona might have been necessary to cope with the schools rigorous military discipline, decrepit buildings, and desolate atmosphere. During the winter months, the dormitories, which were poorly heated, caused the students to suffer from "convulsive shivering, stiff joints, chapped skin, and chronic chilblains." The classrooms, equipped with stoves, were overcrowded and overheated and these horrible situations were compounded with an unforgettable "dunghill smell of January mud, unwashed bodies, and stale food." [12] "The prison-like school even had cells for solitary confinement, which had held political prisoners during the Reign of Terror. When banished to a punishment cell the pupil had to do 1,500 – 1,800 Latin lines a day." [13]

Perhaps, the freezing sleeping quarters and stuffy study rooms contributed to promoting men of genius for Voltaire, Molière, Delacroix and the infamous Robespierre emerged from these Spartan conditions. Then, perhaps, their success may have been due to social-class demographics: "The fees were high, which meant that [his] schoolfellows were for the most part the scions of the landed aristocracy and the sons of wealthy industrialists or of landed aristocracy and the sons of wealthy industrialist or of well-paid members of the legal profession. A number of the boarders came from the wealthy families of planters and merchants settled in the French colonies." [14]

So all these men of genius followed a particular schedule of being awakened at 5:30. The students "had to remain silent during meals while a fellow pupil read passages from history books. The curriculum was narrow, with a heavy emphasis on Greek and Latin as well as history and literature, mathematics and modern languages (Edgar studied German). There were forty-five students in each of the rather large classes, and thirty-eight boys slept in each dormitory. With few outings or visits home, the masters, like tutors or parental stand-ins, had great influence." [15]

Degas, the best educated of all the Impressionists, derived two great benefits from Louis-le-Grand: He formed close, life-long friendships with several of his schoolmates and developed a love for literature. Not all students, however, were grateful for their years at Le Grand. An embittered graduate, Maxime du Camp, wrote, "The college is alleged to build character; I did not perceive anything of the sort, but I did see that it made me become bad-tempered, estranged, deceitful."

After completing his schooling at Le Grand, Degas, in 1853 at the age of 18, received permission to "copy" at the Louvre in Paris. (During the 19th century, aspiring artists developed their technique by attempting to replicate the works of the Old Masters.) His father was somewhat uneasy about his son taking up art as his profession – so to assuage his concerns, Edgar also entered law school and inscribed for a course at the Faculte de Droit on the 12 November 1853. Eventually the young Degas informed his father that he could not go on with law and was allowed to continue his vocation as an artist.

While copying the Masters at the Louvre, Degas produced several impressive copies of Raphael as well as studying the work of more contemporary painters such as Delacroix and Ingres. French poet Ambroise-Paul-Toussaint-Jules Valéry recounted Degas 1855 meeting with Ingres. Degas once knew an elderly collector who was a good friend of Ingres and thus, in meeting Ingres, Degas explained, "I do some painting, I am just starting out, and my father, who is a man of taste and an art lover, is of the opinion that I am not a totally hopeless case." [16] "Draw lines …" Ingres told him, "Lots of lines either from memory or from nature." [17] Degas also shared Ingres' belief that an artist should sacrifice social life and devote himself to work. "I'll shut myself up at home," Ingres insisted, "to lead finally a life which, anyhow, I like, retired, calm, entirely disinterested, my last moments given over to the love of art." [18] In 1855 Degas gained admission into the École des Beaux-Art in Paris, placing 33rd on the entrance exams.

While attending the École des Beaux-Arts, he chose Louis Lamonthe, an incisive, dedicated draftsman who'd been a pupil of the greatly admired Jean-Auguste-Dominique Ingres, as his teacher. Lamothe had a passion for drawing and admired Italian masters of the fifteenth and sixteenth centuries, whom Degas had already been copying in the Louvre. A former student described Lamothe as "a poor man fated for misfortune, who was prevented by his timid nature and by his general misery from revealing his capacity as he should have." Like Manet with Couture, Degas studied intermittently for four years with Louis Lamothe.

After just one year of study at the École des Beaux-Arts, Degas left school to spend three years traveling, painting and studying in Italy. When Degas left for Naples he already enjoyed a solid training, despite his young age. The purpose of his visit was to see his Italian relatives but mostly to undertake the traditional tour like almost all French artists.

In Italy, he painstaking painted copies of the works of the great Italian Renaissance painters Michelangelo and da Vinci. It was around this time that Degas began writing his *Notebooks*, which give us numerous insights into his life.

He lived mainly with family in Naples and painted several portraits of relatives. The *dolce far niente* life in Italy gave him so much leisure that he was in danger of never starting. Degas was fond of quoting a passage from Rousseau's *Confessions* in which Rousseau praised the youthful need for indolence, so reflective of Degas, "The idleness I love … is the idleness of a child who is incessantly on the move without ever doing anything … I love to busy myself about trifles to begin a hundred things and not to finish one of them … to begin on a ten-years' task and to give it up after ten minutes." [19]

Given this tendency to idleness, Degas' father felt obliged to keep up his barrage of admonitions. He told Edgar that he would someday have to earn his living and that he would be foolish to ignore the economic realities of life. But he also encouraged his son's talent. Degas' father, very much an esthete and possessing appropriate means, never thwarted the artistic inclinations of his first-born. Even in his childhood, his father took pleasure in commenting on his son's remarkable skill for drawing and painting. The comments by a father, who was a knowledgeable art lover, certainly encouraged Degas. Several encouraging letters were written to his son: "You have taken a tremendous step forward in your art; your drawing is strong; the tone of your color is right." … Even when relatives wondered about his procrastinations, Auguste defended him by saying, "Edgar is working tremendously hard, though he does not appear to be. … I myself think – I am even convinced – that he has not only talent, but genius." [20]

When his son was discouraged, his father wrote, "You have made tremendous strides in art. … My dear Edgar, you have set an excellent course." "Set your mind at rest, and through calm but steady and unabating work, persevere along this path you have chosen. It is yours and nobody else's. Work in pace. I tell you, stay on track, and rest assured that you will succeed in achieving great things. " … "Follow … that path that lies before you, which you yourself have laid open. … You can be sure you will achieve great things. You have a splendid career ahead of you, do not be discouraged and do not torment yourself. You speak of boredom in doing portraits, you much overcome this, for portraiture will be one of the finest jewels in your crown." [21]

His trip to Italy did not impact Degas as he expected. What affected his development most decisively instead was the encounter with the French painter Gustave Moreau whom he most likely met at the French Academy in Rome. The Villa Medici, as the institution is also known, welcomed all French artists and admitted them to the evening life drawing classes. Moreau copied the great artists Correggio, Raphael, Titian and attempted to reproduce their colors as faithfully as possible, rather than the "details" (drawing and composition) of their works. Moreau specialized in painting meticulously ornate and bejeweled scenes from ancient civilization.

The early *Notebooks* confirm the extent to which Degas was solely committed to classical and historical representations. Gustave Moreau was a major influence for the next several years. Moreau's ideal was Delacroix and "his eclectic tastes, his enthusiasm for the Venetians and for the rich pageant of Italian art helped Degas to grow up artistically." [22] Moreau, aware that drawing would be Degas' strong suit, advised Degas to concentrate on color. Gustave Moreau, eight years older, became a kind of mentor to Degas.

When returning from Italy Degas found a spacious studio in the part of town where he was born, and in the fall reunited with Gustave Moreau. Taking a traditional approach, he painted large portraits of family members and grand historical scenes such as *The Daughter of Jephtha*, *Semiramis Building Babylon* and *Scene of War in the Middle Ages*. Degas, upon returning to Paris, was now set out to make a name for himself as a painter and Paris was *the* center of the art world.

Paul Cézanne was born on a cold but sun-filled day on January 19, 1839 in Aix-en-Provence. Cézanne's father owned a business in Aix and seems to have cared only for that business and its money-making revenue. Louis Auguste Cézanne took advantage of the 19th century's addition of a new industry – manufacturing rabbit-fur hats and became a successful haberdasher. His tightfistedness helped him to become quite rich. When in 1848 Aix's Bank Barges collapsed, Louis-Auguste and its head teller Cabassol, joined forces. Auguste put up all the capital, 100,000 francs, and the banker added his expertise and address book to establish a new Banque Cabassol. The bank was a goldmine; Cézanne Sr. amassed an even greater fortune and became even more tightfisted. The two men shared the profits equally; they were each entitled to draw two thousand francs a year for personal expenses. The core of their business was short-term loans and Cézanne had an uncanny skill at assessing someone's credit worthiness. The partnership was dissolved in 1870 on account of their advancing age, but by that time both of them were very rich men.

In 1849 Paul started school at the Jesuit École de Saint-Joseph as a day pupil and like his fellow artists before him, school did not aspire much confidence. In 1852, he entered the College Bourbon in Aix. College Bourbon was a boarding school where the children of the wealthy upper ranks of Aix society went, and thus, banker Auguste deemed it right for his son. Paul was a half-boarder in sixth grade, which meant he slept at home. It also meant a very long day for Paul - his waking hours at school were from 7 a.m. until 7 p.m. One reads from the school prospectus "… for a modest 300 francs per year, dinner and snack are included." This arrangement continued for his first four years.

School music was supplemented by music lessons at home. This was not a success. Henri Ponce, who also taught at the College Bourbon, was his teacher. Cézanne took no interest in his lessons. He loved operas, however, and diligently memorized the songs of Boieldieu's La dame blanch and Herold's Le Pré aux Clercs. Then there was the school band. Cézanne played second clarinet and Zola an off-key one. Academically, Paul did much better, when he was fourteen he won first prize for arithmetic, and gained a first honorable mention for Latin translation and a second honorable mention for history and geography, and for calligraphy. Paul was also good at natural science, Greek, and became a devotee of poetry from Baudelaire to Virgil.

Away from school, Paul, as a youth, did have beautiful moments of exploring the Aix countryside with his friends, Émile François Zola and Baptistin Baille. Mutual interests and lofty ambitions bound this trio, known as *les trio's inseparables*. Paul would later reminisce that this was the best and most beautiful time of his life. With his friends, Paul felt a sense of harmony and happiness, of shared interests in literature, and of ambitious artistic plans for the future.

Chapter Four: Scolarité

In 1848 *Révolution* was imminent once again. Louis-Philippe's government remained a bourgeoisie-dominated affair; subsequently a resurgence by the workers who had manned the barricades in 1830 rebuilt them in 1848. The French Revolution of 1848 began with reasons similar to the July Revolution of 1830. Both of these revolutions were caused by citizens being unhappy about how the country's government was being run and the fact that only a small percentage of the population (about one percent) were allowed to vote. France, under Louis-Philippe, was so utterly dominated by the bourgeoisie that the laborers had little hope of improving their lot outside of violent rebellion. So, again fighting between the French officials and displeased citizens took place in the barricaded streets of Paris.

Several smoldering issues brought about this revolution: The first of which may be attributed to the working class conditions such as low wages for long hours and the sub-standard working conditions in most factories. The next reason for rioting in the streets related to lack of food – people were literally starving because food prices were too high and wages were too low. The food crisis was not just in France for almost all of Central Europe had experienced bad harvests and lack of food supplies. But in France, nothing was being done by the government to help its starving citizens. There were also increased feelings of frustrations against Louis-Philippe and his monarchal government. The unruly mobs of protestors frightened Louis-Philippe into abdicating making way for Napoleon III's Second Republic. Napoleon Bonaparte's nephew Louis Napoleon was elected Emperor of France in 1852, taking the name Napoleon III.

Domestically Napoleon was quite successful. The protestors were seeking change and some important changes did occur: Nine million Frenchmen were now allowed to vote, instead of the previous 200,000. Under Napoleon's rule the economy modernized; the railway system around Paris expanded, and canals and ports improved. In foreign affairs, Napoleon was decidedly less successful. One of his first blunders was to send a French force to Mexico to collect and acquire a fresh dependency in the New World and to topple from power the government of Benito Juarez, a popular lawyer and liberal reformer. Juarez, soon after he came to power, alienated the Catholics in Europe by confiscating church lands and suspending payment of Mexico's debt, which, in the case of France amounted to twenty million pesos. French troops were defeated at Puebla on 5 May ("Cinco de Mayo"). Napoleon sent more troops across the Atlantic bringing a French victory.

Louis-Napoleon also sent Maximilian, brother of Franz Ferdinand, Emperor of Austria-Hungary. Napoleon decided that France needed a Catholic figurehead to act as the king there to legitimize his ambitions. Thus Maximilian was originally brought to Mexico by France as a puppet figurehead. But he was quite independent; he would not be a tool of the French government. He sought a brighter spotlight with him as a liberating emperor of Mexico. French forces took Mexico City and Maximilian proclaimed himself the imperial ruler of Mexico in June of 1863. He succeeded for about two years.

Maximilian's influence, however, rapidly eroded; the Mexican people wanted one of their own to rule. The republic opposition, led by Benito Juarez, only saw Maximilian as a puppet of their enemy country, France. In 1866, France withdrew from Mexico saying that Maximilian could manage on his own and left him behind with no support. Maximilian was unaware of the hatred of the France intervention felt by the Mexican people. Though he was supported by an army of 8,000 Mexican loyalists, Maximilian's fortunes looked bleak.

With the growing reality of a return of the Juárez regime he was only able to hold out for less than one year before his troops were overrun in Querétaro. His wife along with Queen Victoria, King Wilhelm of Prussia and Czar Alexander II of Russia, pleaded with Napoleon III to help Maximilian but their pleas were left unanswered. On 19 June 1867 Ferdinand Maximilian was executed by firing squad. He was 35 years old. Maximilian and Mexico was a serious mistake by Napoleon III.

Always antagonistic toward the Second Republic, Manet painted, *The Execution of Maximilian* - a dramatic rendering of the terrible French humiliation. The Salon for purely political reasons rejected it; the government forbade it to be displayed. Maximilian's fall meant the end of Napoleon's ambitions for Mexico; it was a defeat and to many - a disgrace. There were, however, historic-detail errors in Manet's rendering of Maximilian's execution. Apparently, these were not due to a slipshod effort at historical accuracy; the errors can be attributed to the rather sparse information received by the French people as the government tried to sweep the incident under the carpet and away from truth-seeking Parisians. The French censor confiscated the scandalous painting and had it torn into three parts. It was later salvaged and put back together by Degas, who recognized its power as a work of art. As humiliating as this incident was for France and Napoleon III, closer to home, Parisians had to contend with the serious crop failures in 1848, which led to widespread hardship.

Claude Oscar Monet was just eight years old when the 1848 Revolutions began and he, true to the period, was somewhat of a revolutionary child, particularly when it came to school:

"I was born undisciplined. Never, even as a child, could I be made to obey a set rule. What little I know I learned at home. School was always like a prison to me, I could never bring myself to stay there, even four hours a day, when the sun was shining and the sea was so tempting, and it was such fun scrambling over cliffs and paddling in the shallows. Such, to the great despair of my parents, was the unruly but healthy life I lived until I was fourteen or fifteen. In the meantime I somehow picked up the rudiments of reading, writing and arithmetic, with a smattering of spelling. And there my schooling ended. It never worried me very much because I always had plenty of amusements on the side. I doodled in the margins of my books, I decorated our blue copy paper with ultra-fantastic drawings, and I drew the faces and profiles of my schoolmasters as outrageously as I could, distorting them out of all recognition." [1]

Out of all the founders of Impressionism, we know the least about Monet and what we do know about Monet is what he himself more-or-less orchestrated about himself and told to his interested friends and biographers. Factually, Oscar-Claude Monet was born on 14 November 1840 on the fifth floor of 45 rue Laffitte, in the ninth arrondissement of Paris. He was the second son of Claude-Adolphe and Louise-Justine Aubrée Monet, both of whom were second-generation

Parisians. On 20 May 1841, he was baptized into the local church parish, Notre-Dame-de-Lorette as Claude-Oscar.

Claude Oscar Monet, known only to his parents as Oscar, passed his youth in Le Havre, French for "the harbor." Le Havre was a busy seaport transferring goods from ocean-going ships to barges that would carry their cargo to Paris via the Seine. Oscar's father had been a grocery-store owner in Paris, and perhaps like all father-and-son businesses he wished for his own son to join him in selling cabbages and artichokes to his Parisian customers. But because of the 1848 conditions of rising food prices and lack of customers who had the money to buy them, the family moved to Le Havre when Oscar was five years old. This move would have an apocalyptic significance for Monet for much of his childhood would be spent outdoors on the beaches where he no doubt gained insight into the changing conditions of the sea; the changing weather conditions, and their impact on the hues in the rapidly shifting waters. Monet probably spent more time roaming and daydreaming along these beaches, less than a few minutes from his house, than he did daydreaming in the school classroom.

Monet senior had joined his brother-in-law Jacques Lecadre's ship chandlery business in Le Havre. Jacques and Marie-Jeanne Lecadre, Claude-Adolphe's sister, lived in a large villa with a terrace overlooking the sea, in Saint-Adresse, then a suburb of Le Havre. The Monets having just moved from their fifth floor, somewhat cramped walk-up Paris apartment were no doubt delighted by their new abode - a sizable house just north of Le Havre in the small suburb of Ingouville. While, the house may have been a step up for the Monet family, according to one acquaintance, the couple took in boarders presumably to help make ends meet.

Claude-Adolphe and Louise-Justine was a social and popular couple that knew how to enjoy life. They often gave parties and their guests would often be entertained by Louise-Justine who loved to sing. Mme Monet was a consummate hostess who filled their ornately decorated home with music and cultured guests. Claude remembered that there was always music in the household.

On 1 April 1851, Oscar entered Le Havre "college communal." The school provided a classical curriculum consisting of Greek and Latin lessons, history, and literature. The college also housed a school of commerce and a municipal drawing school. Monet attended two classes each running about two hours, one class in the morning and one in the afternoon. He undertook his first drawing lessons from Jacques-François Ochard, a former student of the revered classicist Jacques-Louis David. David is perhaps best known for painting *Napoleon at the Saint-Bernard Pass* in which he artistically captured a stormy, windswept landscape, a rearing steed, and Napoleon I, heroic and determined, wrapped in a flowing velvet cape as he made his way across the snow-capped Alps. It was in the mountainous peaks that Bonaparte marched his way into greatness – even though he did so wearing a rather poor grey woolen garb and was riding on the back of not a charging gray, but a lowly donkey. Ochard was described as an earnest man who had a keen interest in teaching his young students how to manipulate a pencil or piece of chalk.

There are no school records that tell us about Oscar's performance; we are not even certain when he left or whether he graduated. But Monet made it abundantly clear that school did not pluck any motivational chords. Later in life he claimed he never liked school, that he favored "his drawing pad over his books," and that as soon as he could, he would abandoned the academic world.

Monet's mother died just two months after his sixteenth birthday and his Uncle Jacques passed away the following year on 30 September 1858. Claude went to live with his widowed aunt, Marie-Jeanne Lecadre. Beyond these modest facts, we know little about Monet's activities as a child or what kinds of experiences he had as an adolescent. Considering what we do know, one may assume that Claude's boyhood was essentially that of a vagabond, and he soon acquired a great deal of skill at this game. At fifteen he was known all over Le Havre as a caricaturist and this for him was obviously quite exciting:

"I started selling my portraits. Sizing up my customer, I charged ten or twenty francs a caricature, and it worked like a charm. Within a month my clientele had doubled. Had I gone on like that I'd be a millionaire today. Soon I was looked up to in the town, I was 'somebody'. In the shop-window of the one and only framemaker who could eke out a livelihood in Le Havre, my caricatures were impudently displayed, five or six abreast, in beaded frames or behind glass like very fine works of art, and when I saw troops of bystanders gazing at them in admiration, pointing at them and crying 'Why, that's so-and-so!', I was just bursting with pride." [2]

The majority of these caricatures date from 1856 -1857 when Monet was sixteen and seventeen. Most were done as a way of making money. While they may not be reflective of his artistic genius, they more-or-less show his engagement with the contemporary world as well as his interest in people. Monet's caricatures were displayed in a framing shop with five or six new ones appearing weekly to the delight of those window-peering passer-bys. Alongside his caricatures were paintings by Eugène Boudin, who was a former partner with the shop owner. Boudin was quite a respected painter considered by most to be an expert at rendering life on the sea and its shores. Monet soon met Boudin, who was deeply impressed with the young man's talent.

Monet recalled his first meeting with Boudin, "Without hesitation, he came up to me, and complimented me. In his gentle voice said: 'I always look at your sketches with pleasure; they are amusing, clever, bright. You are gifted; one can see that at a glance. But I hope you are not going to stop there. It is all very well for a beginning, yet soon you will have enough of caricaturing. Study, learn to see and to paint, draw, make landscapes. The sea and the sky, the animals, the people, and the trees are so beautiful just as nature has made them, with their character, their genuineness, in the light, in the air, just as they are.' " [3] Because of Monet's provincial middle-class upbringing it would have been most likely that Claude would eventually join the family business – perhaps Boudin helped to re-route Monet senior's business-partner dream.

Boudin began to paint the sea, his lifelong passion. On the back of each of his paintings he would make careful annotations of the weather, the light, and the time of day. He was also a dedicated landscape painter who was to exert a permanent influence on the budding artist. Boudin helped Monet to develop a keen insight into the bright hues and the play of light on water that will be quite evident in Monet's later paintings as an Impressionist. He also introduced Monet to outdoor painting, an activity, which Monet entered reluctantly but which soon became the touchstone for his life's work. While Boudin received little recognition until 1888 when the French government bought a few of his works for the Luxenbourg Gallery, he was most important to Monet. "If I could become a painter," Monet told French music critic Georges Jean-Aubry, "it is to Eugène Boudin that I owe the fact."

Monet's mother worried about her son working with Boudin whom she believed was bad company and, as such, their relationship may reflect negatively on her son's reputation. Monet further upset the traditional-family cart by boldly announcing to his father that he wanted to become a painter. Surprisingly, his father was not too unsettled by his decision since his son's aunt in Le Havre, Madame Lecadre, did some painting in her leisure time and was willing to let her nephew work in her attic studio. In preparing the attic for his future work place, he discovered a small painting by Daubigny. Because of his effusive admiration for his discovery, his aunt gave it to him. His family gave him moderate encouragement but was partly unwilling or perhaps partly unable to help him financially.

By the time he was seventeen or thereabout, he had dropped out of school for good. Although he was a bit rebellious, a temperament frequently ascribed to young artists, his artistic ambitions were now clear. Monet was just beginning his art and another artist, Renoir, just a year younger was beginning as well. While their temperaments were not similar, they would find that their artistic renderings had much more in common.

The paintings of Monet and Renoir are ephemeral and bubble with a charm and light, which highlight their genius to capture a fleeting moment. Their emotional signification give the viewer a feeling of Sunday lunch in the afternoon on a warm spring day, one of inner contentment. Soaking in these paintings delivers effortless joy that all is right in the world. Indeed they are windows of ideal holidays spent in the imagination of childhood.

The Renoir family had just moved to Paris from Limoges, famous for its delicately decorated, nineteenth-century porcelain and to a lesser extent for its oak barrels used for storing Cognac. Being from a working-class family, Renoir spent his childhood in housing that bordered on the Louvre, where the artisans lived. The Renoir apartment was in the very center of Paris and a very young Pierre-Auguste would observe the protesters seeking change in the Revolution of 1848 – often witnessing the rioting in the streets taking place in front of his family home.

Renoir's life was all about change – rural areas were abandoned in favor of the capital, where people sought every kind of work and the hope of making a decent salary – just as Renoir's parents had just done. When Haussmann's demolition of the Paris streets began, the Renoir family was forced out of the apartment on the rue de Rivoli, and took up residence in a new location, Marais the Jewish quarter, and later to Montmartre. Renoir would grow up in a city being transformed by revolutions, changing governments, and most importantly for him, changes in painting. He would come to know tradition-breaking artists, such as Delacroix and Courbet from his frequent visits to the Louvre and later his Salon's exhibitions.

His life and art would also be impacted by the hardships of the economic conditions of France and of his family. It was therefore imperative that Renoir's works would be Salon worthy - that they would follow the template of subject matter and details so beloved by the traditionalists comprising the selection jury. A painting exemplifying this vein of art would be a still life called

Arum and Conservatory Plants. But there was also a freer, more contemporary side of Renoir and these works were destined for his friends or perhaps connoisseurs of art or just to gratify himself. Swiss painter, Charles Gleyre, when noticing Renoir's work commented, "Young man, you are very skilful, very gifted, but it looks as if you took up painting just to amuse yourself." "Well, yes," Renoir answered, "if I didn't enjoy it, I wouldn't be doing it." [4]

Shades of cultural change, artistically, would certainly be attributed to Eugène Delacroix and his painting *La Liberté guidant le people* – "Liberty Leading the People" used as a poster commemorating the July Revolution of 1830. Delacroix was considered a great artist at the time of this painting. Unlike Delacroix capturing the political scenes of his time, Renoir would become a champion of romantic art, which represented nature, including 'human nature' or actions, as opposed to the tradition of classicism that represented fixed ideas of behavior and standards of beauty." [5]

In 1848 Jean Désiré Gustave Courbet had also caused a stir in the art world with his realistic paintings depicting simple everyday scenes, such as peasants breaking stones for road repairs. In keeping with the Revolutionary theme of 1848, Courbet's aim in painting *The Stonebreakers* was to inform the masses about the harsh existence of peasant workers, so as to encourage people to come to their aid. Thus, while most artists clung to recycling famous and classical themes, Courbet broke from these traditional subjects of antiquity. His break with convention would make it possible for artists such as young Renoir to concentrate on realistic scenes, and perhaps free artists from the "tyranny of tradition." Viewing, studying and copying these paintings, with their sensuality and feminine sensibility, was to be Renoir's elementary school.

His father L'eonard Renoir, a tailor, took his wife, Marguerite Merlet, a seamstress, to live in Paris, thinking that there he would make his fortune. Marguerite was strong and sometimes stern but according to friends, charitably hospitable. She would often make large casseroles every weekend and anyone who turned up was invited to her table. Despite these gratis dinners, life, financially, was a struggle for L'eonard and their five children. It was imperative then for each of the children to earn their own living as soon as they were able.

There was little doubt as to how Pierre-Auguste was to earn his living. The little artist would express his chalk renderings on the walls of their apartment, the floors of the tailor shop, and even drawing on the clothes his mother hung on the line. As a young boy, Renoir had other talents as well. He had a beautiful singing voice and joined the chorus of the Saint-Roch Church. He could have sung professionally, at least according the church's choirmaster, Charles-François Gounod. Gounod was so impressed with his talent that he was set to arrange a musical education, which would eventually include a place in the chorus of the Paris Opera. Renoir decided that filling his class notebooks with drawings was more to his liking; singing was not his forte.

At around the age of thirteen, Renoir entered the workshop of the Levy brothers, who owned a porcelain factory in Paris. At first Renoir just copied decorative patterns of flowers, birds, and musical instruments. Eventually he was assigned to paint these embellishments on the objects themselves such as plates along with drawing profiles of Marie-Antoinette by hand on teacups and vases. He was so good at this task that his fellow workers called him "Little Rubens" after the

Flemish Baroque painter. In addition to his apprenticeship, he attended evening classes in drawing. It appeared that Renoir was quite content with this job and it may have become his permanent occupation except that his future prospects as a painter of porcelain underwent an abrupt change.

Automation reared its ubiquitous head; machines were now capable of painting on these porcelain vases rendering what had been done by hand, obsolete. So young Renoir was deprived of his means of livelihood. He did, however, find another opening painting some elegant or mythological feasts on blinds and fans. By this time he had acquired great dexterity of hand - his own natural gifts were now fully developed. He was able to apply himself to his new trade with superior skill. After three or four years, he had saved enough of his earnings to satisfy new, broader artistic ambitions. A conspicuous element of artistic training among apprentices and art students has always been the copying from reproductions of the Old Masters, and Renoir was no exception to this practice.

At nineteen he registered at the Louvre as a copyist, and he continued for three consecutive years. Renoir wrote: "It is in the museum that you learn to paint... When I say you learn to paint in the Louvre, I do not mean scratching the varnish off the pictures to steal their techniques or to re-paint the Rubens and Raffaels. You have to be a painter of your own time. But in the museum you acquire a taste for art which nature alone cannot give you. It is a painting, not a beautiful scene, that makes you say: I want to be a painter." [6]

Paris did not hold the same charm for Cézanne as it did for Renoir and for the others in the Batignolles group. Cézanne's art was linked in special ways to his hometown Aix-en-Provence in the south of France. Aix is an idyllic town in which one feels progress has bypassed. On almost every corner is a beautiful moss-covered or dauphin-squirting fountain; streets are lined with sycamores and pine trees; flowers burst from window boxes; Baroque basins and old houses with faded shutters abound. The town is watched over by a one thousand meter mountain, Ste. Victoire, an inspiration that was to figure so predominantly in Cézanne's artistic life. Sleepy and provincial, Aix is a town petrified in the sleep of ages, indifferent to everything.

Provence afforded Cézanne with the tranquility and solitude he needed for his work and provided him with ample subjects to last his whole life. He drew "the hills and mountains of Provence, fields shimmering in the heat of the sun, pine forests windswept by the mistral, villages clinging to craggy slops and river, lakes, and the picturesque Mediterranean coast." [7] Cézanne echoed these sentiments in a letter to his friend Victor Chocquet, "This region is full of undiscovered treasures. There has been no one to date who proved worthy of the riches that lie slumbering here." [8]

Aix had a light textiles industry and dyeing works along with several distilleries and outside of town, the Tholonet quarries, the Celony plaster works, and brickworks. The Bibémus quarries, had been supplying the orange stone used for houses in Aix since the time of the Romans. The quarry had a splendid location offering a magnificent view across the red soil of vineyards, the meadows along the banks of the Arch, the dam, and then the Sainte-Baume and Etoile hills and right in front of them the mountain of light, Mont Sainte-Victoire.

Cézanne's father owned a business in Aix and seems to have cared only for that business and its money-making revenue. Louis Auguste Cézanne took advantage of the 19th century's addition of a new industry – manufacturing rabbit-fur hats and became a successful haberdasher. His tightfistedness helped him to become quite rich. When in 1848 Aix's Bank Barges collapsed, Louis-Auguste and its headteller Cabassol, joined forces. Auguste put up all the capital, 100,000 francs, and the banker added his expertise and address book to establish a new *Banque Cabassol*. The bank was a goldmine; Cézanne amassed an even greater fortune and became even more tightfisted. The two men shared the profits equally; they were each entitled to draw two thousand francs a year for personal expenses. The core of their business was short-term loans and Cézanne had an uncanny skill at assessing someone's credit worthiness. The partnership was dissolved in 1870 on account of their advancing age, but by that time both of them were very rich men.

Auguste purchased a marvelous 18th century estate, the *Jas de Bouffan* (sheep barn) for the sum of 85,000 francs; it had once been the residence of the governor of Provence. *Jas de Bouffan* "sat on thirty-seven acres with an avenue of chestnuts in the rear and was situated about one-half mile to the west of Aix in the heart of the Provencal countryside. The family spent weekends and summers there, bathing in the large pool, surrounded by stone dolphins and limes. They occupied only part of the house; the rest lay closed and unused." [9] Residing at the manor was Paul's father, Louis-Auguste Cézanne, and his mother, Anne-Elisabeth Honorine Aubert, Paul and his sister Marie, two years younger than Paul. The two were never close.

Paul's parents were not yet married; that was common enough at the time. There was no stigma attached to the parents, or the children, so long as they were publicly acknowledged by the father. In this instance the birth certificate was the form of recognition of paternity; when the document had Louis-Auguste Cézanne's signature on Paul's birth certificate, he was legally recognized. Auguste and Elisabeth did not become legally entwined until five years after Paul's birth – thus legitimizing his as well as his sister Marie's existence. A month later Paul was baptized in the Church of Sainte-Marie-Madeleine.

Paul's mother, from an early age forward, was interested in Paul's paintings. She even subscribed to special fine-art magazines and these were Paul's initial introductions to art. Elisabeth appeared to revel in her little son's drawings, and they became a source of satisfaction for both Paul and his mother filling her mind and most likely Paul's with magnificent thoughts of artistic success. His mother's favorite picture was her son's drawing *Kiss of the Muse* (1857), which hung in her room and traveled with her whenever she moved between town and country. His sister Marie had no interest in art, and had little fondness for her brother's work. By all accounts, Paul loved his mother dearly and was less afraid of her than of his father.

Marie believed that her father was not a tyrant but was simply unable to understand anybody except "people who worked in order to get rich." He couldn't understand his son who did not believe in his father's pecuniary doctrine. Paul remained close to his mother and often unburdened himself to her; she was privy to almost as many of his secrets as was his best friend Émile Zola. Cézanne found reinforcement in his reading Thomas Couture's handbook of advice for arts, *Methode et entretiens d'atelier* (1867) emphasizing the role of the mother "Yes, in women, above all your mother, you will find your best counselor." [10]

Zola was a grade behind Paul at the College Bourbon. His father had come to Aix to build a dam for a reservoir but had died during the construction work and now the boy was living in a poor part of town with his mother and grandmother who were forever in need of money. Zola became the butt of his fellow-pupils' teasing and jokes. Zola was an easy target because he was so different from the other boys. He had no father; "spoke with a lisp, was terribly thin, and most of all he was from the wrong side of town." He was a "scholarship boy" living on charity - a *boursier*! Thus, he received the taunts of his classmates – "Beggar." "Parasite." Émile later wrote, "My years in school were years of tears," says the protagonist in his *La Confession de Claude* (1865) - Zola's autobiographical first novel. [11] Cézanne took young Zola's part against the Aix boys. The next day Zola brought Paul some apples - *" Cézanne pommes revenir un long chemin"* - Cézanne's apples go back a long way.

Unfortunately, life at the College Bourbon was not an unalloyed pleasure for Cézanne or his fellow mates either. "There was no heating and in the winter, the interminable recitations began in clouds of steam. The ground-floor *etudes*, or study rooms, were depressing places: airless, humid, and dimly lit, with the damp running down the walls. The pond where the boys learned to swim was covered in slime. The school uniform was a trial - stiff and uncomfortable, it consisted of a blue woolen tunic with red border and gold palms on the collar with matching, scratchy blue trousers. School meals were so bad that there were occasional riots." [12] Zola remembered, "a strange codfish stew that poisoned the mold… For the six years I was there, I was hungry." [13] The schoolmasters had nicknames; the deputy headmaster, Snitcher, had a nose like a cannon, conveniently identifiable at long range.

Happier moments were found outside the confines of their ivy walls Zola and Cézanne both loved to swim, naked and free. It was part of the bond between them - bathing, reciting poetry, and howling at the moon. These experiences were packed away inside him, fabulous but unrepeatable; the images were engraved on Paul's memory. *Les baigneurs de Cézanne remonte un long chemin.* "Cézanne's bathers go back a long way." Paul and Émile were joined by Baptistin Baille who later became a distinguished scientist, professor of optics and acoustics at the School of Physics and Chemistry of the City of Paris. These were the beginnings of the most beautiful time of Paul's life.

Holidays were delightful … Paul recalled, "In winter, we loved the cold, the ground frozen with ice which cracked merrily and we would go and eat [sic] omelettes in the neighboring villages, reveling in the clear sharp air. In summer, all our meetings were on the river bank, for we had a passion for water; and we would spend all afternoon paddling about, living there, coming out only to lie naked on the fine sand, warmed by the sun. Then in autumn, our passion switched, and we became hunters; harmless hunters, for the chase was used as an excuse for long strolls … And our loves, in those days, were all the poets. We had books in our pockets and our game bags. For a year, Victor Hugo reigned among us as an absolute monarch. He had captured us with his high style and powerful rhetoric. We knew several works by heart. At dusk, we walked in time to the beat of his verses, echoing like a trumpet blast." [14]

Poets were real presences in Cézanne's world. They were a source of moral support. Baudelaire's *L'Art Romantique* (1868) was one of his favorites. Among many wonderful things, it contained the celebrated essay *"Le Peintre de la vie moderne"* - The Painter of Modern Life - in which Baudelaire tells the modern painter to utilize the following concepts in creating his or her art: "The painter of modern life extracts, from his observation of modern fashion and events, whatever elements they contain of poetry within history. In other words, the artist distills the eternal from the transitory ..." [15]

These were joyous moments, but even at the age of fourteen, Cézanne exhibited gloomy, perseverating thoughts and bouts of morbid depression. Paul was a tempestuous, short-tempered boy, whose thin-skinned irascibility earned him the nickname *"L'ecorche"* (The Man without skin). He was excruciatingly shy when confronted with women and general reticence towards others, made him seem distant. Writing to Zola, "As you know, I don't know what causes it, it comes back every evening when the sun sets, and then it rains. That brings on the gloom." [16] Recognizing the depressive moments that characterized Cézanne's life, Zola wrote, "Paul may have the genius of a great painter, but he will never possess the genius actually to become one. He despairs at even the smallest obstacle." [17]

Fortunately, Zola's prophetic statement did not come true, but becoming a renowned artist was a long time coming. While most artists in Cézanne's time were cash poor, this was not an obstacle for Cézanne. One obstacle was his psychological health for Cézanne suffered from depression, inquietude, anxiety, and restlessness in almost pathological proportions. But as an index of greatness, despite these psychological demons, he was able to achieve artistic greatness. The main obstacle that posed even bigger problems for Cézanne's artist-pursuing life and no doubt a main contributor to his unhealthy psychological states, was his implacably resistant father. Cézanne Sr. was a strict authoritarian who would not tolerate dissension among his troops. A stubborn, domineering personality, Auguste had only one problem in life – his son - who not only wanted to paint, but to make matters worse, he wanted to paint differently from the real painters, the serious artists who exhibited at the official Salon. Cézanne Sr. was the undisputed head of his household; strict and authoritarian, he would brook no contradiction. Most of his life Paul felt paralyzed in front of his father. He would retreat into isolated seclusion and make clumsy drawings and anxiety-ridden paintings.

Louis-Auguste continually coerced Paul to follow a more traditional career line, as a lawyer or banker. Paul rarely stood up to his father and most often tried to comply with his wishes. As such, Cézanne studied law at Aix University for two years. His father, however, did allow Paul to also attend Giberts' drawing classes at the Musée Granet, the Fine Art Museum in Aix in the evenings. He did well in his law studies but his passion to become an artist flourished as he spent every spare minute drawing.

"I've always found Paris incomparably romantic".

Chapter Five: Liberté from Family Ties

As Meissonier continued to work on his *The Campaign of France*, a short distance from the Café Guerbois in the Batignolles district, another artist was preparing a painting of a rather different sort. Édouard Manet did not live in a pretentious mansion; he lived in a three-room apartment in the rue de l'Hotel-de-Ville. One did not enter his atelier through a pillared hall, and up a staircase rich in carved paneling. Théodore Duret described Manet's studio as consisting of a "large, dilapidated-looking room. There was scarcely anything to be seen in it but pictures, framed and unframed, ranged in piles round the walls. As Manet had as yet sold only one or two canvases, all the work that he had done was accumulated here." [1] He was not the consummate socialite that Meissonier was; in fact, only his intimate friends used to visit him. The conditions under which he lived were very favorable to his work, and his production during this period was on a large scale.

Manet was granted permission to copy the Old Masters in the Louvre; its collections greatly enhanced by art plundered in Napoleon's I victories. Manet also, in 1850, began a six-year apprenticeship with Thomas Couture that gave rise to a tangle of contradictions and conflicts. Couture was already famous and held a distinguished place among the masters of historical painting, then regarded as forming the essence of *le grand art*.

Manet chose Thomas Couture for his master, with his father's acquiescence. "No painter ever strove harder to acquire a mastery of craft than Manet. But Manet was possessed of a strong sense of individuality, and was dominated by the impulse to follow an independent course. Couture and Manet were of entirely different characters and subsequently the relationship that existed between master and pupil was riddled with constant collisions and quarrels followed by reconciliations that finally ended in a definite hostility." [2]

Antonin Proust, Manet's fellow student at Rollin, reported that "Couture was all too casual about his teaching duties and left his pupils pretty much on their own. Couture's atelier consisted of 25 to 30 students. As in all studios, each student paid a monthly subscription to study from the model, man or women." Manet recalled, "Couture came to visit us twice a week; he glanced at our studies with a distracted eye, ordered a 'break,' rolled himself a cigarette, told some stories about his master Gros, then took himself off." Manet complained to Proust, "I can't think why I am here; everything we see here is absurd; the light's false, the shadows are false. When I arrive at the studio I feel as though I'm entering a tomb." He did adopt one of Couture's dictums that when painting "one should relate to his own times." [3]

The fact that Manet endured Couture's jibes and arrogance for so long shows not only how diligent he was as an art student was but it also shows the importance he gave to Couture as his mentor. He may have endured Couture's retributions because Manet may have seen Couture as playing the role of a surrogate father: "There was a generation gap in their ages and Couture's view of art was similar to that of his father's. His attempt to measure up to Couture's standards may be a reflection of trying to meet his father's standards of excellence. In his father's mind and subsequently Manet's, he would not be considered a successful artist until he won a prize or his paintings would be selected by the Salon or he had won a prestigious medal. In a family like Manet's, the expectations were obvious, as were the standards of measure." [4]

Thus, Couture became Manet's only source of legitimate approval. "His fellow students might applaud, hang a garland on his easel, offer him a drink to celebrate his return to the studio, but only the master could satisfy his need for approbation. And Couture, doubtlessly irritated by Manet's insubordination, perhaps even resentful of his originality, refused to grant him that. Emulation, the determination to outdo, or defiance, the determination to do differently, enters into every relationship of this kind. For Manet the problem was compounded by the presence of two father figures. Couture he would outdo, on his own turf; his father he would defy and in more than one way." [5] All his life even thought he was a revolutionary artist, Manet craved official honors and never abandoned his desire to be accepted by the Salon. Manet wanted the Italian Renaissance stairway to his studio; he wanted to obtain social acceptance; his coveted goal was to receive the Legion of Honor from the French government; in short, he wanted the success of a Meissonier.

In contrast, Degas despised glory. He was "a man who loved his art like a mistress and guarded it with jealous passion. Degas, the incomparable pastelist, the faultless draughtsman, the bitter, satirical, pessimistic genius, was an isolated phenomenon in this period, a grand creator, unattached to his time." [6] Later in life, Degas was to lead a sedentary life, leaving Paris only for routine summertime sojourns in Normandy or to visit the spas of southwestern France. He made occasional trips to Naples to try to iron out the never-ending financial problems he had with his father's side of the family.

He lived alone, without pupils and almost without friends. Degas wrote in one of his *Notebooks* "It seems to be that today, if one wants to engage seriously in art and make an original little niche for oneself, or at least to preserve the most unblemished of personalities it is necessary to steep oneself again in solitude." [7] He always said he had no desire to marry "What would I want a wife for? "I would have been in mortal misery all my life for fear my wife might say after a grueling day, 'That's a pretty little thing' after I had finished a picture." The glamorous, bejeweled women with bare shoulders and plunging necklines, hauled by their husbands from salon to opera box then on to some glittering dinner party, dismayed him.

Marriage was a viable option for Manet and in 1851when he met and fell in love with the Dutch girl who came to Manet's house to teach piano as part of his mother's cultural enrichment program for her sons. Suzanne Leenhoff was the new piano teacher and has been described as "beautiful and serene, a blue-eyed blond with fair complexion, delicate fingers and a Rubenesque figure." Others were less generous and described her as "matronly blonde, placid, plump, but an accomplished pianist." Suzanne was a compliant young woman of decent background but being newly arrived from Holland, she did not know many others and perhaps was lonely. It's probably safe to assume that she did not have many opportunities to meet eligible, marriageable men.

Manet's secret visits to Suzanne's lodgings in the rue de la Fontaine-au Roi resulted in her being pregnant by April 1951. Manet was uncertain about what to do; he was certain, however, that his father would never find out. Édouard was totally financially dependent on his father at that time and would be so for years to come; he did not want to lose his financial support. While illegitimacy was not a great stigma for most residents of Montmartre, it was not acceptable for the son of a judge - particularly Judge Manet. "Koella Leon Édouard, son of Koella and Suzanne Leenhoff" was born and registered as such on 29 January 1852. "Leon," henceforth, was presented to society as Suzanne's brother, the last-born son of his Grandmother Leenhoff. Four years later Manet was still uncertain about what to do; Leon was baptized and Édouard became his godfather and Suzanne his godmother. Judge Manet never found out his son's secret; Manet was never close to his son.

Leon's paternity has become the crucial mystery of Manet's life. "It would seem that marrying Suzanne (October, 1863) that Manet tacitly acknowledged that Leon was his own son. However, strong evidence suggests that Auguste Manet was Leon's father not Édouard. He knew that his father had syphilis and incorrectly reasoned that he, too, would inherit the disease. The estrangement, fear and barely suppressed rage in his portrait of his parents may have been provoked by the secret surrounding Leon and by Manet's bitter resentment of having to step into the shoes of his hypocritical father who heard paternity suits and was enormously self-righteous." [8]

"Illegitimate children were common among the Impressionist painters; Pissarro, Cézanne, Monet and Renoir all had children out of wedlock and were initially reluctant for various reasons to marry their fertile but uneducated lovers. But they all legitimized their children after marriage." Manet did not. Manet scholar Nancy Locke noted that there was a good reason why Édouard did not legitimize Leon: "In French law of the time, whereas nothing stood in the way of legitimating of children born out of wedlock upon the marriage of their parents, children born to individuals who were already married to others at the time of conception would never be able to legitimized under any circumstances." [9] Manet could have legitimized Leon if Leon were his own son. But couldn't and didn't since Leon's father, Auguste, was a married man. Whether or not he was the father, by the late 1850s, Édouard Manet was living with both Suzanne and her child.

It was also around this time that Manet began to travel abroad. He visited Holland, where he fell in love with Franz Hals, who was the first great artist of the 17th-century Dutch school and was regarded as one of the most brilliant of all portraitists. He then visited Prague, Vienna, and Munich. Then the attractions to the Venetians led him to Italy, visiting Venice, Florence, and Rome. After leaving Couture's studio, he returned to Florence in 1856. The purpose of these trips was to copy the Old Masters and to this period belong some copies of the original Rembrandt at Munich.

Degas spent his free time studying from the Old Masters as well. While he began to study law at the age of nineteen, his free time was spent copying paintings at the Louvre. Like Manet, Degas also began traveling and in 1856 went to Italy. With close family ties and sufficient wealth to travel and study, he spent nearly three years in Naples, Rome, and Florence. He lived with family and painted several portraits of his relatives. His decision to travel was to study the Old Masters. Upon his return, he announced to his father that he wanted to become a painter; his father made no comment.

With his liberation from family ties, in 1854, he abandoned his legal studies and enrolled in the studio of Louis Lamothe, who was a pupil of Ingres, the great neoclassical draftsman. Degas was greatly encouraged (as Manet had been by Delacroix) by visiting the studio of Ingres. Ingres told him "never work from nature. Always from memory, or from engravings of the masters ..." Early works followed more closely the example of Ingres. Degas "showed from the beginning the refined touch of a delicate and highly cultivated artist, raised in a home where questions of art were intelligently discussed." [10]

It was also time for Manet to be his own master and when he returned from his travels, in 1856, he left Couture. He then established himself in a studio in the rue Lavoisier. Manet had had enough of the academic tradition that followed the archaic methods. His canvases would be void of historical painting and the painting of nudes from professional models, which now filled him with detestation. In short, he was abandoning the academic tradition, the conventional methods, "the pseudo-classical ideal, which he had come to hate while in Couture's studio." In 1857, he would begin to paint life as he found it. His models would no longer be trained or professional; he would choose them from the diversified types that his surroundings had to offer. He continued to work to observe and to learn.

Breaking away from tradition described both Manet and Monet's lives in 1857 – both involving independence and seeking their artistic niches. Monet's decision occurred as the result of his mother's death. His Aunt Lecadre took over the care of seventeen-year-old Claude encouraging him to continue his drawing and painting. Claude who had not yet reached his majority nevertheless quit school – a place he had long hated. His resentment of being trapped inside a building and told what to do even for a few hours a day continued to build. He left before his final examinations, greatly displeasing his father, and began to dream of life as an artist in Paris. To pacify his father, Monet agreed to his father's condition of studying art at one of the studios affiliated with the École des Beaux-Arts.

Shortly after his mother died, one most often would find Monet taking his habitual walks on the beaches of Normandy. It was on one of these walks that he again encountered Eugène Boudin. Boudin, fourteen years earlier in 1844, when he was twenty years old, had opened the stationery and framing shop where he later met Monet and introduced him to outdoor painting. He was reported to have told Monet, "Everything that is painted on the spot has a strength, a power, a vividness of touch, and that cannot be recreated in the studio." Monet, approaching his eighteenth birthday, could not have found a better teacher.

"Boudin was neither doctrinaire nor theorist; all that he knew he had learned with his eyes and his heart, trusting them with genuine naiveté. A simple man with a humble devotion to nature and to art, he was well aware of his own limitations having no other aspiration than to express himself with the conscientiousness of an artisan. He was a modest man who knew that his lessons would not be enough to help Monet reach his true potential." [11]

Liberalism from family ties also characterizes Zola at the age of eighteen. He left Provence behind, along with a depressed Cézanne and moved to Paris to embark on his literary career. Soon after arriving in Paris, he sent a letter to Cézanne pleading for him to join him there and pursue his dream of becoming an artist. He wrote to Paul drawing up a structured schedule that he felt Paul needed, "From six to eleven in the morning, you could do live painting in a studio school; then you could have your lunch, and from twelve to four in the afternoon, you could copy a masterpiece to you in the Louvre or the Luxembourg Museum. That would mean nine hours of work. I think that would be enough and with such a program you are bound to make progress." [12]

Cézanne's father, however, was adamant about Paul pursuing a stable career, "My child," his father explained, "think of your future! Genius keeps no man alive. But money does." Cézanne's departure was put off time after time. First his sister Rose was ill, then his father consulted Cézanne's art teacher Gibert, who was of the opinion that Cézanne could study art just as well in Aix as in Paris. Cézanne became increasingly apathetic, neglected his studies, when he was not drawing at chez Gibert, he was painting out in the open or at Jas de Bouffan where he was allowed to set up a studio in one of the rooms.

Paul was then 20 years old. The family occupied only the first floor of the vast residence; the large room with the curved wall on the ground floor was used as a storage area, and beginning in 1859, Paul was given license by his father to decorate the walls of the salon. The house was in bad condition then, which may explain why his father, so opposed to his son's artistic career, allowed him to paint directly on the walls of the large oval room on the ground floor. He decorated the walls with four large panels of each of the four seasons. Spring is symbolized by a young women in a red dress descending the steps of a garden; summer is a seated woman with a sheaf of wheat on her lap; autumn is of a woman carrying a basket of fruit on her head, and winter is a woman seated before a fire under a cloudy sky sprinkled with stars.

These murals appear to have been done over a period of some ten years, starting around 1859. Cézanne ironically signed "Ingres" on the bottom right and added the date 1811 on the bottom left of the panel representing winter. This inscription echoed that of Ingres himself on his *Jupiter and Thétis*, signed and dated in Rome in 1811 and housed at the Musée Granet. By signing these works with the name Ingres, Cézanne perhaps wanted to prove to his father, ironically, that he was no worse than one of the most famous artists of his time.

The pictures were arranged two by two around a central portrait painted by Cézanne of his father in profile, sitting in a chair reading the newspaper. His father begrudgingly admitted to sit for him. Thus the first *Portrait of Louis-Auguste Cézanne, Father of the Artist* assumed center place attended by *The Four Seasons*, the ones that were playfully signed Ingres.

In 1859, the subject matter of Manet's art was much more controversial than Cézanne's rather innocuous *The Four Seasons*. Manet had just completed his *Buveur d'absinthe*; it was his first submission to the Salon. It portrays a familiar street figure from the Breda district, notorious for its brothels. The subject of the painting was thought to have been suggested by a poem of Baudelaire's and also by Manet paying heed to the advice of Couture. At this time, when Manet was still unknown, the only man who visited his studio, who understood and admired him, was the poet Baudelaire. "Baudelaire, along with Couture, often prided themselves on the fact that nothing was too audacious, no one too daring, for their liking. Both discovering Manet to be a fearless innovator, they encouraged him and defended those of his works which were most assailed." [13]

The Absinthe Drinker is a dark image of a figure from the Paris streets, a rag picker, cloaked, top hatted. The man was recognizably from the world of Baudelaire; the poem, *Le Vin des Chiffoniers* first appeared in *Les Fleurs du mal* in 1848: [14]

> A ragpicker stumbles past, wagging his head
>
> And bumping into walls with a poet's grace,
>
> Pouring out his heartfelt schemes to one
>
> And all, including spies of the police

The model in the picture is a man named Collardet whom Manet met at the Louvre; his portrait personifies the moral and physical ruin that results from abuse of absinthe.

Absinthe was quite popular with working-class Parisians but with the advent of the Second Empire it suddenly took on immense popularity. It was so popular that they spoke of the "green hour" after work when they would imbibe this seventy-five proof drink flavored with wormwood, an herb whose toxic properties caused "hallucinations, birth defects and according to some gendarme authorities, rampant criminality."

While the subject matter of the painting was unsettling, what brought the most attentive comments pertained to the "style and technique of the artist." The critics, used to meticulously executed details, thought the painting was terribly incompetent. As such, the jury, composed entirely of men devoted to tradition, was not impressed with Manet's work. To them it was an unpleasant example of the realistic trends that they were trying to stamp out; consequently it was summarily rejected. But to the Café Guerbois group, Manet's unique technical innovations intrigued the likes of Pierre Renoir and Claude Monet and loosened the traditional and conservative reigns of academic painting. But this painting, like *The Execution of Maximilian,* went beyond stokes of color on canvas, it spoke of his "spirit of revolt" against the composition of the jury; it spoke against its partial manner of distributing awards; it spoke against the whole system of hierarchical gradation of artists, and it spoke of his detestation of the Second Republic. Manet began and ended his career by battling traditional art; sometimes including it in his compositions – in order to undermine it.

How fortunate that Degas did not have to suffer Manet's humiliation surrounding his *Buveur d'absinthe*. His "coveted" position was the result of Degas being completely supported by his father's wealth and by the fact that Degas rarely submitted paintings to the Salon. Also, Degas' art was more in sync with the Salon's preferences and *Le Grande Art* than was Manet's. In 1859, Degas began his career as an academic painter of historical themes. He was inspired by Ingres, Delacroix and the Old Masters that he had copied in Italy; he chose exemplary events in human history that would reveal his erudition and launch his career by appealing to the Salon jury and perhaps would make his father and other relatives most happy. But slowly, his subject matter began to change and it appears that the other artists who made up the Café Guerbois' society would become quite instrumental in changing the course of Degas' art.

For most of his career, money was not an issue for Degas; for most of Monet's career, it was. His father did not see any reason to support a would-be painter and Monet's first decades as an artist were spent in misery associated with bohemian life. While his father had given qualified approval and his aunt was encouraging, Monet used his own savings often borrowing from others to help support him. He, however, tried to follow his father's traditional advice of being supervised by an establish artist, which might lead, in time, to acceptance into the state-owned and tuition-free École des Beaux-Arts. And, after further training, awards would follow and he would obtain possible success exhibiting at the biennial Salon, and even garner state or Imperial patronage.

Manet, however, was recently solvent for having sold a painting or two. He was thus able to employ a young boy to clean brushes, run errands, and model for paintings like *Boy with Cherries* (1858-1859). In early 1860 Baudelaire wrote a story based on a tragic incident that occurred to this hired young boy, Alexandre. Manet had accused Alexandre of stealing sugar and liqueurs, and the boy, consumed with shame, hanged himself in Manet's studio. The guilt-stricken painter had to cut down the corpse, face a police interrogation and break the news to the boy's family. In Baudelaire's "The Rope," dedicated to Manet, the painter is the unnamed narrator.

In 1860, France had a lottery system which determined who was called up for seven years of military service. If your family had the resources, they could pay for someone to take your place. In February, Cézanne's number had come up for the draft of the "class of 1859" - twenty-year-olds eligible for call-up. In May he was declared fit for military service. His father purchased an exemption. Monet's lottery number was also called but he refused to allow his father to purchase his release from military service. He was attracted, he later said, by the glamour of the uniform. However, one account has it that Monet's father offered to pay for a substitute if his son came to work for him, an offer rejected because Monet wanted to study art in Paris.

For two of his seven-year commitment, Monet joined *Chasseurs d'Afrique* (First Regiment of African Light Cavalry) in Algiers. Some historians believe that Monet's choice of Algiers for service had been a result of his admiration for the Romantic painter Eugène Delacroix, whose coloristic work had been influenced by a visit to Morocco in 1832. Monet offered a different explanation, "The seven years of service that appalled so many were full of attraction to me. A friend, who was in a regiment of the *Chasseurs d'Afrique* and who adored military life, had communicated to me his enthusiasm and inspired me with the love for adventure. I drew an unlucky number. I succeeded, by personal insistence, in being drafted into an African regiment. In Algeria I spent two really charming years. I incessantly saw something new; in my moments of leisure I attempted to render what I saw. The impressions of light and color that I received there were not to classify themselves until later; they contained the germ of my future researches." [15]

There was enough free time for Monet to draw and he engaged his time mainly drawing caricatures, this time of his senior officers and his friends. But there were more serious artistic moments one of which was discovering the rich palette of colors in the landscapes of Algeria. As he noted, "The impressions of light and color would return to inspire me for many years to come." On a lighter note, one other consequence of his time spent in Algeria was a name change … because of the teasing and taunts he received from his comrades, he stopped using his first name, Oscar, and swapped if for his second, Claude, instead.

Monet did not spend "two charming years" in Algiers; he contracted typhoid after serving one year and was shipped home to convalesce. His Aunt Marie-Jeanne intervened on Monet's behalf. With a rather handsome sum of money, she arranged to get him out of the army for good if he agreed to complete an art course at a qualified academy. Monet's parents also "consented that he should give himself up entirely to painting, stipulated, like his aunt, that he enter the atelier of one of the famous painters in Paris and there pursue those regular studies, which, in their opinion, formed an indispensable apprenticeship to art." [16]

Monet's father tried to do his part by writing to the Municipal Council, hoping that it would do for his son what it had done once for Boudin. "I have the honor to state to you that my son Oscar Monet, aged eighteen years, having worked with MM. Ochard [Monet's art teacher at school], Vasseur and Boudin, wishes to become a candidate for the title of Pensioner of Fine Arts of the city of Le Havre. I hereby beg you to be so kind as to accept favorably my son's candidacy..." [17] Without waiting for an answer, his father gave his son permission to take a short trip to Paris so that he might ask advice of some artists and see the Salon, which was to close in June. Shortly after he arrived, he sent a letter to Boudin:

"I haven't yet been able to go more than once to the Salon. ... I have paid visits to several painters. I showed [a French painter] Troyon two of my still lifes and he told me: 'Don't neglect painting, however; from time to time go to the country. ... Well, my good fellow you have color all right; it's correct in the general effect; but you must do some serious studying, for this is very nice, but you do it too easily; you'll never lose that. Make some copies in the Louvre.'" Troyon who urged him to draw incessantly, "One can never get enough of it. Enter a studio where you only work from the figure. Learn to draw ...."[18] He closed his letter by saying that his parents were going to let him stay a month or two. Monet could not get enough of Paris and the Louvre.

A common sight at the Louvre were artists arranging their easels around the paintings of the Old Masters attempting to capture the greatest that was before them. Instead, Monet, who always traveled with his paints, took his position by the window. Rather than attempting to mimic like the others, Monet painted the view that he saw of Paris. During his visit to Paris, Monet met several painters who would become friends. One of those friends was Édouard Manet, who gave up copying from the masters at the Louvre and now drew from live models. The subject of his most original works was the charming Victorine Meurent - his favorite model.

Models like Victorine lived from hand to mouth. To refuse even a few sous could be the difference between eating and going hungry. The relationship between Victorine and Manet reflected a special parity. Victorine refused Manet's offer of a bonus. Accepting a bonus would have demeaned the relationship by emphasizing her status as a hireling. Her refusal speaks highly of Victorine's independence and personal ethics.

Victorine was born in 1844 in a working-class district of Paris. As the daughter of an impoverished engraver, she had never known anything but poverty. Barely out of her teenage years, she began to model for Couture and the Belgian painter Alfred Stevens, who became her lover. She was eighteen when Manet first saw her in a crowd outside the Palais de Justice. Struck by her unusual appearance and self-possessed air, he asked her to pose. According to Manet's friend Adolphe

Tabarant, Victorine was an exceptional model. She was "exact, patient, discreet, and not given to chattering. Most important, she was [physically uninhibited but] not too vulgar in appearance. She had fine eyes, animated by a fresh and smiling mouth. With that, the lithe body of a Parisian, delicate in every detail, remarkable for the flowing line of the hips and the supple grace of the bust." [19]

By June, Monet had taken rooms in Montmartre and began painting and drawing on his own. In the winter, Monet entered the private academy, the *Academie Suisse,* named after its owner, Père Suisse. The Academie was housed in an old and sordid building on the second floor of a building on the Île de la Cité. Manet would also come there from time to time while he was still a pupil of Couture. At the Academie Suisse, Monet was constantly drawing figures - none of these drawings have survived.

There were few permanent artists at the Academie Suisse; it was mainly comprised of a revolving, fluid grouping of artists who paid ten francs a month to draw from the nude model. Père Suisse, once a model for life classes, had founded the academy to give young art students the opportunity to draw models. In return for their monthly fees, the artists had three weeks of drawing a male model and a fourth drawing a female. A number of famous artists climbed those steps, among them, Eugène Delacroix and Gustave Courbet.

The Academie Suisse was quite perfect for Monet for it did not offer lessons by some professor and his "pedantic splitting of academic hairs." In fact, there was no formal supervision or instruction and no compulsory attendance and no examinations – all of which suited Monet. "The Academie Suisse was a little like a free university of painting – except that there were no professors, no instruction, and no corrections were offered, apart from the commentary of one's peers. Anyone could enroll, and work completely unsupervised in the genre or medium of his choice. Moreover, the *Academie* had a youthful, bohemian atmosphere filled with various kinds of would-be artists none of whom would have a good word to say for the École des Beaux-Arts or the Salon artists - all of them, however, were anxious for recognition by the very establishment they affected to despise." [20] In contrast to this bohemia-type freedom at Suisse's, Monet was actually quite diligent in his studies - attending for several hours when its doors first opened at six in the morning, and returning again in the evening from seven to ten.

Pissarro occasionally dropped in when he was in town, in order to work from the nude or simply to meet some friends. Monet had just missed the arrival of Paul Cézanne at Suisse's. Cézanne, a new strong brooding student from Aix, made his appearance at the Academie Suisse during the afternoons. His fellow students noticed that even at the young age of twenty-two, Cézanne was "intense, clumsy and paranoid;" he seemed suspicious of all the other students. While he seemed to draw with great care and passion, the results were baffling. His manner and accent seemed gauche and uncouth, even to his fellow artists at the Academie Suisse.

Cézanne's days were spent just as Zola advised … working every afternoon at the Academie Suisse. Trial and error were the order of the day in attempting to build a diversified portfolio appealing to as wide an audience as possible. Cézanne was not alone in this approach as his friends from Academie Suisse were also painting a range of pictures, particularly Renoir who produced portraits, still lifes, figure pictures, landscapes, and modern-life scenes.

Pissarro was also experimenting with new approaches to his art. Pissarro came from a family established in Saint Thomas, a small island in the West Indies, which then belonged to Denmark. He was born there in 1830. His father was a French citizen of Portuguese Jewish descent, and his mother, who had previously been married to her new husband's uncle, was Creole. The marriage was controversial, probably due to racial factors, and as a consequence the Pissarro children were compelled to attend the all-black local school rather than the Jewish school. [21] The port of Charlotte Amalie, where he grew up, had a polyglot mix of European settlers and a sizeable indigenous population. Pissarro quickly learned to speak French, Spanish, and English. At the age of twelve he was sent to boarding school in Paris. Five years later he returned to Saint Thomas to work in the family haberdashery and hardware business. He was no more capable of being a haberdasher than was Paul Cézanne.

Like other Impressionist fathers, Pissarro senior would have liked Camille to take over his business. Opposed to such plans, Pissarro went into exile in Caracas, to cut the strings that tied him to the bourgeois life of his parents. For two years, 1852 to 1854, he stayed in Venezuela on his mission of self-discovery. By the time he returned to Saint Thomas, his decision was made: he would be a painter. Pissarro left for France in 1855, never to return to his native land.

Pissarro continued to work in the outskirts of Paris and to drop in at the *Academie Suisse* and "was soon attracted by a young man from southern France whose provincial accent and strange behavior were no less mocked by the other artists than were his sketches full of strong feelings. His uncouth manners and violent absorption in his work made him the laughing stock of his class. Pissarro would be responsible, in part, for ushering in Cézanne's Impressionist period." [22] Pissarro, an older but as yet unrecognized artist, exerted a dominant influence on Cézanne's artistic style but also provided moral encouragement to a shaky and always insecure Cézanne. He became something of a father figure, working painstakingly with Cézanne, who, astonishingly, listened to his advice. From Pissarro, Cézanne learned to move outside the turmoil of his imagination. Pissarro encouraged him to "Lighten your palette," as Diaz had once advised Renoir.

Cézanne had learned from Pissarro emphatic color highlighting, a new brushwork technique and above all a devotion to landscape. And he would never forget it. Cézanne's landscapes now assimilate the principles of color and lighting of Impressionism. During this period, Cézanne's brushwork loosened up; his colors become softer and brighter. But his work would transgress from the Impressionists as he developed his own distinct style. About the only thing that Cézanne and the Impressionists would eventually have in common would be their struggle for positive recognition. Some of Cézanne's pictures could have been taken as Pissarro's – and ungenerous critics accused the two painters of copying each other. Pissarro felt obliged to explain the mutual influence of "Delacroix, Courbet, Manet, and even Legros on all of us …"

Cézanne works develop more substance – meaning his works convey something more solid and durable. There is no longer anything ephemeral in his paintings. Mont Ste. Victoire would become the essence of all that he felt eluded the Impressionists – solidity and permanence. His brush strokes would become blunt and structural not impressionistically soft and round. While

Impressionists were interested in color and light, Cézanne focused on structure and form. These differences would eventually put Cézanne into Post Impressionism, along with Gauguin and Van Gogh.

Chapter Six: The Salon des Refusés

The year 1861 marks the year that Manet's oeuvre first came to the public's attention. He had submitted to the jury the portraits of his mother and father and *The Spanish Singer* reflecting the Parisian love of "all things Spanish." In the 1860s Spanish vogue enjoyed a fresh surge of interest that started with the 1853 marriage of Napoleon III to young Eugenis de montijo (Eugénie) daughter of a Spanish count and the last Empress consort of France.

The Salon accepted both of Manet's pictures. *The Spanish Singer* demonstrates the visible influence that Goya and especially Velázquez had on Manet; "its broad execution, its vivid colors, its pleasing subject and lively attitude" inspired the critics. It was so especially admired by Théophile Gautier, literary and art critic, that it was placed at eye level at the Salon so more patrons of the arts could notice it. Through the success of his first works at the Salon, Manet, then twenty-nine years old, found himself overnight with a reputation that assigned him an enviable place among the "promising young men" of the art world.

Manet also developed a fondness of painting still lifes: "A painter can say all he wants to with fruits or flowers, or even clouds. You know, I would like to be the Saint Francis of still life." [1] Later, the Musée d'Orsay presented a history of Manet's still lifes and noted that throughout his career, from ambitious compositions to whimsical sketches that still lifes represented almost one fifth of Manet's works. While Manet's drawings would generate a great deal of criticism, his still lifes would receive the warmest welcome. "The most vociferous enemies of Édouard Manet's talent grant him that he is good at painting inanimate objects," noted Émile Zola who would become a great literary fan of Manet.

One generally does not associate still lifes with Manet; most likely, we attribute works of oranges and apples to Cézanne. But these types of compositions would be drawn later in his career. Cézanne had just arrived in Paris and had rented rooms in the rue des Feuillantines, near the Pantheon quarter where Zola lived. He had an allowance from his father of 125 francs a month and high hopes of being in Paris. A more down-to-earth Zola calculated Cézanne's expenses: 100 francs – 20 francs for working at an atelier, 10 francs for art supplies, leaving 25 francs for lighting, laundry, drinks and tobacco and other cheap leisures…

Cézanne's first works had very little overt resemblance to his mature drawings. The subject matter is brooding and shows a general preoccupation with the macabre – so apparent in *The Murder* - one of Cézanne's earliest paintings. It is an unusually dramatic piece disturbingly capturing a brutal scene in which two figures, one wielding a dagger, are shown silently attacking a third. The style of his work was frequently as alarming as the subject matter. Cézanne's work from 1861 to 1870 has often been labeled the dark period. His work is unrefined; it's rough and splashed with thick cumbersome brush strokes. The painting's unique style of "combining Courbet's use of a palette knife with Manet's thick outlines and sharp juxtapositions of color - produced undeniably brusque-looking canvases with bold but sometimes indecipherable images." [2]

The subject matter, such as seen in *The Murder*, is antisocial and violent. The expressive portraits and the foreboding scenes of violence and sexual aggression in his paintings seem to mirror the struggles going on within Cézanne – his continuing angst and his quest for liberation from a father who undermined Paul's art at every turn including cutting up his canvases in his absence. Zola noticed the emotional turmoil and apathy that seized hold of Cézanne and wrote, "I rarely see Cézanne … in the mornings he goes to the Atelier Suisse while I stay home writing. He spends the rest of the day drawing chez Villevielle. … He fought for three years to come here, and now he doesn't give a fig for it all." [3]

Zola had found work in the advertising department at a prestigious publishing company, the *Librairie Hachette*. He also began publishing articles on art and politics in various newspapers. He found time to write a collection of short stories and published his first novel, *The Confession of Claude* – sensationalized with raunchy bedroom scenes that attracted a series of lurid headlines. The book was dedicated to Cézanne. Zola boasted in a letter to his friend, "Today I am ranked among those writers whose works cause trepidation." The critics were outraged at the book's flaunting of public religious morals - an offense given to both Flaubert and Baudelaire. This was just the beginning of the many controversies surrounding Zola's work.

In the early sixties, a glance at Manet's early works was in striking contrast to Cézanne's macabre paintings but would become just as sensational. Manet's paintings exhibited in 1863 and 1865 were the real starting point of his career. In 1861, Manet drew a colorful rendering of the happy times in gay Paris: *Musique aux Tuileries*. It is a painting in the court gardens of the Chateau of the Tuileries where the Emperor held his court, the centre of the luxurious life of the period. Here one could observe a fashionable and well-dressed crowd of men in striped trousers and women in gigantic hats and elaborate parasols flocking to the garden where a band played twice a week.

Manet's painting was placed in the window at Martinet's gallery. Louis Martinet was a former painter who became an official in the Ministry of Fine Arts. Because of his powerful position in the art world, his gallery was to become a major venue of the new artists whose works failed to find a place on the walls of the yearly Salons. Those passing by and observing Manet's painting noticed, " that it had no conventional framing devices, the colors seemed to clash, and it had no proper subject. Where was the battle, the tragedy, the shipwreck, the parable?" [4] It is difficult to understand the kind of fury *Musique aux Tuilleries* provoked when it was exhibited in the gallery on the Blvd des Italiens.

Today, Manet's picture happily recalls the costumes and manners of a vanished age; but then, the reaction was one of violence. One spectator threatened to resort to brute force if Manet's painting wasn't removed from the gallery. When he showed his paintings at Louis Martinet's gallery in 1863, visitors had menaced his canvases with their walking sticks, creating a climate of hostility and mockery. Most of the commotion engendered by this painting was due to his "loose handling of paint" and the lack of a highly finished canvas. Then, too, it had a "snapshot" quality reminiscent of the newly invented camera. Despite these criticisms, *Music in the Tuileries* was the first indication that Manet would become the painter of modern life.

Another spectator was Claude Monet, who in 1863, made the discovery of the works by Manet. In seeing the fourteen canvases that Manet was exhibiting at Martinet's in the Blvd des Italiens, Monet, unlike the other more volatile viewers, "was suddenly confronted with a luminous painting in which bold colors were laid side by side without the usual accompaniment of conventional shadows. He was fascinated from the very first by this fearless style innovation." [5] Monet, too, wanted to capture nature's unchanging masks - the brief moments in the pre- dawn before sunrise when the earth is covered with dew and a hazy mist. He wanted his canvases to show the effects of the rising sun on the landscapes below. It was these momentary, ephemeral effects that Monet wished to seize upon.

The Clianteuse des rues –The Street Singer - followed *Musique* in 1862. The dominant color reflective of this more somber painting of a singer, who stands holding a guitar under her arm while eating cherries, is gray. The Museum of Fine Arts in Boston, described this painting: "Manet was inspired by the sight of a woman with a guitar emerging from a sleazy café. She refused to pose for the picture, so Manet employed his favorite model of the 1860s, Victorine Meurent. The style and subject matter seemed crude to academic critics when the painting was exhibited in 1863. But Manet's friend, the novelist and critic, Émile Zola, admired its formal beauties and its apparent confrontation with real life."

Just as the public, critics, and members of the École des Beaux-Arts could not understand Manet's technique and subject matter, Manet as well as Monet were disillusioned with the technique and subject matter still taught in traditional schools. But, when Monet returned from Algiers and resumed his artistic training in Paris, he was obliged to conform more closely to his father's expectations of joining a "traditional-type" school. When Monet was twenty-two, he became a student of Swiss artist Charles Gleyre. His classmates included future Impressionists, Auguste Renoir and Frédéric Bazille. The choice seemed to pacify his father because Gleyre prepared candidates for the examinations of the École de Beaux-Arts.

Monet cut a dashing figure as he entered the Gleyre Studio in his well-tailored clothes with fashionable lace cuffs and he responded immediately to the more socially propitious ambience of Gleyre's studios. There was greater opportunity here for showing off than at Suisse's. One of the women students fancying her chances began to flirtatiously try her luck. "Sorry," said Monet, "I only sleep with duchesses or maids. Preferable duchesses' maids."

Monet did not choose to take up the École-training option but enjoyed the relaxed atmosphere of Gleyre's studio. It was here that Monet met Renoir, aged 21, who had come to oil painting and high art via an apprenticeship in porcelain decoration and Bazille, aged 21, who was supposed to be combining medical studies with painting. Together, the three experimented with colors, painting the effects of light en plein air with broken color and the use of rapid brushstrokes.

Because of Monet's "worldly experience," he gained a sort of ascendancy over this trio. No doubt another reason for his leadership role was that Monet had a clear vision of what he wanted to accomplish and was able to argue clearly and distinctly for his vision of a new and modern approach to painting. It was therefore natural that Monet should take the lead over his new friends. Further, Monet was not a "mere beginner," such as they.

Monet participated as little as possible in Gleyre's class. But so as not to exasperate his family, he continued to appear regularly at the studio, remaining just long enough to execute a rough sketch from the model and present it at inspection. The advice given in 1862 by Gleyre, who was one of the most prestigious of the 19th century Academy painters, was in keeping with his Salon background, "When you draw a figure, young man, you should think of antiquity. Nature, my friend, is all very well as an element for study, but it is of no interest in itself. Style, mark, my words, is all that counts." From that day on, the little respect that Monet may once have had for the teacher, evaporated.

Monet, from the very first day, had taken a role of an open rebel, especially since he lacked both the desire and the capacity to submit his works to the Salon. While Monet was obliged to study under Gleyre, Renoir's case was different. Renoir entered the studio of Gleyre without any idea of revolt and displayed a pacifist eagerness to learn and to do as the others. Monet hated the academic work condoned by Gleyre; he passed through the studio without deriving any profit from it. His natural preference led him towards landscape painting.

Unlike Monet, Renoir worked hard and tried to do as he was instructed to do. Even as late as 1890 Renoir declared himself at the Salon as a "student of Gleyre." The teachings of Gleyre stayed with Renoir throughout his life. The framework of his paintings is based on clearly arranged compositions. Renoir adhered to the tradition of Academic Realism, preferring nudes and portraits as well as narrative genre scenes over pure landscape painting.

It was apparent to Monet that Renoir had great talent - a talent that had distinguished itself so clearly when he entered the studio of Charles Gleyre as an art student. And for Renoir, the most crucial and historically consequential event during this training period was the acquaintances of Claude Monet, Alfred Sisley, and Frédéric Bazille - the core of the future Impressionist group. Artists all in their early twenties soon became friends. In the future, Renoir would receive much support from his new friends – a support that lasted over the next several decades.

Monet found Gleyre, who was essentially traditional with no real interest in the natural world, quite frustrating. One morning at Gleyre's, Monet declared that he had finally seen the light: "truth, life, nature - everything that moved him - clearly did not exist for Gleyre." "Let's get out of here!" he said, one afternoon. They all thudded downstairs and made for the Gare Saint-Lazare. He tried to be true to his father's request, but obviously failed.

Cézanne was also trying to appease his father and remain true to his father's request to be admitted to the École des Beaux-Arts. In 1862 he made his second attempt to pass the entrance exams. Perhaps his father encouraged him or pushed him into sitting twice for the École exam, for to Louis-Auguste, the Beaux-Arts was the passport to the profession, to say nothing of remuneration.

It was a difficult exam: Part one consisted of a practical test: Drawing by observation and drawing from the imagination (a specific theme is given at the time of the examination; candidates are permitted to use color and various materials). The subjects given were mostly drawn from mythology and Greek and Roman history, or from the Bible. Pupils were expected to acquire the knowledge necessary to deal with these subjects, through the courses taught within the École. For example, for the year 1857 the subject of the historic landscape competition was "Jesus and the Good Samaritan." The candidates then also had to write an essay on the thoughts and comments on contemporary art and culture in response to specific questions. The subject of the historic composition was "Saint-Lazarus's Resurrection." The last test of Part One was to demonstrate one's mastery of a second language (English, German, Spanish, or Italian).

Part Two of the exam consisted of an interview: The candidate would present his portfolio of personal works before a jury. The portfolio needed to show varied approaches and use of diverse mediums: drawing, painting, sculpture, photography, film, prototypes, maquettes (scale models). The jury would then ask questions with a view to ascertaining the candidate's motivation for attending the school, interests and concerns, and general knowledge. The entrance exam did not call for knowledge of any one subject in particular, but rather, it tried to evaluate the candidate's ability to think both independently and analytically.

Cézanne failed the exam once again, shattering his dreams of academic success and the prospect of finding a patron. His early years were difficult and his career was, from the beginning, dogged with repeated failure and rejection. The only bright note was being introduced to the famed circle of artists who met at the Café Guerbois in Paris, where he met Edgar Degas. While Cezanne's figures were thought to be unfinished and clumsy looking, Degas portraits were seen as elegant renderings.

Degas was attempting to perfect his style by copying at the Louvre where he first met Manet. Degas was etching a copy of Velázquez's painting of a royal child, the *Infanta Margarita* (1653) when he was interrupted by a voice behind him saying "You have a lot of nerve, and with that method you'll be lucky if you come out with anything." Manet's interest in this work is understandable as his own style was deeply indebted to Spanish art. Degas, however, was completely amazed by the audacity of this man. Degas, who had not yet exhibited at the Salon, was a mere beginner compared to Manet, who, in the fall of 1861, appeared for the second time before the public. Degas was well dressed, of elegant manners, highly intelligent and witty; in short, he was a perfect companion for the worldly Manet. Despite his rude intrusion, they soon become friends. Manet, however, was more attracted to the man than to his art.

Degas' early works reflected his ambition to become a history painter. While his education had prepared him well for classic art, his initial venture away from historical subjects occurred in his early thirties when he became a classical painter of modern life. He had not yet exhibited at the Salon, for the early 1860s were years of misgivings and doubts. Despite his lack of confidence, he was turning out a prodigious amount of work that, to him, seemed never to lead anywhere. His brother, René de Gas, who always closely followed his brother's career, commented "He is working with a vengeance and has only one thing on his mind, his painting. He is so hard a worker, he does not take time out for diversion."

The first meeting of Manet and Degas was one that would be marked by a sharp-edged yet friendly rivalry that lasted until Manet's death. In time, they both discovered they were of kindred spirits: "Both were Paris-born and educated, well-off, cultured and sophisticated. Manet had been to Rio, Degas would travel to New Orleans. Both families had recommended that their sons study law and then encouraged their painting. Both families, once prominent, suffered scandal and decline. Both had studied for five or six years with teachers of the old school, Couture and Lamothe. Eventually rejecting their teachers' conventional ideas. Manet loved to paint around people; it had been said that he would quite readily paint in the Place de la Concorde with a crowd around him. Degas double-bolted his studio door and wouldn't allow any visitors when he was painting. Manet was optimistic and resilient. … Manet and Degas' portraits of their parents reveal their contrasting attitudes to their subjects. Manet's 1860 portrait of his paralyzed father is mercilessly harsh; Degas' portrait of his elderly father listening to Lorenzo Pagans is sweet and tender." [6] Their arguments at the Café Guerbois provoked Degas' competitive instinct and he challenged Manet by boasting: "I shall be at the Institute [of France] before you will Manet!" The other burst out laughing. "Yes sir," continued Degas, "because of my drawing." [7]

Degas had become a regular at the artists' corner at the Café Guerbois where he met Paul Cézanne, also a son of a banker. Unlike Cézanne, Degas looked and acted the part of a plutocrat's offspring and of being raised in the first arrondissement. Throughout his life, it was said that he used the informal *tutoiement*, tu, the linguistic marker of intimacy and equality with only three people outside his family. His charmed upbringing, however, together with his sharp tongue and love of the Old Masters in the Louvre, had quickly made him a natural friend and ally of Manet and Cézanne.

It took Degas much longer to hit his stride. In Renoir's estimation, "If Degas had died at the age of fifty, he would have left behind the reputation of an excellent painter, nothing more; it was after the age of fifty that his work grew and he became Degas." Degas passed slowly from classicism to modernity. Degas grew to share Manet's disdain for the presiding art establishment as well as adopting his belief that artists needed to turn to more modern techniques and subject matter. Degas, who never liked outbursts of color, was by no means and Impressionist from this point of view. As a draughtsman, he expressed all by precision of planes and values; a grey, a black and some notes of color sufficed for him.

Degas had a love-hate relationship with the Impressionists: "He was never on particularly close terms with the Impressionists proper, though Monet owned a superb nude drying herself by Degas … He was friendly with Renoir until the 1890s when he took umbrage at the fact that he should have sold one of his pictures. … Renoir, though admiring him, considered that his character was bad and that he ran people down. Degas shared Pissarro's interest in print-making … despite provocations, was always generous about his acerbic friend." [8]

Degas was quite interested in his appearance; he loved clothes – Manet as well. It would be a few years hence that Henri Fantin-Latour would paint the *Portrait of Manet* showing Manet as the quintessential Parisian *flaneur*. Manet was handsome, charming and when he met his friends at the Café Guerbois, he was always fashionably dressed in his carefully tailored jacket, a top hat, frock coat, gloves of yellow suede, a walking stick and, according to a friend, "intentionally gaudy trousers." Armand Silvestre, a contemporary critic, described Manet as "a kind of dandy."

A flâneur was an archetypal character who emerged in the mid-nineteenth century. The most celebrated and imitated of all the dandies was Beau Brummell. "Brummell's name remains alive today; it is harder to recall the person behind it. He was, as his reputation suggests, a model and dictator of fashion - the person whose manner of dress and behavior all those who aspired to social recognition had to follow." [9] A flâneur was "characterized by exquisite manners and by impeccable dress, on which he lavished a great deal of time. He was abreast of all current events and current gossip. A flâneur promenaded on the boulevards where he displayed himself while recording all that went on. By the early 1860s the Parisian flâneur had absorbed many of the leading characteristics of the dandy. Manet was a notable example of the flâneur. In his dress, exquisite manners, his savoir-faire, and his devotion to shocking the bourgeoisie, he epitomized this urban species. Degas was too much the lone wolf that he deviated from this type, but he shared many of the flâneur's qualities and represented them in his paintings. For example, in his portrait of James Tissot, Degas shows his painter friend as the dandy he was, a flâneur-dandy who's been out for a stroll, and who dropped in on his friend for a moment." [10] Baudelaire because of his friendship with Manet gave memorable expression to key concerns of the flâneur in his poems and essays.

In 1863 Manet married Suzanne - thirteen years after their affair began and eleven years after Leon was born. Perhaps if Suzanne had been the choice of his heart or had Manet been truly in love, and if Suzanne had made a more favorable impression in society, Manet may have made his marital commitment earlier. Most likely that marital commitment would have been celebrated with its customary rites such as a marriage bans – a formal announcement of the intent to marry and certainly some kind of ceremony. At a bare minimum, a husband was expected to provide little more than security and position and it was this bare minimum that Suzanne received after the marriage. It was also in 1863 that Manet submitted his painting *Le déjeuner sur l'herbe*.

Arguably, Manet suffered more rejection than the others and true to form his *Le déjeuner sur l'herbe* was rejected. He wasn't alone, however, for only 2,217 works were accepted out of the more than 5,000 submitted, a failure rate of almost sixty percent. Napoleon III heard the cries of the artists' and felt their outrage that so many paintings were being rejected. The emperor descended on the Palais de l'Industrie on the Champs-Élysées to sample the rejected work. Count Nieuwerkerke was also summoned. The Emperor made a sensational decision, which was announced two days later in the official *Moniteur*:

"Numerous complaints have reached the emperor on the subject of works of art that have been refused by the jury of the exhibition. His Majesty, wishing to leave the public as judge of the legitimacy of these complaints, has decided that the rejected works of art be exhibited in another part of the Palais de l'Industrie. This Exhibition will be elective, and the artists who may not want to take part will need only to inform the administration, which will hasten to return their works to them. This Exhibition will open on May 15 (the Salon proper to open on May 1). Artists have until May 7 to withdraw their works. Beyond the limit, their pictures will be considered not withdrawn and will be placed in the galleries."

The jury's decision would stand but now a provision was made for an exhibition of the rejected works in another part of the building – the annex, opening two weeks after the main event. The extraordinary exhibition was elective and would be called *Salon des Refusés*. Manet's painting was included in the Salon des Refusés.

The jury of judges would view each submitted painting placed around the Palais des Champs-Élysées in alphabetical order. Votes by the Salon's jury were taken by a show of hands for or against – the majority prevailed. If a canvas received a unanimous positive vote, it was accorded the Number One appraisal. This meant that when it was displayed at the Louvre it would receive an "on the line" placing, which meant eye level to the viewers.

When paintings were rejected by the committee, they were carried away by white-coated attendants and a most humiliating red "R" was stamped on the back - "Rejected." These paintings that failed to receive a positive majority of votes were carried away to the *depotoir* (rubbish dump). It wasn't exactly a "rubbish dump;" it was an out-of-the-way room into which few Salon-goers ventured. Most assuredly that red R was nothing short of disastrous; not only did it signify the refusal by the Salon, it also hampered just about all chances of selling a painting to a private buyer. Then, too, artists who might have sold their paintings a few days before sending them to the Salon most often had to make refunds when the jury rejected the canvas and emblazoned it with the "Scarlet Letter." Works by Manet, Monet, and Renoir spent time in this humiliating obscurity; their work not meeting the jurors' particular favored style of painting.

Many of the jurors deciding the fate of the artists' submissions taught at the École des Beaux-Arts. They preferred smooth finishes in which all the brush strokes were effaced. They looked for detail and sanctioned historical or mythological works. Many of the Batignolles Group favored landscapes and painted in unmixed, vibrant colors and abandoned the use of dark and somber hues. Their work featured less detail and aimed for an overall aesthetic impact; what Corot called the "first impression" rather than a precise depiction of Meissonier minutiae. The qualities of their unrecognized greatness are found in their lithe touches of paint, giving their artistic renderings a light and ethereal quality. They were interested in painting modern life, not in painting ancient history. Art critic Étienne-Joseph-Théophile Thoré summed up the aims of many of these rejected painters: "Instead of seeking what the connoisseurs of classic art call 'finish,' they aspire to create an effect through a striking harmony, without concern for either correct lines or meticulous detail." [11]

From the very day of its opening the Salon des Refusés attracted an enormous crowd; on Sundays there were record numbers of three to four thousand visitors. People were, of course, more attracted by the sensational features of the rejected works, which the press described as hilarious, than by the staid pictures of the Salon proper. Manet's *Le déjeuner sur l'herbe* received the most attention and criticism along with instant notoriety. *Le déjeuner* is a drawing of a girl in the woods, wearing only the shadow of the leaves, surrounded by fully dressed male students. She stares directly at the viewer and it was the brazen "facingness" of the painting that was disconcerting.

For the idea of *Le déjeuner* Manet turned to the Old Masters. "Raphael's grouping of three river gods and Giorgione's *Concert champetre* (now attributed to Titian) have long been recognized as the sources for the composition of *Le Déjeuner*." [12] The female nude was a matter of frequent occurrence with the masters of the Renaissance. Manet, like other artists of his time 'borrowed' subjects from other artists. Many of his works, if not based directly on Old Masters, were at least inspired by remembrance (Manet had traveled extensively), by reproductions, prints etc. As Degas later explained it: "Manet drew inspiration from everywhere, from Monet, Pissarro, even from me. But with what marvelous handling of the brush did he not make something new of it?" [13]

It may be doubted whether Manet's painting would have provoked such criticism had it not been painted in broad contrasts and frank oppositions, with a tendency to simplification. His "vulgarity," in the eyes of the public, lay probably even more in his execution than in his subject matter. Ernest Chesneau, writer and critic, found the painting lacking in perspective and draftsmanship as well as being morally objectionable. It was Manet's "renunciation of the customary slick brushwork, his fashion of summarily indicating background details and of obtaining forms without the help of lines, by opposing colors or by sketching his contours, if necessary, with decisive brushstrokes in color, which helped to model volumes instead of limiting them, that were responsible for the almost universal disapproval he met." [14]

Le Déjeuner sur l'herbe (1863) created one of the first of many public scandals for Manet. The critics not only objected to Manet's technique, they objected to Manet's inclusion of a nude figure in a modern setting. "While a classical, mythological or exotic nude was acceptable thanks to the distance of time or cultural space, a naked woman in a resolutely contemporary setting was considered obscene." [15] In this "shocking" picnic in the grass, Manet "portrays the new subculture of leisure, yet the painting remains elusive in its jarring combination of a modern naturalist vision with classical reference to Italian Renaissance masters. The tension between the dressed middle class men and the naked woman that further foregrounded the very modern fact that this was a prostitute - in many ways a symbol for modernity." [16]

It was in the same year, 1863, that Cézanne had shown a still life, largely overlooked in the same Salon des Refusés because of Manet's *Dejeuner*. Cézanne was convinced that the Salon was "the only battlefield on which an artist can reveal himself at one stroke to both the critics and the public, and in this he apparently set out to surpass Manet at his own game by outraging the public with themes taken from Manet, but crudely rendered." [17] Cézanne's admiration for Manet's painting was later contaminated by his resentment over Zola's effusive praise of Manet.

Renoir also submitted a painting to the Salon, which was accepted, but it also did not win him any recognition or acclaim. But a watershed moment was soon to occur recorded by his closest friend Albert André: In the Fontainebleau Forest, Renoir was painting in his old porcelain-decorator's blouse and some rowdy young boys were making fun of his costume. They were driven away by the heavy cane of a man with a wooden leg, who then looked at Renoir's canvas and said: "It's not badly drawn, but why the devil do you paint so black?" The stranger was Narcisse Diaz de la Pena, who might have been attracted by Renoir's unusual attire because he himself had begun his career as a painter on porcelain. Diaz immediately took a great liking to Renoir; Renoir's admiration for the man thirty-six years his senior, grew when he came to know him better. Aware of Renoir's precarious financial situation (at Gleyre's studio he had observed Renoir often picking up the tubes thrown away by others and squeezing them to the very last drop), Diaz put his own paint-dealer's charge account at the disposal of his young friend and thus discreetly provided him with colors and canvas. It was a defining moment for Renoir, who decided that from now on he would take the risks with color, which Gleyre had always tried to discourage. [18]

The critical onslaught had not subsided since Manet's showing of *Le déjeuner sur l'herbe* at the Salon des Refusés but the unflappable Manet continued to believe that the Salon was the real field of battle and in 1865 submitted another painting - *Olympia* (1863). This painting would be even more shocking and controversial. The scandal it caused at the Refusés would be much worse.

Chapter Seven: A Dozen Men and Two Women – Morisot and Cassatt

To borrow a famous literary line – "It was the best of times and the worst of times." In the 1860s, the best drawings were being rendered by a handful of artists. Manet's painting of *The Spanish Singer* reflects the vogue in Paris for the art and culture of Spain during Napoleon's Second Empire. Monet, even when depicting something as unexceptional as a wheatstack, sought different ways to render the visual experience. Degas was experimenting with the vivid use of color on his artist images of ballet dancers and women at their toilette. Renoir was perfecting *plein air* painting. Cézanne was seeking less ethereal subjects, capturing the beauty of Mont Ste. Victoire. Then again, it was the worst of times particularly for female artists like Berthe Morisot and Mary Cassatt. Females were not allowed to enter the most prestigious and principal Parisian art academy– the state-owned and tuition-free *Ecole des Beaux-Arts* - the *exposition officielle* for the *Salon de Paris*. Their entrance was barred until 1897.

Most women faced social mores and attitudes that were limiting factors on their aspirations that transcended marriage and family. Societal roadblocks existed that prevented most women from procuring roles thought to be only obtainable by and capable of the masculine gender and that included the world of art. A woman musician might be tolerated, or a novelist, if she wrote under a pseudonym, and about rather innocuous "family" subjects. But an actress or a dancer was tantamount to a prostitute. As for a woman painter, Renoir made clear the view of most men of his generation, "I regard women writers, lawyers, politicians, like George Sand, Mme [Juliette] Adam and other troublesome females as monstrosities and nothing but five-legged calves. The woman artist is simply ridiculous, but I do favor the female singer and dancer." [1]

Nonetheless, in the 1860s, a good many female painters from various social strata were studying art - painting, drawing, and copying. They were even exhibiting at the official Salon, with some fifty women or so exhibiting during any given year. Their careers were often sidetracked, however, because no studio would accept a woman as a student. A drawing master, even an established painter, might teach talented ladies privately in her home. But studios like those of Couture and Gleyre, to mention a few of the most respected, would not entertain the thought of a woman's presence, no matter how gifted she might be. Moreover, a woman was not able to study anatomy or work from nude male models or for that matter even fully clothed male models, except relatives. Women, of a certain elk, did not have the liberty of patronizing Parisian cafes such as Café Guerbois, nor could they roam the boulevards at will. This, perhaps, explains why most women painted flowers, landscapes, and portraits of women and children. Art, for most women, could only be a "decorative pastime."

While few women were singled out for acceptance by the Salon, one of those represented most consistently, a specialist in "light-suffused riverscapes and woodlands" was a most fascinating figure, Berthe Morisot. She gave professional vision to landscapes and to woman's domains: domestic interiors, park-like estates, vacation villas. Her most recognizable work were scenes such as a young girl studying her reflection in the mirror and fixing her hair most likely for the hundredth time – a young nanny reading a princess story to her young charge and perhaps daydreaming of herself as the heroine. Each of these paintings comprised her best-known work of mothers and children. The placidness of these paintings, however, belies Morisot's shocking determination.

Morisot was the reserved, soft-spoken, daughter of Edme Tiburce Morisot, an official in the French government and his exquisitely pretty and highly intelligent wife, Marie Cornélie Mayniel, daughter of an official in the French government. Berthe's father had studied architecture at the École des Beaux-Arts before going on to a career in the civil service. Berthe lived with her parents, sisters and brother in the affluent Paris suburb of Passy. The couple's daughters, Berthe, Marie-Elizabeth, and Edma started taking art lessons when quite young. Their teacher was M. Geoffroy-Alphonse Chocarne, an academic, genre painter of mediocre talents. These lessons, however, were part of their *haute bourgeois* education; girls from privileged classes did not aspire to recognition outside the home. So, their art lessons were simply to cultivate a cultural appreciation for art. Humoring his daughters' interest in art, their father had a studio built in the backyard.

The art lessons continued, but not with Chocarne; soon Berthe and Edma moved on to another rather minor artist, Joseph Guichard. One could say Berthe began her artistic career at the age of seventeen when Guichard opened the young girl's eyes to the greatest teacher of them all – the Louvre. It was here, against the conventions of her society, that young Berthe was captured by the world of art and soon made a life-long commitment to that world. By age twenty, she met and befriended the important landscape painter of the Barbizon school, Camille Corot, a pioneer in plein air painting who was known primarily for his tranquil landscapes many created in the Forest of Fontainebleau. Just three years later, astonishingly, she began to exhibit at the Salon. In her earliest pictures, Morisot's work appears to be "bathed in brightness and sunlight, and demonstrates her freedom of touch and originality." and demonstrated her freedom of touch and originality."

Morisot was not only well bred and intelligent she was also dramatically attractive. She became equally famous for her art and for her beauty. She was described as being elegant and aloof; she had a voluptuous figure, black hair, dark eyes, and complexion reflective of her Spanish heritage. She met Édouard Manet in 1868 and felt an immediate rapport with him, his work, and his family. The feelings were mutual; Édouard Manet was beguiled by her beauty and was taken by her artistic talents. Manet, who hated professional models, in 1868, asked and convinced Berthe to model for a painting entitled *The Balcony* – inspired by Goya's *Majas on a Balcony*. The painting was an exterior view of two women and a man idling on a balcony with a boy in the background behind them. Morisot made regular visits to his studio.

Berthe seemed to vacillate between art and marriage. At one point she said, "Men include to believe that they fill all of one's life, but as for me, I think that no matter how much affection a woman has for her husband, it is not easy for her to break with a life of work." At the age of thirty-three, and professionally established, she married Eugene Manet, the brother of the great painter. Berthe, however, still continued to paint and exhibited at various private galleries, where the works of the Batignolle's Group were first to be seen. Morisot would become one of the mainstays of the Impressionist movement and would participate in all but one of the group's eight independent shows.

Like Berthe Morisot, Mary Cassatt was relegated to the category of "feminine" artists because of her usual subject matter — women, children, and domestic scenes. An American, Mary would become French through her assiduous participation in the exhibitions of the Impressionists. She is one of the very few painters who Degas advised. She is a pastelist of note, which at that time, was a genre almost abandoned. Cassatt, because of her boldness, caused astonishment by those whom she met.

It seemed that Mary, even as a young girl had expressed a serious interest in becoming an artist. Finally, at the age of sixteen, her parents were reconciled to Mary's choice of study and reluctantly acquiesced to her artistic desires. "Mame," as she was called by her family, enrolled in the Pennsylvania Academy of Fine Art (PAFA). The serious art world was for males only as Mary was soon to discover even at this micro-level of the art world. The faculty and its male students were rather patronizing toward Mary and the only other female student, Eliza Haldeman, Mary's best friend. Both girls wistfully thought of Paris and its bright lights that represented an intoxicating beacon of artistic freedom. They were not alone, for in a few years, the number of Americans living in Paris would be estimated at 7,000 – one of seven was artists or art students.

After overcoming her father's objections (her father declared he would rather see her dead than living in Paris as a "bohemian") Mary persisted. She always persisted. Her father then gave his consent and was not known to have ever regretted it. Mary moved to Paris at the age of twenty with her mother and family friends acting as chaperones. She began her study with private art lessons in the Louvre. Having obtained her permit to copy paintings in the Louvre, she joined the thicket of easels clustered around popular paintings. Under the tutelage of a highly regarded teacher, Jean-Léon Gérôme, she studied and copied the paintings of the masters. It is a measure of Mary's artistic skill at the time that she was accepted by one of the most sought-after teachers in Paris. Her friends back home who knew of Gérôme's reputation were amazed. Mary spent diligent hours copying the works of Correggio and Parmigianino as well as making friends - the Louvre often served as a social gathering spot for young artists as well.

Many artists continued to leave the Academy style of art and like the Batignolles Group were seeking to find new ways of capturing reality on canvas. Mary, however, continued to follow the more Salon-accepted traditional artistic style. Over the next decade, as her rejections grew in number in spite of the obvious flowering of her abilities, with increasing frustration and bitter mood, she continued to dance faster and more hopelessly to the Salon's tune and submitted Neo-classical works – somewhat reflective of her Victorian upbringing.

As a young girl, in the 1850s, Mary's home life, like Morisot's, reflected a lifestyle with her mother engaging in self-contained activities like reading and embroidery. Mary was the fourth child who for five years was the youngest child bequeathed with all the special rights due to the baby-of-the-family. Mary's education, consisting of classes in sewing, homemaking, and music, was to prepare her to follow in her mother's cultured footsteps. It was during this decade that the Cassatts traveled to Europe and spent several years living there to service two purposes: to find a proper school for Mary's older brother, Alexander, and to find a specialist to cure her brother

Robbie's injured knee joint. Mary's linguistic skills profited from living in various cities from Paris to Heidelberg that would be quite useful to her in her later years. The Cassatts enjoyed living in Europe and had the monetary means to rent beautiful villas and apartments replete with ample servants that made their stay work and stress free.

Unlike Morisot, Mary's looks were plain, she did have a strong and intelligent face but her chin was a bit angular for her to have been considered pretty. Her gray eyes were large and alert, and she had the slender figure and perfect carriage for her well-tailored ensembles. "Miss Cassatt's tall figure, which she inherited from her father, had distinction and elegance, and there was no trace of artistic negligee, or carelessness, which some painters affect," wrote Louisine Elder [Havemeyer] of New York, who would become a wealthy friend of Cassatt's. Louisine continues, "Once having seen her, you could never forget her – from her remarkable small foot to the plumed hat with its inevitable tip upon her head and the Brussels lace veil without which she was never seen. She spoke with energy, and you would as soon forget her remarks when she conversed as to forget the motion of her hands." [2]

At the age of twenty-one, traveling with another young Philadelphia painter, Eliza Haldeman, Mary had returned to Europe to study and paint. Here in Paris, she entered the studio of a distinguished portrait painter, Charles Chaplin, one of the few French masters who held classes especially for women. She made copies of masterworks at the Louvre, painted in the countryside, and generally worked hard and steadily.

Both Morisot and Cassatt had initial successes at the Salon. Berthe made her debut at the 1864 Salon with two plein-air landscapes, and managed to exhibit her work at the next four consecutive Salons. Successes were not unconditional since her paintings tended to be hung near the ceilings – almost invisible to the viewing public. Mary, who in 1868 was studying with Thomas Couture, an academic and historic painter, had a painting accepted by the Salon in that same year. Her *A Mandolin Player* clearly showed the influence of Couture's spirited and un-academic style. In *The Mandolin,* a young child with a melancholy expression is starring away from the viewer as she methodically plucks the strings of the instrument. While it was a huge thrill for Cassatt to have a painting accepted by the Salon, fearful of her father's disparaging words, the painting was submitted under the name of Mary Stevenson. Both Berthe and Mary were determined that they would be professional, not merely "a woman who paints," as was the expression, despite the continued frustration each were about to experience with the Salon.

Cassatt's friendship with Morisot was intimate and competitive. They came from similar upper-class backgrounds and did not have to sell their pictures to support themselves. Morisot spoke softly and quietly; Cassatt's voice was loud and harsh. Morisot expressed her personal feelings; Cassatt repressed hers. Morisot was emotional, troubled, and filled with doubts. Cassatt was determined, confident and single-minded about exhibiting and selling her work. Morisot was sympathetic and discreet; Cassatt was brusque and frank with a keen intellect and sharp tongue.

As the careers of Morisot and Cassatt were beginning to flower, in mid-October 1864, Monet was spending a few days with his family in Sainte-Adresse. He was trying to appease them following their expressed dissatisfaction at his long absence. He then executed some studies painted near Cap de la Heve. One of his best was *The Pointe De La Heve at Low Tide;* once again, Monet demonstrated his taste for the coastal landscapes of Normandy.

In 1864 Gleyre closed his studio advising Monet and Renoir to continue their work. They along with Manet, Cézanne, Sisley, and Bazille were entirely on their own. Monet had not engaged another renowned painter to the extreme displeasure of his family and a heated discussion ensued. Monet was asked to leave and not to come back in a hurry. Monet was faced with the serious threat of having his allowance cut off and a serious position considering the debts he had incurred during his stay in Honfleur. So he worked on repeating his best studies, with variations, including his view of Sainte-Adresse.

In 1864, Emperor Napoleon arrived for a tour of the Louvre with his wife Eugénie and the Prince Imperial, his eight-year-old son Napoléon Eugène Louis Jean Joseph Bonaparte, known as Lou Lou. The Emperor had celebrated his fifty-sixth birthday a week earlier. He had come to see Meissonier's painting *The Champaign* but also viewed two renderings by Manet - *The Incident in a Bull Ring* and *The Dead Christ with Angels.* They were the first of several paintings by Manet with a religious theme.

After *The Dead Christ* was already on its way to the 1864 Salon, Manet realized that he had made a grave mistake; he depicted Christ's wound on the wrong side. He wrote to Baudelaire of his mistake, and the critic instructed him to correct the position of the wound in the painting before the exhibition opening, adding, "Take care not to give the malicious something to laugh at." Manet did not repaint the wound, and the malicious laughed.

Manet's submissions to the Salon of 1864 were again condemned by critics. The Metropolitan Museum of Art noted that the critics "found errors of perspective in his *Incident at a Bullfight* and a lack of decorum in *The Dead Christ and the Angels*. The latter picture, in particular, was denounced for its realistic touches, such as the cadaverous body of Christ and the seemingly human angels. It was argued that the painting lacked any sense of spirituality; the figure of the battered Christ was said to more closely resemble the body of a dead coal miner than the son of God."

Manet was hardly prepared for such a critical mauling, particularly from his friend, Pierre Jules Théophile Gautier. Referring to his *Incident in a Bullring*, he gave Manet the Spanish sobriquet – "Don Manet y courbetos y Zurbaran de las Batignolas" -and then proceeded to lampoon his drawing with "his amateurish stab at conveying on canvas the recession of three-dimensional space in the bullring – with the result that the bull, placed in the background, looked like it had shrunk." The flaws were particularly outstanding because next to his painting was one by Meissonier, with a masterful example of how the impression of a receding three-dimensional space could be created. *The Campaign of France* showed Napoleon and his generals riding diagonally across the picture plane, in a flawless escalation of scale, perspective, and minute detail. But this sort of finicky exactitude was merely the stock in trade of the technically flawless but creatively barren alumni of the École des Beaus-Arts. After the failure of his works at the Salon, Manet was determined to take inspiration not from Old Masters in the Louvre so much as from, as both Baudelaire and Couture had been exhorting, the everyday life that surrounded him.

Pierre-Auguste Renoir was a painter of everyday life in keeping with his proletarian background as a legitimate member of the bohemia class, the poor son of a tailor, a slum dweller, a porcelain worker when still a boy, and then a resident of Montmartre where he lived among an assortment of proletariat shop assistants, restaurant employees, laundresses, models, concierges, and workers. He frequently took his models from among them including several figures in his *Moulin de la Galette* and the young performers in *Little Circus Girls*.

Renoir's first successful submission to the Salon in 1864 was *La Esmeralda*, which was inspired by a character from Victor Hugo's *Notre-Dame de Paris* and the following year his portrait of Sisley's wealthy father was also accepted. The greater part of Renoir's career, however, was to depend on patronage by and portraitures for the bourgeoisie. Victor Chocquet supported Renoir´s work when others ridiculed it, and he collected a considerable number of the artist's paintings. Renoir painted Chocquet's portrait several times and his depictions were often regarded as his greatest male portraits. He seemed to capture the spirit and passion of his supporter. Beginning in 1865 and lasting until 1874, Renoir was frequently the guest of Jules Le Coeur, a wealthy painter who owned several homes in different parts of the country. Renoir eventually painted several portraits of his family.

Renoir would paint without interruption over a period of forty years. He spent a great deal of time sketching on the Seine river banks with his friend Monet and during these meetings the two young artists developed their famous technique and experimented with the bright colors that later became central to Impressionism. His early works captured real life scenarios and his themes were always pleasant and non-serious. A master at depicting facial expressions, Renoir tended to paint youthful portraits of his associates, most of whom were artists and writers.

Early on in his career, Renoir was greatly influenced by Manet, an artist who, like most of the Batignolle's Group was also influenced by Courbet whose realism was also evident in Renoir's first few paintings. Soon after he had entered Gleyre's studio, Renoir had fallen in with Henri Fantin-Latour, whose studio was nearby. Fantin-Latour would take him off to paint, lavishing advice: "The Louvre! There is only the Louvre! You can never copy the Masters enough!" [3] When Renoir was granted permission to copy at the Louvre, he was exposed to the works of Rococo masters such as Boucher, Fragonard, and Watteau. This inspired him to create a classic form while retaining the luminous palette.

"Renoir is the most lyrical, the most musical, and the most subtle of the masters of this art. More than Manet, and even more than Morisot and Monet, Renoir surrounded contemporary Parisians with flowers and gardens. He was more of a landscapist than Manet, and more of a figure painter than Monet, so combining the two genres came naturally to him. He received great inspiration from a range of artists and periods that led him to produce a technique that was individual and ever changing." [4] Renoir dedicated himself to his work and collaborated with his fellow students to develop a technique that went on to spawn modern art - Impressionism. Renoir created some of the most famous and frequently reproduced work in the history of art. Renoir spent a great deal of time studying the paintings of Camille Corot and Eugène Delacroix; he was also influenced by Edgar Degas's sense of movement.

Degas had dismissed Lamothe, and began to focus his attention on works by Eugène Delacroix, known as a "master of color." "Frequently Degas would work on canvases for years without really finishing them, while on other occasions he managed to execute elaborate studies amid a bustling, noisy household. This gave rise to some uncertainties among his relatives as to whether or not he would make a commitment to his work and finish the works he had started. In response to one relative's doubts, Degas's father noted with a sense of confidence that 'our Raphael is still working, but has not produced anything that is really finished.' " [5] It was not until the 1870s when Degas would paint *The Orchestra of the Opera for Desire Dihau*. His friend Dihau had commissioned Degas for a painting showing Dihau, the bassoonist, as the central figure. Degas actually finished the painting making his family quite satisfied. Dihau had taken the painting off to Lille, thus making any further retouching impossible. "It's thanks to you that he has finally produced a finished work, a real painting," the family told the musician.

During the 1860s Degas remained largely unknown to the public. Among a limited number of artist's circles, he enjoyed an undeniable reputation for his manners, cultivation, and urbanity. He had achieved a degree of celebrity among other habitués of the Café Guerbois - Bazille, Renoir, Sisley, Pissarro and Cézanne, among others. Along with Manet, he would become a leading figure of the Impressionists, particularly in organizing a series of independent exhibitions. Within this select circle of artists, he enjoyed an undeniable reputation not only for his manners and tremendous refinement, but for his uncompromising views of art and his already notoriously caustic witticisms. The history painting *The Misfortunes of the City of Orléans* (Musée d'Orsay, Paris) was the first of Degas' paintings to be accepted by the Salon in 1865. The painting made allusions to the plight of women in the American Civil War.

Probably due to Manet's influence, in 1865, Degas suddenly began to paint entirely new subjects and in a very different style. "He moved from the historical to the contemporary world, from the neoclassical line of Ingres to more lively and psychologically incisive work and started to portray the social life in racecourses, theaters and cabarets of the Second Empire under Napoleon III. He chose his new modern heroines from ballet dancers, café singers, and circus performers. His new victims were from absinthe drinkers, laundresses and prostitutes." [6]

Like Degas, Cézanne was somewhat of a loner as well – a loner with a charitable heart. He was walking back from the Gare Saint-Lazare with a landscape under his arm after a day's painting in the country when a young man stopped him in the street and asked to see his work. He propped his canvas against a wall, making sure the light was perfect, not too much sun or shade, and the stranger was delighted, especially by the green of the tree. "If you like, you can have it," said Cézanne. Well, I can't afford to pay you," replied the stranger. "Take the painting, I insisted." But these brighter moments were also accompanied by dark periods that would increase in frequency as Cézanne became older. Zola felt that one way to help Cézanne escape from these torments of depression was to paint a portrait and he suggested himself – based in part on vanity and in part to keep Cézanne's mind occupied.

On varnishing day when hundreds of painters descended on the exhibition hall for one last touch-up of their paintings, one could hear the scraping of ladders and smell the penetrating odors of

The Opera Orchestra, c.1870, Degas, Edgar (1834-1917) / Musee d'Orsay, Paris, France / Giraudon / The Bridgeman Art Library

varnishes, turpentine, and drying oils; Paul Cézanne was not there. As ever, he failed to have a canvas accepted. But Cézanne had been persistently going to the Palais des Champs-Élysées each March, as another friend wryly observed, "Carrying his canvases on his back like Jesus with his cross." [7] Cézanne had fewer illusions concerning his chances to be admitted. He actually enjoyed the idea of his works making "the Institute blush with rage and despair," as he wrote to Pissarro on March 15, 1865. The Salon rejected everyone of Cézanne's submissions from 1864 to 1869.

Claude Monet, however, had both of his 1865 Salon submissions, *The Mouth of the Seine at Honfleur* and *The Pointe de la Heve at Low Tide,* accepted. He began working on these paintings a year earlier when he was just twenty-three and an art student. Financially, Monet needed to have a success, so both submissions were highly calculated in style and composition to appeal to the classic-oriented tastes of the Salon's jurors. The subject matter was traditional – a fisherman and peasants gathering seaweed - and not a hint of the modern world. The paintings rightfully earned Monet important notices in the press.

With such praise, most artists would try to capitalize on their success by painting similar kinds of pictures. Monet, however, only a few weeks after his triumph, began an entirely new group of paintings that pointed him in quite a different direction, demonstrating his desire to expand his repertoire and to step boldly to the forefront of contemporary art. As Charles Baudelaire put it, to paint "the eternal in the transitory."

Stimulated by Salon success, Monet's enormous undertaking for the summer of 1865 was the 20 x 15 foot canvas entitled *Dejeuner sur l'Herbe* influenced by Manet's similarly titled picture of two years earlier. It was intended to be both a tribute and a challenge to Manet whose painting was the subject of much sarcasm from the public as well as the critics when it was exhibited in the Salon des Refusés in 1863. "Manet became a hero to Monet and his circle who were attracted by the persistent intensity of his choice of modern subjects and his suppression of detail." [8] Manet was viewed by his contemporaries as the first painter of Modern Life.

Monet's *Le déjeuner sur l'herbe* consists of fashionably dressed men and women enjoying a picnic in a secluded but richly foliated corner of the Forest of Fontainebleau. His models were Bazille who posed for four of the six males – recognizable from his lanky form, mustache and bushy muttonchops while Monet's future wife, Camille-Leonie Doncieux, at the age of eighteen, modeled for two women in the center of the picture.

The project was abandoned in 1866, just before the Salon where Monet intended to show it, opened. Later, in 1920, Monet related what happened to the painting: "I had to pay my rent, I gave it to the landlord as security and he rolled it up and put it in the cellar. When I finally had enough money to get it back, as you can see, it had gone mouldy." [9] When he got the painting back, he cut it up into three pieces. Two fragments are in the Musée d'Orsay; the third has disappeared.

It is not surprising that many of the submissions to the Salon of 1865 received little attention, mainly because Manet's painting of *Olympia* was in the same exhibition, which thoroughly scandalized Parisian society. It was Manet's second nude portrait of Victorine, the startlingly *Olympia,* a companion piece to *Luncheon on the Grass*, and also painted in 1863. Just as the earlier picture had parodied Titian, *Olympia* (a common name for prostitutes) boldly alluded to another masterpiece, Goya's *Naked Maja*.

Manet presents Victorine in the guise of a Parisian prostitute, whose unabashed gaze confronts the viewers as if those viewing were her customers. A courtesan lying in bed undressed, a Negress approaching her with a bouquet, and a black cat, caused the tremendous stir. It is a powerful work of strong color, broad design, and intense sentiment.

The Louvre is filled with paintings of female nudes but they were always painted in the guise of nymphs or goddesses; so the blatant modernity of *Olympia* was something the Parisians were not used to. Viewing a nude goddess in the guise of religious paintings was perfectly acceptable, but a contemporary prostitute awaiting her client was not. The storm of abuse unleashed by *Le Dejeuner* pales in comparison with Manet's submissions to the salon of 1865: "Never has a painting excited so much laughter, mockery and catcalls as this *Olympia,*" wrote the critic Louis Auray, in his review of the show. [10] "Nothing can convey the visitors' initial astonishment," wrote the correspondent for *L'Epoque*, "then their anger or fear." Manet did not fare better with Théophile Gautier a leader of the romantic poets in their fight against tradition: "With some repugnance I come to the peculiar paintings by Manet. It is awkward to discuss them but one cannot pass them by in silence. … In many persons' opinion it would be enough to dismiss them with a laugh; that is a mistake. Manet is by no means negligible; he has a school, he had admirers and even enthusiasts; his influence extends further than you think. Manet has the distinction of being a danger. *Olympia* can be understood from no point of view, even if you take it for what it is, a puny model stretched out on a sheet. The color of the flesh is dirty, the modeling non-existent. The shadows are indicated by more or less large smears of blacking. …here is nothing, we are sorry to say, but the desire to attract attention at any price." [11]

Even the model Victorine did not escape criticism being called a "female gorilla," " a coal lady from Batignolles." "She is thin, tough and scrappy; she has armpit hair and dirty feet, while the presence of the bed with its rumpled sheets, a bouquet from a client and the cat all point directly to an unromantic view of her trade." [12] Manet was given the title of "Apostle of ugliness." Théodore Duret noted, "Even the black cat in the picture, which was a purely accidental feature due to the whim of Manet, was singled out as the object of a special attack, and helped to prejudice the picture. A black cat, it appears, is the symbol of lewdness. Manet had a fondness for cats introduced this one for sake of its pictorial effect and also in order to have a bold black note to enhance by the contrast the prevalent tones of white and pink." [13]

There were defenders of *Olympia*. Alexandre Astruc was Manet's vociferous defender when *Olympia* was being stoned by all the other critics. "Manet! One of the greatest artistic figures of the day. I will not say that he has been awarded the triumph of this Salon … but he is its sparkle, its inspiration, its flavor, its marvel." [14] Astruc was also one of the group that congregated at the Café Guerbois.

In the past, Chennevieres and Nieuwerkerke had been forced to post guards in front of Ernest Meissonier's paintings to protect them from their crushes of admirers. "At the 1865 Salon, guards were posted to protect *Olympia* from the malicious designs of indignant spectators." [15] When even these proved inadequate, the painting was removed from its original location and suspended high above the heads of the visitors – so high, in fact, that a critic for *Le Figaro* claimed that "you scarcely knew whether you were looking at a parcel of nude flesh or a bundle of laundry."

Initially, Manet was doubtful about exhibiting the painting, but Baudelaire helped him to overcome his doubts when he wrote: "You complain about attacks? But are you the first to endure them? Have you more genius than Chateaubriand and Wagner? They were not killed by derisions. And, in order not to make you too proud, I must tell you, that they are models each in his own way and in a very rich world, whilst you are only the first of the decrepitude of your art." [16]

Baudelaire did not give wise encouragement to exhibit this painting of *Olympia*, at this point in time, anyway. In 1865, French politicians and police were busy trying to quell the spread of pornography ... the photographers who produced nude pictures for the painters of académies soon branched out to supply a much wider market with a book entitled *The Squalor of Paris* with "cynical photographs boldly showing insolent details." Soon, prostitutes capitalized on this new form of advertising, distributing photographs of themselves in enticing poses on their calling cards. Against this backdrop of police raids on suspected pornographers, and angry petitions to authorities and heated debate on the floor of the Senate, Manet exhibited a work such as *Olympia*. [17]

It was not a propitious time for crowds to be confronted with a painting of blatant prostitution. There were five thousand registered and thirty thousand unregistered prostitutes in Paris at the time who serviced a large proportion of the male middle classes in the *maisons closes*. The shock that stood before the painting was the shock of the familiar. She was all too real. [18]

Manet was now famous or infamous. Degas said that he was "as well known as Garibaldi," a hero in the age of the Italian unification. "When Manet went out into the street, people turned round to look at him or pointed him out as though he were some curious beast." [19] Zola, however, was impressed by Manet's modesty and gentleness, his energy and intelligence, and, above all else, by his strength: "I was in the presence of a committed fighter, an unpopular man who did not tremble before the crowd ... but tried instead to tame it, to impose his personality on it." [20] But these vile reactions did hurt Manet deeply, and for a while he stopped going to the Café Guerbois, and instead, took long, solitary walks, nursing his wounds. But he persevered; "It is my fate to be vilified," Manet confessed, "and I accept it philosophically."

Dejected by the critical response to his art, Manet traveled to Spain in August 1865 where he took his fill of Velázquez and Goya. He was most forcefully affected by the bullfights and the paintings of Velázquez. During this journey he made the acquaintance of Théodore Duret. The two men went to bullfights, looked at the pictures by Velázquez in the Museo del Prado, Madrid, and visited Toledo to see the cathedral and the paintings of another great Spanish artist, El Greco. "I saw in Madrid some thirty or forty portraits or paintings, all of them masterpieces; he [Velázquez] is greater than his reputation and he alone is worth the exhaustion and the unavoidable discomfort of a trip to Spain." [21]

Manet, as a good Parisian, became too exasperated with Spanish food to stay in the country. Spanish olive oil was more pungent than fragrant and for those Parisians accustomed to a butter-based cuisine, or more delicate olive oils, food was offensive to the nose as to the palate – at least for Manet. Adding insult to injury, when he returned to France, the customs-officer saw the Manet label on his luggage and quickly fetched his wife and child so they, too, could see this person about which so many bad things had been written.

Despite all this negativity, Manet was contemplating on having his own show. He would not, however, abandon the Salon and would continue his efforts to exhibit there. He still believed that the fight for Naturalism should be taken into the enemy camp.

Chapter Eight: The Exposition Universelle

It was one of the best pictures that any artist had ever painted that year, Zola thought. This picture would put Monet at the head of this new group of artists, now sometimes called *Les Actualistes*. In Zola's words, "Monet cannot paint a landscape without including well-dressed men and women. Nature seems to lose its interest for him as soon as it does not bear the stamp of our customs. Claude Monet loves with a particular affection nature that man makes modern." [1] This painting was different, more daring than his others. It was not somber in tone but Monet appropriated bright tones that adapted to the landscape. It was 1865 and the painting was *Le dejeuner sur l'herbe*, very different from that of Manet's exhibited in the Salon des Refusés in 1863.

But it was another painting done by Monet in 1866 that would grant him national fame. This painting, however, had little to do with lithe colors but his technique would make him famous. This painting is *La femme à la robe verte - The Woman in the Green Dress*, also known as *Camille*. The model is Camille Doncieux, his favorite model featured in several of his pictures, who will later become his first wife. The portrait is of Camille wearing a dress striped in green and black with a long silk train. Over her dress she is wearing a jacket with fur trim and on her head is a small hat.

Woman in the Green Dress attracted a great deal of attention at the Salon where it was hung. Its success made Manet aware of this younger near homonym before he met him. The beginnings of the relationship between Manet and Monet were not exactly amicable. Since the works of the Salon were now hung in alphabetical order to prevent favoritism, Monet's works found themselves in the same room with Manet's. When the latter entered this room on the opening day, he had the disagreeable surprise of being congratulated by several persons about his portrait of Camille.

"Having studied the signatures of the two pictures attributed to him, Manet at first thought it was a cheap joke; his anger was conceivably not lessened by the fact that the pictures continued to have more success than his own works. He left in a rage and openly complained to some friends, 'I am being complimented only on a painting that is not by me.' " [2] Andre Gill, the renowned newspaper cartoonist, wrote as a caption to his caricature of the painting, "Monet or Manet? Monet. But it is to Manet that we owe this Monet; bravo Monet, Thank you Manet."

Camille also was praised by Émile François Zola in an article published in the daily newspaper *L'Evenement* entitled *The Realist at the Salon*: "I confess the painting that held my attention the longest was *Camille* by M. Monet. Here was a lively, energetic canvas. I had just finished wandering through those cold and empty rooms, sick and tired of not finding any new talent, when I spotted this young woman, her long dress trailing behind, plunging into a wall as if there were a hole there. You cannot imagine what a relief it is to admire a little, when you're sick of splitting your sides with laughter and shrugging your shoulders. ... Here is a strong character, a man among all these eunuchs." [3]

Boosted financially by his successes at the Salon, Monet moved to Sevres. He needed to complete a large format work en plein air in order to break with the traditional creative process once and for all. To this end he painted *Women in The Garden*, in which he, allegedly, devised a trench and pulley system that allowed him to hoist the canvas, despite its considerable size, to the desired height for painting. This painting marked a return for Monet to the image of bourgeois women in *Le Dejeuner sur l'Herbe*, notably with Camille among the figures.

In his report on the Salon Zola wrote: "The sun fell straight on to dazzling white skirts; the warm shadow of a tree cut out a large grey piece from the paths and the sunlit dresses. It had the strangest effect imaginable. One needs to be singularly in love with his time to dare to do such a thing, fabrics sliced in half by the shadow and the sun. The faces are left vague and cannot be considered portraits." [4] Monet's style was evolving, as he gradually abandoned large areas of solid color in favor of using small touches to give detail to the painting. Rejected by the Salon, this work was displayed in a shop and then purchased by Bazille for a high price.

While Camille had been a favorite of Claude's, in her eponymous painting, she wasn't a favorite to Monet senior. In fact, when Monet's father discovered that Camille was pregnant, he promptly cut off Monet's allowance. A bleak situation, indeed, making it impossible for Monet to support himself anywhere but at home in Le Havre. Despite Bazille's paying Monet 2,500 francs for *Women in the Garden*, a truly tangible sum as factory workers at the time earned that much as an annual salary, it was being paid in installments. Monet only received fifty francs a month, so he was not able to feel instantly solvent. In fact, he cried poverty, which was his constant lament over the next several months. Most of his letters pleading for money, and becoming increasingly more desperate, were written from his aunt's house in Sainte-Adres where Monet had relocated for the summer and fall in 1867, presumably to save money.

Monet had depended on his father to support his lifestyle and replenish his finances and was now attempting to transfer that responsibility to his friend Bazille. It hardly seems to have occurred to him that Bazille might not have limitless funds. Bazille sent more money. Monet spent it. Monet finally left Paris and left pregnant Camille under the watchful eye of Renoir and Bazille. It's difficult to contemplate why Monet would leave her at such a critical moment in their lives. It is possible that money was a secondary issue and the primary one was his relationship with his father. When Monet had first spoken to his father about his deep relationship with Camille, his father was furious. To the elder Monet, it was just another example of how negligent his son was and how he was traveling down the wrong path. To stay in his father's good graces, Monet had to follow a better, more righteous path.

Not only was Camille left without a sou to her name, there was nothing set aside for the expected child. In desperation Monet again wrote to Bazille, his best friend and financier, that he needed money, *immédiatement*. He even audaciously told his friend that if he did not receive a reply soon, that he would never write to him again. During this period of roller-coaster finances, Monet lived in various places around central Paris - Ville d'Avray, Le Havre, Fecamp and Etretat, lodging with family or friends, sometimes borrowing empty apartments and houses. He seemed to be just a few steps ahead of the predatory creditors seeking him for non-payment of rent. "In 1866, he fled Ville d'Avray after slashing over 200 canvasses to prevent their seizure and forced sale. That, however, did not prevent them from being seized and sold in lots of fifty at thirty francs a lot." [5] . Monet also suffered the blow of rejection of his large painting *Women in the Garden* by the Salon jury of 1866.

Manet was a regular frequenter of the Café Guerbois along with the regulars including the cultured and tranquil Fantin-Latour, who had been a friend of Monet's for nearly ten years. At the 1864 Salon, Fantin-Latour depicted Monet among a number of persons assembled to do honor to Delacroix – *A Homage to Delacroix* (Musée d'Orsay). It was the first major work by an artist closely linked to the Impressionists; however, the critics saw it as nothing but an aggrandizement of realist painters. They further criticized it for its harsh colors and it's photographic-like style.

There was one critic found brave enough to defend and explain the new naturalistic art and that was the young Zola. Before going on to write a series of naturalistic novels about the Rougon-Macquart family, he would become the crusading journalist of the Impressionists – mainly the champion of Manet's work. Émile Zola met Manet in 1866, when he came to interview the painter for a newspaper article in *LÕEvénement*. Before the creation of the daily *Le Figaro*, the *LÕEvénement* was the leading republican and liberal journal, which was popular among literary and society Parisians. Though he had no special expertise beyond his enthusiasm, Zola had been commissioned by M. de Villemessant, who was on the lookout for new writers, to write an account of the Salon of 1866. When Zola took up art criticism he wrote especially about Manet. Zola began by championing Manet's "striking originality, his radical break with academic art and his Baudelairean commitment to painting scenes from contemporary life."

His second article was devoted to an enthusiastic eulogy of Manet and his works. The artist, whom the Salon that year had rejected, Zola declared to be a great painter, predicted that some day his pictures would find a place in the Louvre, and asserted his infinite superiority to the painters of the traditional school, then at the summit of their fame and popularity. The readers, who were not sympathetic to Manet and his works, were incensed by Zola's article.

Maybe Zola's enthusiasm was based on kindred spirits for Manet's naturalism, his desire to show modern life in a truthful light. Perhaps it resembles Zola's *Nana* (1880) in a literary work similarly portraying the unadorned life of a prostitute. But Manet's *Woman with a Parrot* (1866) striking in its simplicity, and cool, detached emotion, captured Zola's heart and commitment to Manet and his works. Zola writes in *Le Figuro,* "The pattern formed between the figure in pink and the dark grey background creates a contrast that carries as much weight as the subject itself. In painting the fabric of her gown, Manet appears more interested in the surface application of pigment (note the discernable brushstrokes) than in creating something that looks like real fabric." [6]

On an impulse, Zola collected the articles he had already published and brought them out in a book form, entitled *1866 Mon Salon*. Most of the new painters were included Manet, Monet, Pissarro, Renoir, though not Cézanne and their opposition to the dismal taste of the Salon was described. In a lengthy foreword, Zola once again recalled the youthful times he had shared with Cézanne (doing so for the last time) and encouraged his old friend to persevere. It reads like a letter of farewell "For ten years we have been debating questions of art and literature. We lived together, and – do you remember? – often daybreak found us still immersed in discussions, discussions in which we would examine the past, scrutinize the present, and try to locate the truth, since all our endeavors were aimed at fashioning an infallible, total belief. We moved awesome mountains of thought." [7]

When Zola championed Manet, he tried to demonstrate his seriousness with a willingness to put his money – had he had any – where his convictions were. "I am so certain the M. Manet will be one of the masters of tomorrow that I believe I could make a good speculation, if I had any wealth, by buying up all his canvases today. In fifty years, they will be sold for fifteen or twenty times as much." [8] The then impoverished Zola was unable to test the force of such predictions, but there were others who did, notably the pioneering art dealer Paul Durand-Ruel. When he succeeded his father as head of their family business in 1865 Durand-Ruel first championed the so-called Batignolle's school of landscapists, who had preceded and influenced the Impressionist through painting nature by direct observation outside of the studio, en plein air.

In 1866 Manet submitted two pictures to the Salon, the *Fifre* and the *L'acteur tragique*. The jury rejected both. This refusal was the outcome of the indignation produced by the works exhibited in the previous infamous year of the *Olympia*. In the summer of 1866, following his exclusion from the Salon, he had invited the public to his studio to see his rejected works for themselves. He told Zola, "He was determined to take at least forty-old pictures I can show, and have already been offered sites and very good locations near the Champ-de-Mars. I'm going to go all out and, with the support of people like you, it should be a success." [9]

The year 1866 was not a banner year for Cézanne either. However, one of the most important works was painted in 1866; it was Cézanne's portrait of his formidable father. *The Artist's Father* is one of Cézanne's "palette-knife pictures," painted in short sessions between 1865 and 1866. The painting's realistic content and solid styles reveal Cézanne's admiration for Gustave Courbet. "Here we see a craggy, unyielding man of business, a solid mass of manhood, bodily succinct from the top of his black beret to the tips of his heavy shoes. The uncompromising verticals of the massive chair are echoed by the door, and the edges of the small still life by Cézanne on the wall just behind." [10]

Cézanne still felt caged among his family. By 1866 he had been toiling at painting for at least five years. A number of canvases had come to nothing. Constant rejection made him even more bitter and cantankerous and it showed when he joined the company in the Café Guerbois. He remained a solitary dissident, as his visits to Café Guerbois were to show saying of his fellow artists, "They are all bastards! They're decked out like lawyers!" [11]

The future to Cézanne seemed to always consist of gray clouds and black skies. He walked a solitary path and remained on the fringes of Montmartre society. "I don't believe," concluded Renoir, "that there is a single case comparable to that of Cézanne to be found in the entire history of painting. … right from the very first day he wielded a paintbrush, he remained as secluded as if marooned on a desert island. To be passionately devoted to art, yet at the same time so utterly indifferent to his own work once it was finished." [12]

"Cézanne had been working right up to the last minute to meet the 1866 Salon deadline. On the last possible day for submitting, a wheelbarrow arrived outside the Palais de l'Industrie, pushed and pulled by Cézanne and Oller, his Cuban friend from the *Academie Suisse*. When both paintings were rejected he headed straight back to Aix complaining to Pissarro about the 'rotten' family he was being forced to rejoin, all of them 'boring beyond measure.' Cézanne was determined, however, to make his views of the Salon felt. He wrote to Nieuwerkerke, protesting that the Salon should be open to every serious artist and protesting that the Salon des Refusés, which did not take place in 1865, be re-established." [13] No reply was forthcoming. Cézanne would find his niche and paint many landscapes around Aix including some sixty views of Mont Sainte-Victoire, but these studies of the Provence landscape would not develop until the 1870s.

Degas painted a portrait of Manet and Suzanne, done in the summer of 1866. Madame Manet playing the piano while her husband lounged on the sofa. While Degas, for once, was satisfied, Manet felt the profile of his wife was so unflattering that he took a knife and cut off the offending right hand section of the picture and destroyed it. Degas was enraged and for several months the two did not speak. The rift healed and Degas claimed "one cannot stay vexed with Manet for very long." Degas' clashes with Manet, a long-standing friend, were legendary; for a while, following one such encounter, they would pass each other in the Café Guerbois without so much as a word or greeting.

Despite these verbal disagreements and Salon rejections, in the summer of 1866, discussions at the Café Guerbois continued. The artists argued about the relative merits of Delacroix and Ingres; they discussed naturalism and plein-air painting, and grumbled the loudest about the state control of the arts, police censorship of literature and journalism, and the control exercised over the Salon by outdated and prejudicial juries. Cézanne who had returned to Paris from Aix in February joined them occasionally. When Zola came along, the discussions were political. Even though Manet was an ardent republican along with Monet, the conservative son of a grocer, both kept their mouths shut.

In 1867, the confrontation between the old and the new was made very graphic in the huge World's fair devised by Napoleon III as a proof of France's rise to new prominence in industry and the arts. The fair, ostensibly dedicated to progress and peace, was built on the Champ de Mars, the military parade ground in front of the *Ecole Militaire* on the left bank. Few visitors probably did not pay any attention to the ominous portent in Prussia's exhibit - that of a huge Krupp cannon.

Three years after his election to the presidency of the Republic, in 1848, Napoleon III had broken his solemn oath to the constitution, eventually proclaiming himself Emperor. Only through the use of absolute power could he maintain himself against a republican opposition on the one hand and various royalist factions on the other.

Napoleon had called for another *Exposition universelle* - Manet, Monet, Cézanne had all submitted works but they had been rejected – only the works of Salon medalists were on display. But it was an exciting affair: "Above the grounds hovered a double-decker balloon the height of modern technology, in which Nadar, the celebrity caricaturist and photographer, took visitors a dozen at a time, for flights above the grounds. Along the Seine ran newly built excursion boats carrying 150 passengers at a time. A huge pavilion with all the leading countries, presented their exhibits of gleaming machines, the latest in modern military technology, and exotic oriental fabrics. The Americans exhibited an amazing new invention – the rocking chair." [14]

The Exposition was not organized to protect the future of French art but to reflect the stars of its immediate past – Daubigny and, of course, Meissonier. Concurrently, on another site, there was a pavilion to showcase the work of younger artists. However, of the three thousand submissions to the Salon, two thousand were refused, a rigor paralleled by the jury for the exposition's exhibit, which accepted only 550 works, whereas twelve years earlier, 1,872 had been admitted. Painters everywhere were up in arms; the Café Guerbois buzzed with indignation.

After being rejected from the Salon of 1866 and learning in May that he was to be excluded from the *Exposition Universelle* of 1867, Manet decided to try another path to success. He would imitate Gustave Courbet and would hold his own private show. Manet borrowed 18,300 francs from his mother about fifty thousand in today's value. A note in his mother's hand details his income over the four years since his father's death in 1862, all of which he had spent; "79,484 francs divided by four years comes to nineteen thousand seven hundred eighty-one francs per year. I think it is time to stop this ruinous slide." Undaunted, he built his own wooden shed-like structure just outside the grounds and mounted a one-man show of fifty paintings – almost the whole of his work. He also included once again *Le Dejeuner sur l'herbe* and the *Olympia*, which had already given mortal offence. The male portion of the visitors complained that Manet's women were neither pretty nor attractive while the feminine viewers scrutinized and condemned the fashion of their dresses. His show was a disaster and was hardly mentioned in the press.

Manet had not bothered to submit any work to the 1867 Salon. Among the thousands of canvases returned to their owners with a red stamp on the back were ones by Renoir, Pissarro and Cézanne. The latter was cruelly mocked in *Le Figaro* (which dubbed him, Monsier Sesame) as someone whose paintings were "worthy of exclusion from the Salon." Also among the 1867 refuses was Claude Monet. His eight-foot-high painting begun at Ville-d'Avray, *Women in the Garden*, was turned down by the jury, as was a seascape called *Port de Honfleur*. Rejection came as an unpleasant shock for Monet after his previous triumphs at the Salon in 1865 and 1866.

Rejection of any of his paintings was inopportune in view of Monet's precarious domestic situation. Camille Doncieuz had given birth to their child, a son named Jean, on 8 August 1867. "It pains me to think of his mother having nothing to eat." Camille suffered through the winter of 1867 with barely enough money for coal. Monet experienced huge financial embarrassment and was obliged to reduce the price of his pictures to a hundred francs and it was only with great difficulty that he was able to sell enough to keep him from absolute ruin. Then to make matters worse, Monet suddenly had to stop painting outside because of eye trouble.

While it was the winter of discontent for Monet and his family, it was love in bloom for Renoir. Around 1867, Renoir met Lise Tréhot, a seamstress who became his model. She served as the model for such works as *Diana* (1867) and *Lise* (1867). The two had become romantically involved. According to some reports, she gave birth to his first child, a daughter named Jeanne, in 1870. Strangely, Renoir never publicly acknowledged his daughter during his lifetime. Renoir submitted *Lise* to the Salon of 1868. It was the portrait of a girl, full length and of life size, in a white dress, with a sunshade in her hand. Duret remarks, "His figures glow with color upon a brightly painted surface full of combinations of tones; they form part of a luminous whole. Lise Trehot was unusual for full length portraits was a convention normally reserved for royalty." [15]

Cézanne was back in Aix as he tried to cope with his own life by fleeing Paris for the remoter reaches of Provence, where memories of a happy childhood remained fresh. [16] Even after his friends departed, he still liked to go walking in the countryside, either alone or with fellow-students at the Aix Art School. These moments provided Cézanne with the relaxation he needed after the shock of Paris noted in a letter to Joseph Huot, a school friend from Aix: "I had expected that the boredom that was overwhelming me would relax its grip once I left Aix. But in fact I have merely changed my domicile, and the boredom has moved with me. I have left my parents, my friends, and my routines behind, but that is all. And yet I am out and about almost all day long. I have seen (I known this sounds naïve) the Louvre, the Luxembourg and Versailles. Of course you are aware what tedious stuff is in those wonderful buildings. It is staggering, extraordinary, overpowering … Just don't' go imagining that I shall become a Parisian." [17]

Cézanne's mental conflicts, the tension of the family situation, his problems with his art, and the upheavals he experienced all seem to culminate in his picture entitled *The Orgy*. "There was a respectable tradition behind this painting of an orgiastic banquet, from Veronese's *Wedding at Cana* to Delacroix's *Death of Sardanapal*; but it also reflects Cézanne's personal need to work crises in his own life (with his father for instance) out of his system." [18]

It was quite evident that Paul was not happy in Paris; he often lamented, "I was wasting my time in every respect." He was an outsider and no doubt due to his maudlin demeanor, was not befriended by the Impressionists. Cézanne, however, returned periodically for short visits to Paris – spending a time equivalent of eight years in the art capital. But, he never felt at ease amongst the other Impressionists or in the demi-monde of the Paris salons. The bare landscape of Provence afforded Cézanne with the sense of calm and tranquility.

Zola was disappointed by Cézanne's growing lack of courage; he himself, after all, had to contend against far greater difficulties. He was scraping by on proceeds of poorly paid, proof reading work. He tried in vain to set Cézanne to work but Cézanne simply dodged his friend's reproaches, and repeatedly changed his lodging, only to return to Zola out of the blue. His wretchedness began again after his departure from Paris and taking a job as clerk in his father's bank. He did not stay long; fitted out a studio at Jas de Bouffant, resumed painting, and thought of his time in Paris. True he was relatively free of financial worry, but the humiliation of having to account to his despotic father for his every move must have been trying.

Like Cézanne, Cassatt's inflated image of the Parisian art world deflated as she saw this world being ruled by sycophants striving to receive recognition. She and her American friend, Eliza Haldeman, decided to leave the artificial environment of the classroom and engage in genre painting in the French countryside. Genre art is characterized by a potpourri of subjects having to do with pleasant scenes of daily life – usually showing peasants and the lower classes. On trips to the countryside, Mary learned to use nature and local villagers as models for her genre paintings.

Mary had not been dragged through the mud by the critics; Manet's record of rejections by the Salons was worse than any of his great contemporaries with the possible exception of Cézanne. But now most of his exhibitions were ignored in what appeared to be a conspiracy of silence. The excitement of 1863 and 1865 may had been a novelty, not to be renewed. Eager for official recognition, he perversely preferred to assault the salons directly rather than join the flanking movement.

Arguably the most important figure in Manet's personal and artistic life as of 1868 was one who could never sit and argue at the tables of the Café Guerbois. A respectable woman did not cross the threshold of cafe establishments, and Berthe Morisot was eminently respectable. Manet did not give lessons but his influence on Morisot was apparent. Duret noted, "Morisot was influenced by a number of artists but came to adopt her own manner of painting in bright tones without the intervention of the traditional shadows. But while her work shows a deviation from Manet, she always preserved her own originality. She had great charm and delicacy of perception. Her painting is refined, free from dryness, which usually mars the work of women artists." [19]

In spring, the attacks against the Impressionist in the French newspapers were becoming a regular event. The infamous spotlight turned again to Manet with critics branding him as a "rebel, unbalanced, uncultured, uninstructed." The press could not find terms forcible enough to express the contempt, which they felt for his pictures and subject matter. But at least Manet could luxuriate in his reputation as the leader of the group of younger artists who clustered around him at the Café Guerbois. Manet had the personal qualities of a chief, to all his contemporaries, he was a "man of spirit, an ardent worker, and an enthusiastic and generous character."

Over a period of twenty-three years, Manet submitted thirty-seven paintings to the Salon and twenty-six were accepted, but most of them were mocked and condemned when exhibited. The conservative Salon juries, extremely reluctant to accept anything different or new, demanded and got variations on a limited range of subjects, treated in a convention manner. To the critics, art was a solemn thing, and involved national pride: epic events, history, religion, nobility, and sentiment. They couldn't grasp what the members of the Batignolle's Group were painting.

Manet "joined one movement, then freed himself of it, then invented another and recommenced to learn painting at the point where anybody else would have continued in his previous manner. He had all the pictorial gifts which make the glory of the masters: full, broad composition, colouring of irresistible power, blacks and greys, which cannot be found elsewhere since Velázquez and Goya, and a profound knowledge of values. He has tried his hand at everything: portraits, landscapes, seascapes, scenes of modern life, still-lifes, and nudes have each in their turn served his ardent desire of creation." [20] "Each time I paint," Manet said to Stéphane Mallarmé, an intimate friend, "I throw myself into the water to learn swimming."

At the beginning of 1868, Manet went to England and had invited Degas to go with him but he declined. In writing Degas from London, Manet said that he " missed the lively conversation at the Café Guerbois. I envy your discussions and being able to debate whether or not it is advisable to put art within the reach of the lower classes by turning out pictures for sixpence apiece."

The year 1868 did not start under too favorable auspices for Monet. It was still about money; he had left his aunt, and there was not even coal for Camille and the baby. He remained depressed and wrote Bazille "…all this is not enough to give me back my former ardor. My painting doesn't go well, and I definitely do not count any more on fame. I'm getting very sunk. To sum up, I've done absolutely nothing since I left you. I've become utterly lazy, everything annoys me as soon as I make up my mind to work; I see everything black. In addition, money is always lacking. Disappointments, insults, hopes, new disappointments – you see, my dear friend. At the exhibition at Le Havre, I sold nothing. I possess a silver medal (worth 15 francs), some splendid reviews in local papers, there you are; it's not much to eat. ... I have sold the Woman in Green [Camille] to Arsene houssaye [inspector of Fine Arts and editor of L'Artiste] …" [21] Houssaye paid 800 francs for Camille.

But by the end of 1868, a rare period of stability occurred for Monet as a result of a portrait commission given by the Baudiberts, a prosperous Le Havre family. Camille and Monet were able to set up home at Etretat. But his highs were once again followed by lows. He submitted *Magpie* to the Palais des Champs-Élysées along with *Fishing Boats at Sea* and both paintings were rejected. Monet was furious. "That fatal rejection has virtually taken the bread out of my mouth."

Monet's submissions aside, the protests and petitions that were launched in the spring of 1867 seemed to have born fruit when the results of the 1868 jury's decisions were made. More than five thousand works of art - paintings, sculptures, engravings, photographs had been submitted, of which more than 83 percent were accepted, including 2,587 paintings. The successful artists included Pissarro, Renoir, and Degas.

By 1868, Degas had become a prominent member of a group of avant-garde artists and was still adding his satirical wit to the discussions at the Café Guerbois. He also fulfilled his youthful promise and had his work accepted by the Salon jury for four years running. *The Misfortunes of the City of Orleans* in 1865, *The Steeplechase* in 1866, *The Bellelli Family* in 1867, and *Mlle. Fiocre in the Ballet* "La Source" in 1868. Ballerinas were favored, "the petticoats of pink or white tulle, the graceful legs covered with flesh-coloured silk, the arms and the shoulders, and the hair crowned with flowers, offer motives of exquisite color and of a tone of living flowers. His colour with its pearly whites, subdued blues and delicate grays, always elevates everything he does and confers upon him a distinctive style." [22] He began to be noticed in the press, and more importantly, his art might have followed a more traditional path but for that chance meeting with Manet in the Louvre in 1862 that made him alter his direction from historical to characteristically contemporary themes.

Degas' work can be divided into several great series: the racecourses, the ballet dancers, and women bathing count among for the most important. In fact, Degas "is one of the most perfect painters of horses who have ever existed. He has caught the most curious and truest actions with infallible sureness of sight. His racecourse scenes are full of vitality and picturesqueness. The dancers go much further still in the expression of Degas' temperament. They have been studied at the foyer of the Opera and at the rehearsal, sometimes in groups, sometimes isolated. Some pictures, which will always count among the masterpieces of the nineteenth century, represent the whole corps de ballet performing on the stage before a dark and empty house. By the feeble light of some lamps the black coats of the stage managers mix themselves with the gauze skirts." [23]

Both Monet's 1869 Salon submissions had been rejected. His allowance was not sufficient for him to support himself, Camille and Jean. He was planning to return to Paris hoping Monsieur Gaudibert, a wealthy Le Havrais and his first patron, would purchase his most recent work. But the following evening before leaving, he was so dejected that he actually flung himself into the Seine. He was too good a swimmer to drown, and he immediately chastised himself for his act of cowardism.

In early 1869 Cézanne also returned to Paris. "His life suddenly took a new turn. His friend the painter Armand Guillaumin, a government clerk who painted pale violet and orange landscapes and sketched brilliantly in charcoal, had a young girl modeling for him. Hortense Fiquet was tall, with black hair, dark eyes and a sallow complexion, a girl from the Jura who had come to Paris with her mother, in search of work. Until now, Cézanne had had something of a love-hate relationship with women, chasing them out of his studio, like Degas, when he could not succeed in transposing their attractions into his work. … Hortense was born in Saligny, but she arrived in Paris as a small child. Her father, probably a bank clerk, had abandoned the family and Hortense made her living sewing handmade books and on occasion by modeling. Her mother had died just before she met Cézanne, so she was very much alone in the world." [24] Childlike and inexperienced, Hortense was barely nineteen and Cezanne was thirty.

Chapter Nine: Bismarck Strikes

It's hard to imagine the medieval city of Paris with its dung-smelling, sewer-less streets lined with high buildings casting deep shadows over narrow-winding cobblestone or mud-packed roads. "Much of Paris in the 1830s still had filthy, foul-smelling streets running every which way. Ancient stone buildings, some black with centuries of smoke and soot, crowded on all sides. Wagons and drays and shouting vendors with pushcarts clogged the way. People could be seen living in the most wretched squalor. And, yet, there were the famous bridges on the Seine, the gardens and palaces and the gilded dome of the Invalides amongst the appalling poverty." [1]

Galignani's Paris Guide, 1827, directed tourists to the Royal arrondissements that contained the Palais Royal, the Louvre, the Palace and Garden of the Tuileries. Tourists were cautioned about the Pays Latin, the Latin Quarter, on the Rive Gauche. The intrepid tourist who traveled here would have encountered the ancient College of the Sorbonne, École de Medecine and several major hospitals as well. There were students everywhere. The University moved from the Notre Dame area to the left bank and the hillside was covered with dingy wooden structures, shacks really, where the students lived. The *Paris Guide* warned tourists of the horrendous conditions; the streets were unpaved and the gutters were filled with sludge flowing down the middle of the street. James Fennimore Cooper having lived in the city for some years, still struggled to adjust to the "dirt and gilding … bedbugs and laces." [2]

"Jardin des Tuileries was once a clay quarry for tiles (tuiles, hence the name Tuileries) – the garden was initially created in 1564, for Catherine de Medici in front of her palace to remind her of her native Tuscany." [3] Those visiting Paris know that navigating around the city meant encountering vast distances between the hallowed tourist sights. Aching arches were a common plight after a day of seeing the city now and then. However, in the 1850s if walking became too much, there were "streamlined omnibuses," which were actually giant horse-drawn public conveyances that went to all parts of the city.

What we see today as we walk down the large boulevards flanked by elm trees is vastly different than the Paris of 1850; credit for this transformation is given to the Prefect of the Seine Georges-Eugene Haussmann. His renovations began in 1853 and lasted until 1870. Napoleon III actually spearheaded much of the transformation of Paris. Pointing to a large map of Paris and with Haussmann looking on, Napoleon criss-crossed Paris proper with lines drawn in four colors. Zola commented that Paris appeared as if it had been "cut up with an axe." Nevertheless, these were the new streets Napoleon wanted created. The different colors indicated the level of urgency for the various projects. Haussmann would work singled handedly answering only to the Emperor.

As the construction continued, some saw the destruction of cultural Paris. Entire blocks were being demolished and along with them the old charm of Paris was demolished as well. The twisted and narrow lanes were now replaced by less picturesque streets lain out in geometrically straight lines. Entire communities of humble craftsmen and workers had been driven out of the capital, and they had taken with them the village atmosphere. Haussmann tore down twelve thousand buildings and replaced more than three hundred miles of twisted alleyways and haphazard streets with eighty-five miles of wide thoroughfares. Napoleon asked for wide boulevards not for aesthetic reasons but he reasoned it would be more difficult for the ever-revolutionary Parisians to build barricades on these wider streets.

"Houses were razed, whole streets were suppressed, hills were leveled, roads cut and paved, and row upon row of apartment buildings were erected, imposing patterns of modernity that are still very much in evidence. There was now an extensive network of long, tree-lined streets – the ubiquitous boulevards; there were four new bridges and two reconstructed, 27,500 houses were pulled down in the Department of the Seine, and over 102,500 were built or rebuilt, and there were new public squares and parks." [4]

"In 1848 Paris had only forty-seven acres of Municipal Park mostly along the Champs-Elysées, plus private gardens open to the public on certain days, the Tuileries, the Luxembourg Gardens, and the Jardin des Plantes." [5] These were all turned over to the public and new parks, squares, and gardens were created, totaling, by 1870, 4,500 acres. Haussmann envisioned a network of large squares and crossroads around the centre, a sewer system, many parks, gardens and other innovations. He succeeded in implementing most of his projects.

Haussmann remained in power for seventeen years when the Parisians and Napoleon had enough. His great power had once earned monikers like "Haussmann the First" and "Vice Emperor." Now Haussmann was under increasing attack for the ruthlessness of his projects. He was finally dismissed by Napoleon in January 1870. Urbanization happens to most cities; it often becomes synonymous with renewal and regulation. The wide boulevards made logical sense with their convenience. Along with urbanization were demarcations or special zones; in Paris, the rich were concentrated in the west of Paris, and the poor were more evident to the east. These divisions were sharpening. While most peasants ate to appease their hunger, the wealthy French now dined to gratify their souls in beautiful cafes on tree-lined boulevards serving palate-pleasing entrés - so stark in contrast to pitiful men, women, and children with begging eyes. On the surface, Paris was glittery and gold.

The effects of the reconstruction plan went far beyond the physical appearance of the Parisian streets. This "new" Paris, this altered one, with its festive cafes and restaurants, hidden squares and quays, theaters existed along with the more humble patronizing less haute bourgeoisie districts of rag-pickers and absinthe-drinking souls. Both these sides of the streets were painted by Manet, Monet, Degas, Renoir, and Cézanne – the renovated Paris with images of women in fashionable millinery stores, men at the racetrack, petite rats de l'Opéra de Paris and the repercussions of Haussmann's renovations – displaced rag pickers and the shop girls. This changing face of Paris unfolded during the changing face of art. This contemporary history and its evident subtleties had its impact on the lives and art of all the Impressionists.

The renovations impacted Degas and his work on two levels. The first relates to his painting of historic subject matter. Degas saw historic paintings as a challenge and, like Paris, he wanted to modernize the field. In his words, "the flame of contemporary life could illuminate the ancient past." In *Semiramis Building Babylon*, Degas achieved a fresh solution to a historical subject. The scene of the painting is Semiramis accompanied by various warriors, standing on a terrace, surveying the construction of Babylon, the city she founded on the river Euphrates. The painting is inspired with new color, subjects, and modes of execution. On the second level, interestingly, this painting is also an implicit criticism of contemporary town planning. "Degas' Babylon, with its borrowings of Italian architecture, stood in direct opposition to the sweeping modernization plans of Baron Haussmann in Paris, where entire historic quarters were demolished to make room for large boulevards and modern tenement buildings." [6]

Despite the discontinuation of vast renewal projects, the 1870s witnessed a flurry of activity in all areas. The Batignolle Group would be busy organizing artistic exhibitions, engaging in highly diverse artistic output, creating numerous technical innovations and, simply falling in love.

Berthe Morisot was now in her late twenties/early thirties, and Manet had became obsessed with her striking beauty, magnetic presence and elegance that he less than modestly felt perfectly matched his own. Manet expressed his love for her, and revealed that love in a series of eleven portraits. These emotionally charged portraits are arguably among Manet's greatest works. The sheer number and beauty of these portraits naturally arouses one's curiosity about the intimate relations of Manet and Morisot. She was certainly in love with him. But that could not be. She married his brother and most likely Édouard encouraged the marriage to bring her into the family and maintain their close connection. [7]

Despite her marriage Berthe continued to paint and was now tackling a subject that had been previously explored by both Monet and Renoir. The subject was a contemporary woman in a park, enjoying a leisure activity; the painting was entitled *Reading* or *La Lecture*. Featured in the painting are Morisot's sister Edma and her mother. When Berthe completed *Reading* in March 1870, she asked Manet's opinion of it. Instead of telling her what had to be done, he grabbed a paintbrush and began to retouch it. It appears that he got quite carried away and tried to make her work his own. Morisot recalled, "Manet found it very good, except for the lower part of the [mother's black] dress. He took the brushes and put in a few accents that looked very well; mother was in ecstasy. That is where my misfortunes began. Once started, nothing could stop him; from the skirt he went to the bust, from the bust to the head, from the head to the background. He cracked a thousand jokes, laughed like a madman, handed me the palette back; finally by five o'clock in the afternoon, we had made the prettiest caricature that was ever seen. … and now I am left confounded. My only hope is that I shall be rejected… Though terribly upset, she was unable to protest and when Manet insisted, she entered it in the Salon." [8] It was accepted.

Manet had sent two paintings to an exhibition sponsored by the *Cercle de l'Union Artistique*, which opened on 18 February 1870 on the Place Vendôme. Duranty, writing in such journals as the *Review of Paris*, *Paris-Newspaper*, *Gazette of Fine Arts* and others, had written just one very brief sentence about the two paintings Manet had submitted: "Monsieur Manet has exhibited a philosopher trampling over oyster shells and a watercolor of Christ supported by angels."

Credit: Portrait of the Artist's Mother and Sister, 1869-70 (oil on canvas), Morisot, Berthe (1841-95) / National Gallery of Art, Washington DC, USA / The Bridgeman Art Library

This casual insolence from a friend seems to have been too much for Manet. Encountering Duranty a day or two later in the Café Guerbois, Manet struck him in the face and loudly demanded satisfaction. Things escalated very quickly. Seconds were quickly assembled, with Zola agreeing to represent Manet. The duel was set for four days later, at eleven o'clock in the morning on 23 February, in the wild privacy of the Forest of Saint-Germaine. It is quite miraculous that Duranty and other critics had not been marched before this to the woods in hopes of painters finding satisfaction. According to the police report: "There was only one engagement, but this was so violent that both epees were damaged. Monsieur Duranty was slightly wounded above the right breast when his opponent's epee glanced off a rib. In consequence of the wound, the seconds decided that honour was satisfied and that there was no point in continuing the duel." [9]

Paul Alexis, an habitué of the Café Guerbois, phrased the situation in a slightly comic way and suggested that both parties were "completely ignorant of the art of fencing … Manet and Duranty threw themselves upon each other with such savage bravery that, when the four astonished seconds had separated them … their swords appeared to have been turned into a pair of corkscrews. Manet informed Suzanne that he had "run his sword through the wag's shoulder," while Duranty boasted in a letter, "I would have killed him if my sword had been straight." [10] That very evening they had become the best friends in the world again and were sipping their absinthe at the Café Guerbois; this evening the talks had turned to politics.

Napoleon III, ruling the Second Republic of France was, by most accounts, less than a prepossessing character. He was described as "a ringmaster who has been sacked for getting drunk;" he had the appearance of a "melancholy parrot;" " he was vulgar-looking without the slightest resemblance, except for height, to his imperial Uncle." [11] Napoleon was made emperor in 1852 after a long, hard climb up a rather rocky slope. Twice he tried to overthrow the government and twice he failed. The throne, regarded Napoleon, was his birthright. His first attempt in 1836 resulted in his being exiled to America. In August 1840, Louis-Napoleon made a second attempt. He and his band of fifty-six conspirators – this included many of his royal staff, butlers and such - chartered a Thames pleasure boat from London where he had been living in Carlton Gardens. They made way for France with his nine horses, two carriages, and several crates of wine. Napoleon was forced to land at Boulogne-sur-Mere where he beat a hasty retreat. Apparently his presence on French soil had failed to incite a popular uprising against the king. Upon his return, his landing craft capsized in the Channel, the invasion ended with Louis-Napoleon clinging to a buoy and awaiting rescue. [12]

The water-sogged would-be emperor was arrested. The second-attempt was just too much for the French government; losing its patience, Napoleon was, in 1840, sentenced to life imprisonment at Ham – a medieval chateau in northern France. Napoleon III never lost faith that he would rule France. He spent his time reading volumes on politics, history, and economics. He referred to this time as being spent at the "University of Ham." After six long years, he escaped from Ham in 1846. The prison was undergoing several repairs; Napoleon donned a workman's uniform and simply walked out the front gate.

Soon his destiny drew nigh and in 1848 the "Year of Revolution," King Louis-Phillippe abdicated his throne, as his Bonapartist rival crossed the Channel to France. In December, the former

President of the Second Republic, found himself enjoying the splendors of the Élysée Palace. Four years later, he increased his powers in a bloody *coup de'etat*. And one year later, on 2 December 1852, he proclaimed himself Emperor Napoleon III. His reign lasted almost eighteen years; his fall from power was quick and ignominious.

At present, Napoleon had grave concerns. In the autumn of 1868, a military coup had disposed the queen of Spain, and a new head was being sought for the crown. The leading contender was a cousin of Wilhelm I, King of Prussia. His chancellor, Otto von Bismarck, felt that a member of Wilhelm's family on the Spanish throne would provide a bulwark against any future war with its powerful rival, France. If that were to pass the French army, preoccupied with defending its border with Spain, would be unable to throw its weight against Prussia. The French government rightly feared that Spain and the Germans could easily form a pact of "blood and iron" and thereby isolate or at least threaten France on two sides. This made the threat of Prussia's power more real, since France, geographically linked to Prussia in the northeast and Spain in the south, would thus effectively be encircled by Prussian powers.

Unbeknownst to King Wilhelm I, Bismarck was flexing his power and began actively supporting the king's cousin. When Queen Victoria and Napoleon III heard of this, they expressed their disapproval. Wilhelm obliged their concerns and intervened against his cousin's acceptance. The candidate withdrew to the Kaiser's great relief. Napoleon, however, wanted more. He requested some kind of guarantee that Wilhelm would publicly oppose any renewal of his cousin's candidacy. Wilhelm refused. Chronicling these events, Bismarck sent to the newspaper his famous "Ems telegram," making public on 13 July, an awkward but secret negotiation between France and Germany and was written in language that was guaranteed to infuriate Napoleon. And it did. France's honor was at stake. Was France ready for war? It appeared that Napoleon and his court was more concerned with setting an example of splendor. It was a court devoted to extravagance in jewelry and lavish gowns embroidered with satin and silk. Be that as it may - on 15 July, the French army was mobilized; four days later they declared war against the powerful Prussian fighting machine.

Political events between the years 1870-1871 were turbulent ones for Paris, and the Franco-Prussian war would leave Paris besieged and defeated. Its National Guard consisted of an armed militia of Parisian citizens; it was hastily expanded from twenty-four thousand to ninety thousand and then, through compulsory registration to three hundred and fifty thousand. The guard was poorly organized; the men were poorly trained and paid a paltry sum of 1.50 francs a day. Under these conditions, France could not possibly defeat the Prussian army.

Manet's patriotism was stronger than his dislike and distrust of the government, and he felt obliged to defend his country. At the outbreak of the war he volunteered as an artillery lieutenant in the National Guard, and signed up as a gunner. Manet was intensely patriotic and was disheartened by Zola's desertion to Marseilles. Manet had no intention of deserting his country. Manet was also aware that Paris could soon become dangerous; he sent his mother, Suzanne and Leon to Oloron-Saint-Maried well out of range of any action. He tried to persuade the Morisot women to go as well but to no avail.

Manet's commanding office was Colonel Meissonier, seventeen years his senior. Since they were placed at the two opposite poles in the world of art, it seemed natural that they had never before had any dealings with each other. But surely, each knew of one another. Meissonier was frequently a member of the Salon juries and at the very least he must have known Manet as the creator of the most controversial works ever painted since Delacroix. Now, however, military service suddenly brought them together, and the struggling young artist found himself placed under the orders of the older painter, who not only outranked Manet but was then at the height of his art career. Colonel Meissonier had not deigned to acknowledge Lieutenant Manet as a fellow artist, and his attitude towards Manet was that of "formal politeness." Meissonier avoided any approach towards friendliness. Manet sensitive to matters of etiquette was quite hurt at Meissonier's treatment of him and never forgot it.

Due to the outbreak of the Franco-Prussian war, the Cassatt family returned to Philadelphia. Upon returning home, Mary did place a few paintings in a New York gallery, where she gathered a score of admirers, but no purchasers. In 1871, dejected Mary wrote, "I have given up my studio & torn up my father's portrait, & have not touched a brush for six weeks nor ever will again until I see some prospect of getting back to Europe." Mary's parents made it clear that they would not subsidize the expenses of her art. Even though they were relatively well off and would support her in their comfortable home, they refused to spend any money on her studio, models, art supplies or trips to Paris.

Thus, she was overjoyed to receive great news from the Archbishop of Pittsburg, who commissioned her to paint two of Correggio's paintings. He advanced her enough money to travel to Parma, Italy. This, perhaps, was the shot of adrenalin that she needed, "O how wild I am to get to work, my fingers fairly itch & my eyes water to see a fine picture again." [13] Six months after arriving in Parma, she was hailed as one of the best artists working in the city. Her friend, Emily Sartain wrote to her family back home "All Parma is talking of Miss Cassatt… and everyone is anxious to know her – the compliments she receives are overwhelming." Upon completing her commission, and with the money she earned, she traveled and studied in Spain, Belgium, and Rome, eventually settling permanently in Paris. By virtue of her wit, talent, and charm, Mary gained entrée into the inner circles of the French intellectuals – normally closed to aliens. She chose the life of an expatriate because she craved the cultural values of the French.

"Degas like other citizens volunteered for the National Guard. He was posted to defend a fortification north of Bois de Vincennes on the outskirts of Paris, under the command of his friend Henri Rouart." [14] Degas must have derived consolation in finding that Henri Rouart, his old school friend with whom he had lost touch, commanded his section. Eager to serve his country, he complained that he had not yet heard a cannon going off. "He is looking for an opportunity to hear that sound because he wants to know whether he can endure the detonations," Mme. Morisot wrote. [15] Degas originally joined the infantry but after discovering that he couldn't see the rifle target was sent to artillery. He finally became a gunner in the ring of fortifications that circled Paris. Degas, secure in his fort and with no taste for military duties, could draw, read, and enjoy the autumn silence. His Italian biographer related that as food became scarce "he often had to return to his father's house to satisfy his hunger with sewer rats which could be bought."

"The cold affected Degas, who was compelled to sleep in a hut with a leaking roof, and as a result he claimed that his eyesight worsened. He was not the only artist to have suffered, Gustave Moreau contacted rheumatism, which continued to trouble him for the rest of his life." [16] Fellow painter Henri Hertz claimed that Degas used to pay a daily visit to the field hospital established near the Etoile, where he would give the patients news of his part of the city and Degas was much esteemed for his sympathy for the wounded.

Monet had missed the duel between Manet and Duranty as he was living in London. After the outbreak of the Franco-Prussian War, Monet took refuge in England in September 1870. To avoid the conflict and possible military service, since he had been placed in the reserves at the time of his marriage, Monet received a passport on 5 September 1870 and left France for England, settling in London until May 1871. It was there that he was introduced to Paul Durand-Ruel, who temporarily moved his gallery to London because of the Franco-Prussian War. Monet recalled, "Without Durand we would have starved like all Impressionists. We owe him everything … He risked everything more than once to support us." [17]

While in London, he studied the works of John Constable and Joseph Mallord William Turner, both of whose landscapes would serve to inspire Monet's innovations in the study of color. At that time Monet became interested in the paintings of William Turner in London museums. Turner's influence on Monet remained noticeable, especially in some later "more vividly chromatic paintings of the Thames," which he made during his later visits to London in the 1890's and 1900's. Turner was the most original and imaginative figure in the history of English landscape painting. Michael Bockemuhl in his biography noted that Turner's painting style changed over the years from accurate, topographical watercolors; after visiting Italy, his landscapes were more classical and serene. His next works were more powerful as he tried to capture the violence of storms and raging blizzards.

In the spring of 1871, Pissarro joined Monet in England; each seemed quite happy to find each other and began to meet frequently. Camille Pissarro and Claude Monet were both dedicated socialists who hated the Second Empire. But their time in London was spent furthering their knowledge of art. Pissarro later remembered: "Monet and I were very enthusiastic over the London landscape. Monet worked in the parks, whilst I, living at lower Norwood, at that time a charming suburb, studied the effect of fog, snow and springtime. We worked from nature. … We also visited the museums. The watercolors and paintings of Turner and of Constable have certainly had influence on us. … we were struck chiefly by the landscape painters who shared more in our aim with regard to plein air, light, and fugitive effects." [18]

Renoir, Cézanne and Bazille were all eligible to fight. Bazille joined the infantry and was killed during the Battle of Beaune-la-Rolande on 28 November 1870. He died a hero's death by taking command of his unit after his commanding officer was killed. Renoir had previously been exempted from military service, but he nevertheless had to report to the recruiting office, where he was found fit for duty. Though profoundly a pacifist and terrified of gunfire, he was offered a place on the staff of General du Barrail.

Cézanne was a draft dodger; he packed up a few things and tramped over the hills to L'Estaque and there he remained for the duration of the war. The authorities were looking for Cézanne but the investigation was not being carried out with any particular vigor or earnestness and was abandoned when a search of Cézannes' property the Jas de Bouffan yielded nothing. After the war, in the latter part of 1871, when Paris had cooled, Cézanne returned and would find an apartment for himself in the Fifth Arrondissment.

During the war, Cézanne began painting self-portraits and over a period of some forty years, he painted twenty-six self-portraits. Rembrandt also had a lifelong preoccupation with self-portraiture, characterized as a necessary "process of identity formation." Perhaps it was just easier for Cézanne to be his own model for his relations with other models was less than stellar. The sitter for one of his portrait paintings, *Portrait of Antony Valabrègue*, was a friend from Aix. "Paul is a horrible painter as regards the poses he gives people in the midst of his riots of color," wrote Valabrègue. "Every time he paints one of his friends it seems as though he were revenging himself on him for some hidden injury." [19] The jurors at the Salon recoiled at the sight of this painting, prompting Paul to write to a member of the jury explaining that he could not accept "the illegitimate judgment of colleagues whom I myself have not commissioned to appraise me." At least Cézanne's father, Louis-Auguste, was enjoying some success. He had some 470 men and 240 women in his employ in hat making, and many more in associated activities, the most important of which was rabbit farming. Hat-making was heavily dependent on rabbit farming; the skin made the felt.

Paul's art was successfully evolving, in part, through a mutually helpful association with Pissarro. The two had been painting outside Paris at Auvers, and Cézanne was assimilating the principles of color and lighting while loosening up his brushwork; yet he retained his own sense of mass and the interaction of planes, as in *House of the Hanged Man* (1873; Musee d'Orsay, Paris).

On 2 September, the head of Napoleon's troops suffered a disastrous defeat at Sedan in Northern France about six miles from the Belgium border. The main French army was forced to capitulate and the emperor himself was taken prisoner and an army of eighty-three thousand men surrendered. Krupp's cannons then rumbled towards Paris, not as an exhibition piece, but for the purpose of bombardment and siege. The Germans bombarded Paris, gradually starving the city as it endured the bitterest winter in living memory. Not all the Germans had left before the city was cut off, but most, more than 20,000 had departed in safety, thanks to numerous French officials and those who ran the railroad.

With the ground frozen as hard as granite to a depth of a foot and a half, the Prussians were able to bring up the biggest of their Krupp cannons, and on 5 January 1871, the 109th day of the siege, they commenced bombardment of Paris itself. Four days of continuing fog, rumors, and bombardment followed. Elihu Washburne, the United States Minister to France, wrote, "The first blood has been shed and not a person can tell what a half starved … Parisian population will do." [20]

Manet was preparing for the worst; writing to a friend, Eva Gonzales, "I think we poor Parisians are going to be caught up in a terrible drama." And he was right. Women queued for food in pouring rain, and smallpox had begun to spread. Mules and horses were being eaten. Supplies of salt had run out and children were dying of scurvy. Gas supplies were short and had been cut off in all public buildings. Paris was strewn with the wounded who were dying of septicemia, often complicated by gangrene. Three or four hundred shells a day rained down on the streets of the city.

Manet's September letters were almost wholly given over to the Siege of Paris (19 September 1870 – 28 January 1871) and news of the attacks: "… on the 14th the bridges were blown up; on the 21st Paris was hit by twenty-five thousand shells and fires were raging all over the city; on the 24th people were getting used to the incessant shelling and, in response to Bismarck's outrageous demand of surrender, were determined to hold out; by the 30th *café au lait* was a memory, as were eggs and cheese; what little milk there was went to the young and the sick; butcher shops were open only three times a week and were cleaned out before the last in line was served, the first having arrived at four in the morning." To protect himself, Manet concocted a bulletproof vest made of two hundred sheets of tissue paper, and he tried to buy revolvers, at the rate of one hundred francs apiece. The city was being well fortified, and as of five in the morning those not on duty were out in the streets training to become 'real soldiers.'" [21] By mid October the streets were empty after ten pm. The Café Guerbois closed at 9:30. A week later smallpox broke out in this district.

Paris fought bravely on, but not for much longer. Food shortages became acute. Cats began to disappear; dogs' heads were sold at the butcher. Families were tempted by rat pie. "Paris had become an armed camp. There were soldiers everywhere encamped all about the Arc d Triomphe and down the Champ-Elysées – more than 300,000 … Streets and avenues were filled with tents, baggage wagons, and horses. The Tuileries Garden had become an artillery park." [22]

With the passage of days the toll of disease – and especially of smallpox - mounted steadily. "By the eighth week, 419 would die of the disease. After nearly two months of siege, the gas that made Paris the City of Light finally gave out, along with the food and firewood. An order appeared that instead of only one in three street lamps lighted at night, it would now be one in six." [23]

The cold winter had arrived. Elihu Washburne wrote in his diary: "December 3 - 77th day of the Siege … there has been no fighting at all anywhere today. There was a very light snow last night and this evening it rains a little. The suffering of the troops on both sides must have been fearful these last days. The French are without blankets and with but little to eat, half-frozen, half-starved, and raw troops at that … I have just come from the American ambulance where I saw a poor captain of the regular army breathing his last and his last moments were being soothed by some of our American ladies who are devoting themselves to the sick and dying." [24]

The Germans fired some 12,000 shells into the city over twenty-three days in order to break Parisian morale. It had "little effect on the spirit of resistance in Paris." [25] Bismarck ordered the city to be bombarded with heavy caliber Krupp siege guns. This prompted the city's surrender on 28 January 1871. In January, after a four-month siege of the capital, the interim French government had to sign a humiliating armistice with the new German empire. The surrender of Paris, and the end of the war was announced on the morning of the 131st day of the siege. In January 1871 the moderate republican government on National Defense sought an armistice with the German Empire.

The Germans did not enter the city for several days. For France it had been the most ill advised, disastrous war in history with total defeat coming in little more than five months. Paris sustained more damage in the 1870–1871 siege than in any other conflict. The cost to France in young men killed and wounded in battle was 150 thousand. For the German Empire it was 117 thousand, death toll in Paris 65,591. France was subjected to a staggering war indemnity of five billion francs and forced to cede to Germany the provinces of Alsace and Lorraine, a point of extreme humiliation to the French that was only to fester.

In a victory parade, the German army marched into Paris and down the Champs-Elysées on 17 February 1871. "The city looked as if closed for a funeral. Shops and restaurants along the path were shut tight. No omnibuses or carriages were to be seen. Early afternoon, the Royal Guards of Prussia with glittering bayonets, surrounded the Arc de Triomphe. Then came the main body of the army marching by for two hours." [26] On the third of March, after an occupation of 48 hours, the conquerors marched away.

Chapter Ten: Is Paris Burning?

The Siege of Paris resulted in Prussian forces defeating the French, which helped to establish the German Empire and to create conditions for setting up the Paris Commune. After the armistice on 28 January the National Assembly elected a moderate leader, Adolphe Thiers. On 8 February 1871 the government's National Assembly was formed with Adolphe Thiers elected Head of Executive Power. The Assembly was a monarchist majority elected by rural France against the republican spirit of the metropolis, and it therefore alienated the working people of Paris immediately. Further alienation occurred when Thiers wanted to disarm the populace. He ordered the army on 18 March to remove cannons from the northern districts. This provoked a spontaneous uprising. Rioters in Montmartre refused to surrender their weapons to French troops; they seized and hanged the two generals commanding them. The violence that began at Montmartre marked the start of the insurrection that became known as the Paris Commune.

Renoir was back in Paris on 18 March 1871, when the insurrection broke out, and found himself threatened with compulsory enrollment decreed by the Commune. Soon, the government's leaders abandoned the city for Versailles. In charge were a radical mix of Marxists, Socialists, and old-style Republicans who formed a loose federation in Paris known as the Commune. Each was angered at what they regarded as betrayal and incompetence; this radical government took over the city. Renoir decided to leave Paris. Unable to join his mother in nearby Louveciennes, all exits from the city being blocked by federal guards, he remembered previously meeting the Police Commissioner of the revolutionary government. He had no difficulty obtaining a pass to leave the capital, which he did along with 700,000 others, mostly better-off Parisians, who ceased to support the Commune. The Commune became an increasingly working-class regime.

The Paris Commune was now in charge of Paris. Thousands of Les Amis de l'Ordre marched toward the National Guard, which stood ready at the Place Vendôme to stop them. Someone opened fire; from which side was never determined. Instantly the street was filled with gunfire and screaming and a dozen or so were dead. Elihu Washburne wrote that the situation was already worse by far than during the siege. In a city of two million people there was "no law, no protection, no authority, except that of an unorganized mob. On 28 March with great to-do the Commune officially installed itself at the Hotel de Ville. Military bands played. Red flags flew everywhere and the crown exceeded one-hundred thousand people." [1]

The new French government responded to this new crisis by laying siege to Paris for four months, shelling the city's fortifications and working class districts and cutting off the city from food and supplies. The roar of cannon fire was heard again, exactly as during the German siege, except this time it was the French firing on the French.

"Paris is on fire!" This was beyond any description. Communards, defending their "workers' republic," torched all the symbols of authoritarian order – the administrative center of the municipality of Paris, and many "records of every kind, birth, marriage, and death certificates, police records, went up in flames." Paris was burning … flames raged through the night. The

Hotel de Ville had been set on fire, along with the Palais Justice and the Prefecture of Police. After nearly a month of no rain everything was a tinderbox.

"A vast column of smoke covered Paris; at night an eerily luminous red cloud hung over everything, like a volcanic eruption. Still the shooting went on. The Tuileries was reduced to ashes; the Louvre survived." [2]

Mme Morisot described the condition of the city: "Paris in flames is beyond imagining ... Bits of charred paper and other still legible fragments wafted in the wind all day long, a column of smoke covered Paris; at night a red glow, horrible to see, looked like an erupting volcano ... It is said that the insurrection is over, but the firing continues without interruption." [3]

The Paris commune lasted just seventy-two days but it had a great many victims and consequences. There were food riots and widespread unemployment. Thousands of demobilized soldiers wandered the streets in search of food and shelter and most of them were living on the one franc 50 centimes daily pay of the National Guard. The first acts of the Assembly abolished this payment. The workers were incensed. The government had starved them, surrendered their country, and now seemed to be about to ruin them. Manet lamented, 'Doddering old fools, not excepting that little twit Thiers who I hope will drop dead one day in the middle of a speech and rid us of his wizened little person.' " [4]

The nearer the end came, the more the atrocities accelerated. Forty thousand prisoners, divided into lines of seven or eight and tied to one another by their wrist with string, were marched to Versailles to be sentenced to death by the government. Paris was badly damaged (the most famous loss was the Palace of the Tuileries), thousands of communards were executed without trial, and the political and psychological scars that resulted were palpable for decades.

When the Commune finally fell, French troops marched into working class districts. Reprisals began in earnest. Association with the Commune was a political crime, punishable by death. In one week, 21 May to 28 May 1871, Parisians saw an apocalyptic week of bloodshed and violence known as *La Semaine Sanglante* - "Bloody Week." Some Communards were brutally slain at what is now known as the Communards' Wall in Pere Lachaise Cemetery. Somewhere between 5,700 to 7,400 Parisian men, women, and children were massacred. Thousands more were jailed or exiled - their property confiscated. Paris was in a state of devastation. "There never was such a hell upon this earth as this very Paris."

The Siege of Paris and the Commune created such an upheaval in the national life that it was impossible to hold the Salon in 1871. But when peace had been restored at home and abroad, a spirit of emulation, a kind of ardor for work, seized hold of the people, and they returned to their several occupations with a sense of the necessity of overcoming the recent disasters.

It was now more than ten years since most of the group had arrived in Paris and signed up at Suisse and Gleyre's studios. At the beginning of 1872, there was no secure prospect of regular purchasers or dealers; the group seemed more likely to disperse than to consolidate but things were about to change. Manet asked Alfred Stevens to help him to dispose of some of his pictures and with this object he sent him a still life piece and a seascape. Stevens showed them to M. Durand-

Ruel, a dealer who was just beginning to buy the works of the new school.

 M. Durand-Ruel did just what Zola had spoken of doing - buying up everything Manet had. Durand-Ruel bought twenty-three canvases for which he paid a rather large sum - a total of thirty-five thousand francs. A short while later he bought sixteen thousand francs worth of paintings. By 15 February, Manet had received fifteen thousand francs on account. The next afternoon, he was in the Café Guerbois, "Do you know of a painter who can't make 50,000 francs a year from his pictures?" "You," came the reply. "Well, you're wrong," said Manet. [5] He had just sold over 50,000 gold francs worth in a single week. Théodore Duret noted, "It was only after he had passed through long years of pecuniary sacrifices and financial strain that his perseverance and courage in hazarding his capital at last received just reward." He would not have cash in hand, however, as Durand-Ruel always paid artists in installments. Following the same practice with other members of the school, he assured their survival while at the same time preparing enormous profits for himself. Durand-Ruel did more than purchase Impressionist paintings, he "worked to hasten and further it, holding exhibitions and sponsoring art journals devoted to publicizing new styles - educating a new audience rather than simply satisfying the tastes of an already existing market." [6]

 It seemed as if the tide had turned at last and the dark days of struggle were over. Such hopes, however, proved illusory. "Durand-Ruel had dead stock and even made many enemies of connoisseurs, picture dealers, critics and even the press took up arms against him. Astutely, he chose to move forward and to make further purchases and thus, in acting as paymaster to Manet and his friends, to take a part in the fight that they were waging for recognition. Monet benefited from Durand-Ruel's decision; of the 12,000 francs he earned in 1872 for the sale of thirty-eight paintings, 9,800 francs (for 29 paintings) were through Durand-Ruel." [7]

Renoir had managed to escape to Louveciennes, not far from the capital, to which his parents had moved. In June, after the end of the civic upheaval, Renoir returned to the city. Sadly, one of Renoir's friends Realist painter Courbet, one of the leaders of the Commune had been condemned for his participation in the Commune and for the destruction of the Vendôme Column. Although Renoir first started exhibiting paintings at the Paris Salon in 1864, recognition would not come for another ten years, due in part, to the turmoil of the Franco-Prussian War. Toward the end of 1871, almost all the friends were back in Paris or its vicinity and began again to meet at the Café Guerbois. Slowly after the war, the artistic and intellectual life of Paris began once again to resume.

When Jean Frédéric Bazille died in battle, Renoir was literally homeless. In 1871, however, Renoir was introduced to Captain Paul Darras who asked him to paint portraits of himself and his wife Henriette. With the money, Renoir was able to rent his first studio on the right bank near the Louvre and south of the Café Guerbois. Theodore Duret, whom Renoir had met at the Café Guerbois, and the dealer Paul Durand-Ruel, whom Monet introduced to Renoir early in 1872, were to have a later and strong influence on Renoir's career.

In May 1871 Monet left London to live in Zaandam, a town in the Netherlands, in the province of North Holland, where he made twenty-five paintings. He also paid a first visit to nearby Amsterdam. In October or November 1871 he returned to France. Monet took a studio shortly thereafter and not far away from Renoir. Camille and Monet were married in June of 1870.

It was not until after the war that Cézanne began consistently to concentrate on landscape paintings. He particularly liked painting views of L'Estaque, a small township near Marseille; one such painting was *Le'Estague under Snow*. According to biographer Hajo Düchting these pictures "lack the serene charm of Impressionist paintings by Sisley, Renoir or Pissarro. The colors are muted, light and dark are strongly contrasted, and the unsophisticated scenes, which may seem calm, are nevertheless turbulent and dramatic. There are no people in them, yet a certain tension implies that something terrible is about to happen. When Cézanne opted for the country, and landscapes, his decision was fundamentally the result of an inner development connected with the frustrations of Paris and his sense of rejection both as an artist and as human being." [8]

In the fall of 1871 Monet returned from England and settled in Argenteuil near Paris. While Monet was not terribly productive in England, his visit did impact his career on several levels. He met other important people, Daubigny and Pissarro, and visited museums enabling him to view the work of artists that were poorly represented in France, such as J.M.W. Turner. Moreover, his visit to England provided him with an economic windfall for Daubigny introduced him to the Parisian dealer Paul Durand-Ruel. Daubigny insisted that the dealer purchase works from this up-and-coming artist.

Monet was quite happy in Argenteuil, a small village on the Seine, and here he painted some of his best-known works. Argenteuil, about four miles downriver fromVilleneuve, was so closely identified with Monet that it derived much of its subsequent recognition from his pictures. He had settled there at the end of 1871, not long after his return from England, to avoid the Franco-Prussian War, and then to Holland, where he sat out the Commune and its aftermath.

Argenteuil offered all the advantages of a suburb but its main attraction for the painters was the broad river with sailing boats and picturesque bridges. "Monet had rented a little house close to the water, and whenever Renoir came to stay with him they put up their easels with the same views, studying the same motifs. They both now adopted a comma-like brushstroke, even smaller than the one they had chosen for their earlier works, a brushstroke that permitted them to record every nuance they observed. The surfaces of their canvases were covered with small dots and strokes none of which by themselves defined any form." [9] Out of 175 surviving paintings that Monet did at Argenteuil, 75, by far the largest single category, are devoted to the boat basin adjacent to the highway bridge.

Monet had worked directly from nature. He had fitted up a boat while he was living at Argenteuil in order that he could paint his views of the Seine at his ease. He had arranged it on a special plan, with a little cabin in the stern, where he could shelter when it rained, and a tent in the bow. Although he never mentioned the fact, it seems possible that Monet was helped in the construction of this boat by an Argenteuil neighbor Gustave Caillebotte, an engineer, was a specialist in ship building and owner of several yachts. He also painted in his spare time. The common enthusiasm for painting and for navigation soon created between the two men a bond, which Caillebotte immediately extended to Renoir. In 1872, Renoir painted a portrait of Claude Monet during the summer when he visited the Monet family at their house in Argenteuil. He chose the moment when his friend was reading a newspaper and smoking his pipe. A few years later he painted Monet at work in his garden. And still another time inside the house holding a palette.

The reciprocity between Monet and Renoir was equally important, and had a longer history. It had been a veritable partnership. "In Argenteuil from 1873 to 1875, they frequently pursued the same motifs: ducks on the edge of the river, Monet's garden, the meadows near the village, and sailboats on the river." [10] In 1874, they painted a pair of sailboats. Their use of small, broken brushstrokes enabled them to translate the outdoor light into brilliant contrasts of orange-blue, red-green and yellow-purple sun-flooded patches.

It was in 1872 that Pissarro proposed that Cézanne join him in Pontoise so that they could paint from nature together; the younger artist gladly accepted. He, Hortense and Paul, moved to L'Estaque, a short distance from Pontoise. In early 1873 Cézanne met Dr. Paul Gachet a neighbor. Dr. Gachet had acquired a beautiful house on a hillside overlooking the Oise Valley, where his ailing wife and their two children went to live, while he himself continued to practice in Paris, spending three days a week with his family.

Dr. Gachet was a fellow art lover and often accepted pictures as payment for his advice and treatment. While Dr. Gachet brought Cézanne's *A Modern Olympia,* Cézanne's private situation was still difficult, and without the support of his friends he would have found it hard to get by. In Paris, Dr. Gachet became one of the regulars of the Café Guerbois and became a close friend of the Batignolle Group. Cézanne received a warm welcome at Dr. Gachet's home and because of the moral support he received from Gachet and Pissarro, Cézanne's confidence and courage was restored.

Degas also was beginning to feel more confident about his own talents. Durand-Ruel sold three of his works. Once again, Degas embraced Ingres' influence on his drawing, while at the same time retaining his fondness for Delacroix's colors. In Degas' body of work, portraits outnumbered by far all the other genres. His father, who cautioned his son that this genre would enable him to earn an adequate living, may have fostered the drawing of portraits. Although Degas expressed occasional boredom with painting portraits, he actually demonstrated unflagging interest in this genre from the very onset in Lamothe's studio.

His brother René's visited Paris during the summer of 1872 and inspired Edgar to return with him to America. The following October, the brothers left together for New Orleans via New York. The artist enjoyed a thirty-four hour stay in New York and wrote to Tissot on 19 November, that New York "has some charming spots" and Degas was impressed by the way in which steamers from Europe arrived as if they were "omnibuses at the station" … "we pass, carriages, even trains, on the water; it's England in her best mood." In a letter dated 4 November, shortly after his arrival there, Degas wrote to his friend Dihau in Paris: "All day long I am among my dear fold, painting and drawing, and making portraits of the family … Family portraits must be done to suit the taste of the family, in impossible lighting, with many interruptions, and with models who are very affectionate but a little too bold; they take you less seriously because you are a nephew or cousin." [11]

In a way the city of New Orleans was much like Aix in that time seemed to have bypassed this city. In fact, in "Esplanade avenue, nothing had changed since the days of the plantations. The avenue was lined with palms, elms, live oaks and magnolias, and palatial houses built by the early Creole dynasties. The houses had ornamental cast-iron gates and fences; lawns were planted with flowers and magnolias; many houses had two-storey verandas with elegant columns. The entire extended Degas family seemed to live on this avenue. Degas was given a room in Michel's apartment, which had a second-floor gallery running the length of the house's façade." [12] One of his finest paintings, *The Interior of a Cotton Broker's Office at New Orleans*, resulted from Degas' visit to America.

When he returned to Paris, he was frequently at Mary Cassatt's studio to talk and comment on her work. With her excellent French, she could converse readily and comfortably: "It became an open friendship, but apparently no more than that. By nature contentious, he was not an easy man to get along with, and there would be long spells when she would have little to do with him." [13] The American art student Walter Gay, who greatly admired Degas' work and received "much good advice" from him, later said that Degas was extremely hard to know, "He was very difficult, very witty, but his wit left a sting." Degas' anti-social reputation extended to his treatment of models, with whom he still sometimes got impatient, shouting at them when they lost the pose, or making insensitive comments about their bodies. He never stopped seeing the models' bodies as material to be posed and rearranged in the service of art.

Mary Cassatt had returned and found Paris bitterly cold and smothered in fog. It had been less than a year from the final siege and only six months since the Bloody Siege. In "The Hotel de Ville seemed like a Roman ruin … the fog was so thick everything was lost at fifty feet off, " wrote Cassatt's friend Emily Sartain. "I could scarcely see the pictures in the Louvre, it was so dark." [14] In Paris, 1872, *Galignani's Messenger* carried an article in which a distinguished Italian art critic, Parmetto Bettoli, wrote the following upon seeing the copy of the Correggio masterpiece *L'Incoronata*, done by the young American: "I must candidly confess that when I am called to criticize feminine essays in the *Fine Arts* or *Belles-Lettres*, my eulogisms are generally qualified by the restriction embraced in the phrase, 'It is not bad for a woman.' But as regards this picture I find myself in a very different position. The copy of this great work, executed by Miss Cassatt, betrays such a surprising knowledge of art that a male artists, no matter how great his experience, might feel honored at having the authorship of this work attributed to him." [15]

It was the dawn of a new Republic and Paris would soon have a new startling addition. To add to Montmartre's charm, construction began of a white cathedral, the Sacre Coeur Cathedral began in 1875. It was funded by public subscription to give thanks that the brick and mortar of Paris received relatively little damage from the war with Prussia. Sacre Coeur would be built high up on the Butte so that one could view almost the entire, beautiful city of Paris. Montmartre is a hill composed of gypsum, a soft white mineral, and had the building been placed directly on the hill, it would certainly have collapsed. Thus Sacre Coeur sits on eighty-three large shafts over one hundred feet deep, filled with concrete. While the soft stone may have been a poor foundation for building Sacre Coeur, it did have two somewhat positive qualities: it dissolves slowly in water and when heated it can be easily be ground into a white plaster. Montmartre's slopes honeycombed with craters, some of them quite deep from the old gypsum mines became so famous that the white powder eventually received the name plaster of Paris.

Chapter Eleven: Fleeting Impressions of Contemporary Life

The artists who would soon be known as The Impressionists were noteworthy for their rejection of Romanticism representing nostalgic views of the past and for their whole-hearted plunge into celebrating modern Parisian life. The Impressionists revolted against academic art of the 1830s and 1840s and spurned most of the art of the realist Barbizon painters who followed Romanticism. While the Impressionists soon left behind the traditional bourgeois world of the mythological past and biblical scenes, they also retained some of its characteristics associated with Barbizon artists, such as Charles-François Daubigny and Constant Troyon, who shared the recognition of the landscape as an independent subject.

As the new group of artists with their innovated subject matter and style evolved, there were many names that attempted to describe them and their art: The Batignolle's Group, Romantic Naturalistists, Actualistes among others were considered to be appropriate epithets for their vanguard art. Manet, Monet, Bazille, Sisley, Renoir, Morisot, Cassatt, Cézanne and Degas were identified as the distinct group forming a new artistic movement. Barbizon subjects such as floor strippers, wounded cuirassiers, witches, and Nazarenes, were replaced by brilliantly colored singers, circus performers, and fashionably dressed Parisians enjoying their galettes. Their canvases now captured Parisian leisure and entertainment, boating, concerts, racetracks, and theater. Gradually the grouping of Manet and his like-minded friends took place at the Café Guerbois that provided them with an invaluable forum to exchange ideas and to formulate their pioneering techniques.

One of the most striking things about the art of the Impressionists is color – color that can be seen even in shadows that were once simply defined in blacks and grays. These artists could look at shadows, which were once thought of as lacking light, and learned to catch all their colorful nuances. A shadow is not the absence of light, but light of a different quality. As Théodore Duret pointed out, "they perceived that in winter sunshine the shadows thrown upon the snow appear to be blue, and they painted them blue accordingly. They had also discovered that in summer the light under the trees gives the ground a violet tinge, and therefore in painting woods they made the ground violet." [1]

Renoir studied reflections of sunlight under foliage and found that the shadows actually assume colors in which violet predominates. "The light, broken up in filtering through the trees, throws a general shadow of violet tone on the ground and over the figure." In his painting *The Ball* at Montmartre's Moulin del la Galette, the whole canvas is conceived in a general violet tone. The novelty of blue and violet shadows had produced a great outcry. "The fact that such effects had never been seen in pictures before was sufficient to lead to the conservative prejudices of the beholders to reject with contempt." [2]

Manet, interested in Renoir's painting, was struck by his "daring method of painting colored shadows in the open air." As such, Manet painted the lion-hunter *Pertuiset* in the summer of 1880 under the trees of the Elysee des Beaux-Arts, Boulevard de Chichy. He, too, noted Duret, discovered that "shadows when seen in the open air are variously colored, according to the effects of light, and, without hesitation, Manet painted them variations of blue, violet, lilac – colors parallel to nature." [3] Manet, like the other Impressionists, saw the unexpected tones that played in the rendering of foliage. On close inspection, they were astonished to find the leaves were striped with orange, red, blue and yellow touches and rendered them as nature did. If one were to stand away from the painting, the eye puts together the picture, and the freshness of the green foliage appears to be represented with infallible truth. But if one stands too close, the image can be lost and all that is found is a smattering of colors. Instead of painting firm, well-defined contours, Manet conveyed his forms with short, broken brushstrokes interspersed with vivid strokes of color.

Renoir had said, "No shadow is black. It always has color. Nature knows only colors...white and black are not colors." In nature no color exists by itself. The coloring of the objects is a pure illusion: the only creative source of color is the sunlight which envelopes all things, and reveals them according to the hours, with infinite modifications.

The Impressionists believed that white reflected all colors, so all surfaces that appear white must include colors as well. This meant that black, the opposite of white, is the absence of color. "Using the theory of complementary colors, violet was considered to be the color to use as a shadow because it is the opposite of yellow, the color of sunlight."

Monet avoided black as well; to make a color close to black he mixed many colors together with the exception of white or yellow. Monet said that "when painting objects, try to forget what objects are being painted, instead, think of it as a little square of blue, and oblong of pink or a streak of yellow. After a while, an image can be seen." [4] Most of the Impressionists worked with oil paint rather than other mediums because of the importance of color. Drawing was not an important as the color itself, which showed the emotion the artist wanted to represent. For example, Joris-Karl Huysmans examining Monet's seascapes noted the symphony of colors that determine the mood of the painting: "the tumultuous landscapes, of abrupt seas, violent with ferocious tones, vicious blue, raw violet, harsh green, of rock-work waves with solid crests, beneath skies in rage…" [5]

In Cézanne's work, color had the power to link "near and far, hard and soft, coarse and tender." He both adopted and adapted Impressionist techniques of color. Ambroise Vollard, friend and art dealer, revealed that Cézanne continued to paint studies from nature in brilliant colors, but he gradually simplified his application of the paint to the point where he seemed "able to define volumetric forms with juxtaposed strokes of pure color." For Cézanne, the answer to all the technical problems of Impressionism lay in a use of color both more orderly and more expressive than that of his fellow Impressionists. Cezanne's use of color may account, in part, for his remarkable development.

Technological advances of being able to paint in nature was attributed to the portability of paint in tubes, which had just come into existence. Second, synthetic colors were invented during the time of the Impressionists, which gave way to new rich and bold colors. The Impressionists frequently used these synthetic paints because of the brilliance of color. "In translating the purity and brilliance of their vision they eliminated every trace of earth color, burnt sienna, and black from their palettes; they sought to achieve warm greys, blues, greens, and violets using only pure colors, applying them in stabbing dots." [6]

While their paintings were not spontaneously achieved, what they strove to capture was. Impressionism is about capturing the fleeting impressions of life in everyday scenes. Each painting, however, was carefully conceived, artfully crafted, and skillfully completed. If there is one more than another to whom the evolution of the essential features of fleeting impressions is especially due, it is Claude Monet. He more than any other invested the fleeting aspect of the moment, the ephemeral, the coloring of the seasons, of light, of weather, as dominant forces in any rendering of nature. The Impressionists wanted to paint exactly what they saw as if they were seeing it for the first time, or as if it were their first impression. The often-remembered story is that from Monet's painting entitled *Impressionism: Sunrise* art, critic Louis Leroy coined the term "Impressionism," which he intended as disparagement. The Impressionists, as we know, turned this scornful critics label, after some painful twists and turns, into a badge of honor. There are so many innovating things about their paintings, another one, of course, is the Impressionistic brushstrokes.

Unlike the Realists before them, Impressionists used dramatic brushstrokes to give the essence of the image; texture was added through the thick application of the paint. Rather than enamel-like smooth images, Impressionists were the first group of artists who did not try to hide brushstrokes; indeed, their brushstrokes were "bold, unrefined and obvious." "Most other painters used thin glazes and fine brushes made from sable to cover their traces, in effect brushing themselves – their labors and their personalities – out of their work." [7] The brush strokes of the Impressionist often times blurred the image giving it a hazy look as in *Impressionism: Sunrise*. When the artists used their brushes in this way, it was also a way to contribute to the mood they wanted to create within the painting. Impasto is the term used for "the technique of applying oil paints thickly and liberally so that it keeps the marks left by the brush. Monet, Renoir, Pissarro, and Cézanne were some of the Impressionists who used this technique. Often times, they would use palette knives for various tasks, however palette knives were good for applying thick layers of paint, or Impasto, to create the texture they desired." [8]

The subject matter for most of the Impressionists is carefree and fun and characterized by a lack of chaos and violence. The subject matter is somewhat reminiscent of the musicals rendered by Hollywood during the Great Depression. Here the carefree lighter pallets of the Impressionist's sun-struck surfaces were in direct contrast to the revolutionary times during which these artists painted. Subject matter given new priority by the Impressionists included contemporary landscape settings, to modern city scenes, especially the commercial leisure of city and suburb, of cafes, swimming and boating resorts, beer gardens, dance halls, parading carriages.

Impressionists turned resolutely towards the aspects of contemporary life, and to draw style and emotion from their own epoch; imitating the style of the past, but by extracting the immediate expression of each epoch. One of the reforms due to their conception has been the suppression of the professional model, and the substitution for it of the natural model, seen in the exercise of his or her occupation. Their paintings reflect a return to nature and simplicity. The basis of all their pictures has been a series of landscape and figure studies made in the open air, far from the studio, and afterwards coordinated.

In the course of their careers each of the artists was able to find subjects that would ignite their passions. With Mary Cassatt, the subject of her signature work and style developed rather slowly after her long apprenticeship in Europe. She did not produce a major painting until the late 1870s when she was over thirty, and once she found her mature style, she didn't change it. She mostly painted domestic interiors, with no clear sense of place; and male subjects, apart from members of her own family, were rare. Her themes centered around taking tea, going to the opera, riding in a carriage, women dressed in large hats with elaborate gowns, and mothers and children "physically close and psychologically absorbed in one another." She confined herself to the drawing room and nursery, the garden and the river and usually ignored the urban landscape.

While her subject matter differed, she was one of the founding members and subsequently shared in the praise and criticism of the Impressionist group. Mary welcomed the chance of being a member of this group whose ascetic, critical, and opinionated attitudes were in sync with her own. She was not an additional addendum to the group but rather threw her art and soul to its cause.

One of the first, and most important works Mary painted as an Impressionist was a portrait of her mother, *Reading le Figaro*. In the 1879 Impressionist Exhibition, many critically acclaimed Mary's works. One art critic wrote, "There isn't a painting, nor a pastel by Mlle. Mary Cassatt that is not an exquisite symphony of color. Mlle. Mary Cassatt is fond of pure colors and possesses the secret of blending them in a composition that is bold, mysterious, and fresh." [9] This review and others were clipped from the newsprint and mailed to family by none other than Mr. Cassatt – her father.

Mary may have been well aware that people and critics may have wondered about her chosen subject matter. Similarly, early on in her career, she was well aware that her ambitions of becoming an artist clashed with the expected role of women as wives and mothers. Eliza's father underscores this when he said to both his daughter and Mary, "You will get married and settle down into a good housekeeper like all married women and send off your paints to the garret! There is a prediction for you, and one founded upon universal experience." [10] While Mary tightened her resolve not to give up her art career and not to marry, her friend Eliza did marry fulfilling her father's prediction.

Mary more than likely saw the paradox between being unmarried and childless and making mothers and children her main subjects. She also must have seen the inevitable motivational speculations of her making maternity her predominant theme. Scholars really don't know what her inner motivations were but the fact that she persevered in rendering these themes may be a testimony of her courageousness – one that more trepid artists would not have taken.

She was also intrigued by the human form and became interested in depicting Parisian bourgeoisie women. Her work was frequently characterized by depictions of women in ordinary tasks - especially with children. Art connoisseurs describe her brushstrokes as lithe and her pastel pigments typical of the Impressionist style of Renoir and Degas. These early portraits would be the first of her works in what art historian Griselda Pollock claims to be a discourse on "the ages of women: infancy, childhood, youth or coming of age, adulthood, maternity, maturity, and old age." Degas, upon seeing some of Mary Cassatt's later work, was said to have stated, "I am not willing to

Reading Le Figaro, 1878 (oil on canvas), Cassatt, Mary Stevenson (1844-1926) / Private Collection / Photo © Christie's Images / The Bridgeman Art Library

admit that a woman can draw that well."

In the early1870s, Renoir painted traditional images like *Bather with a Dog* or *Woman in Algiers*. He did so with the jury of the Salon in mind. His strategy proved successful and both paintings were accepted for the Salon in 1870. Clearly, Renoir's subject matter was people; he was mainly a portrait painter. Like Mary Cassatt, Renoir loved painting children. He enjoyed their exuberance and natural radiance.

Some writers have insisted that Monet's primary concern was not what he painted but how it appeared under different lighting and weather conditions. Duret commented that it was the sunshine that flickered across the surface of the Seine or the façade of Rouen Cathedral, for example, that was more significant than the river or the building. It was the atmosphere that wrapped the wheatstacks or infiltrated the sites Monet selected along the Normandy coast rather than those agrarian constructions or the specific locations on the English Channel. To support this one looks at the paintings themselves which are clearly focused on the multiple ways in which nature – the presence of light, air, wind, and time - reveals its many wonders. However, as Duret points out, the sites and subjects were important and carefully considered by Monet.

The study of water played an important role in Monet's subject matter and in his development of the style. "Just as snow scenes had permitted the artists to investigate the problem of shadows, the rendering of water offered an excellent opportunity to observe reverberations and reflections. Thus they could further develop their knowledge of the fact that so called local color was actually a pure convention and that every object presents to the eye a scheme of colors derived from its proper hue, from its surroundings, and from that atmosphere conditions." [11]

The subject matter of Manet's work gave us a glimpse of modern Parisian life, however, *Music in the Tuileries* seemed to have been quite repellent to the art-viewing public. Once again, however, his execution gave viewers pause. His brushstrokes seemed "clumsy, lacking of clarity and were clearly visible." The work looked lackadaisical and incomplete because in places the undercoat of white primer and the weave of the canvas could clearly be seen. It was something of a surprise to the public when they were confronted by a canvas showing a cast of characters, not dressed in Roman togas, but was dressed much like themselves with gentlemen wearing top hats and frock coats.

This was the time when most gentry class males wore top hats, which appears to be a 1797 "invention" by an English gentlemen, Mr. John Hetherington. At least he was the first to be seen wearing a top hat on one of London's most fashionable streets – St. James. This unspectacular event turned into one that was indeed spectacular. Upon seeing Mr. Hetherington and his Top Hat, horses bolted, ladies fainted, and men began throwing rotten fruit at this unsuspecting soul. Unfortunately Mr. Hetherington, was arrested for disturbing the peace and was fined five hundred pounds, a veritable fortune is those days and a considerable sum even today.

Figures generally do not hold a dominant place in the Impressionist landscapes; the landscapes are pure and the figures are introduced as only accessories. Manet had hitherto been first and foremost a figure painter. When he came to devote himself more to open-air work, he still gave primary importance to the figures with the landscape usually serving merely as a frame or a background. In 1874, Manet secured the type of women he wanted and persuaded his brother-in-law Rudolph Leenhoff to sit for him. He then took them to Argenteuil, and posed them sitting side by side in a boat, with the blue water as a background. The painting was exhibited in the Salon of 1875 under the title of *Argenteuil*. He intended to make a sensation with this picture, and he completely succeeded, though not in the way that he wished. The *Argenteuil* was destined to rank with the *Dejeuner* and *Olympia* and *The Balcony*, as one of the pictures, which was most violently and generally condemned.

Degas' subject matter was almost exclusively on the female performer. Beginning in 1875, he devoted about forty pastels and prints to this theme. From the early 1870s onward Degas began to focus more and more on the theme of ballet dancers. He had already included some of them marginally in his orchestra paintings. Scenes of rehearsals or rather moments of relaxation during class were to become his favorite subject for a number of years. Rarely would he depict actual performances. Equally small in number are works showing individual dancers; the artist preferred to study the interaction of figures in space.

In Degas' view a good landscape could only be painted inside the studio. He firmly believed that a work of art was pure artifice, totally outside nature and requiring "as much cunning as a crime." Ballet provided him with the ideal motif. Nothing could be less natural. Degas' technique and content were normally quite different from Pissarro, Monet, and Renoir. Their paintings were "sketchy, rather than finished; painterly and loosely handled rather than linear and smooth; directly, sometimes rawly retinal rather than studio-cooked; unemotional without ideas rather than expressive and intellectual; devoid of story rather than anecdotal." [12]

"Degas' attitude toward nature, the countryside and plein air painting was also strikingly opposed to theirs. He almost never painted or even mentioned the peasants in the countryside; they simply didn't interest him. A confirmed Parisian, he called the excursions of the urban crowd, 'hygienic outings.' He insisted that 'boredom quickly overcomes me when I even look at nature,' that he felt 'stifled and dazed by the amount of air.' He painted landscapes and seascapes, but preferred to re-create them in his studio rather than paint outdoors. He believed that an artist must transform, not capture, what he sees. Degas would go to the race courses, at Auteuil and Longchamps, but it was in his own studio, twiddling his little wooden horses about in the light, that he succeeded in reconstituting nature." [13]

Degas was also simply fascinated by the world backstage. The girls in the corps de ballet were lowly paid working girls, usually with ambitious mothers, who lived in shacks on the hillsides of Montmartre and the wealthy boulevardiers who frequented the Opera sometimes corrupted them. "The young ballet dancers began their arduous training at the Opera at the age of seven or eight. They gave up their chance of a formal education and could scarcely read or write. Yet, they attended dance classes six days a week, and spent afternoons and many evenings rehearsing their next performance. Unlike the girls who toiled in the dreary factories and mills near the racetracks on the outskirts of Paris, the dancers had glamorous work and a potentially promising future." [14] The *petite rat* was a student of the school of dance, and she was called that because she was a child of the house: "She lives there, because she gnaws there, jabbers there, splashes there, because she corrodes and scratches the décor, frays and ears the costumes" … that she has received the name of *petite rat*.

At the age of ten the less-talented girls were ruthlessly rejected and the others began their slow progress from student rats to almost unattainable stratosphere of premiere *danseuse*. "Rigorous annual and biannual examinations were held to determine this advancement, followed by appropriate adjustments to the dancers' level of pay." [15] In the 1880s this ranged enormously from 700 to 30 thousand francs a year. Seamstresses and lace-makers earned 600 to 900 francs, teachers 4,200 francs.

Sexual favors were part-and-parcel of their trade and the dancers made sure they were paid top price. Laundresses, without rich guardians or protectors, were even more sexually vulnerable than the dancers. In the 1870s there were about 70 thousand laundresses in Paris, many of whom were the mothers of the aspiring ballerinas. They picked up the dirty linen and delivered the clean and could be seen trudging to and from the houses of their Parisian clients.

Degas was given free run of the theater, stalls and boxes from which the performance was viewed but also the wings of the stage, its maze of corridors, the dancers' dressing rooms and the green room where the abonnés congregated with the dancers before, during and after the performance. [16]

In addition to subject matter differences, the Impressionists had social differences as well. Though Paul Cézanne came from a prosperous family in Aix, he adopted a defiant pose, exaggerated his southern accent, and wore clothes of a pauper - battered old hat, blue worker's overalls and a coarse coat spattered with brush marks. Approaching Manet in the Café Guerbois, he aggressively explained, "I am not offering out my hand, M. Manet, I haven't washed for a week." Cézanne's refusal to extend his dirty hand could have been a deferential gesture to the elegant Manet or, perhaps more likely, a self-conscious mockery of Manet's dandyism.

The Impressionists were preoccupied with contemporary emotions and substituted character for classic beauty or said differently of emotional beauty for formal beauty. The substitution for beauty, a novel notion, with that of character, renders the painting more moving, than to search for an exclusive beauty, based upon rules, and inspired by the Greco-Latin ideal. To many art connoisseurs, the substitution of character for beauty was the essential feature of the movement.

In summarizing the Impressionist movement, Frederic Chevalier writing for the conservative magazine, *L'Artiste* made the following generalization: "The disturbing ensemble of contradictory qualities which distinguish the Impressionists – the crude application of paint, the down-to-earth subjects, the appearance of spontaneity, the conscious incoherence, the bold colors, the contempt for form, the childish naiveté that they mix heedlessly with exquisite refinements, all of this is not without analogy to the chaos of contradictory forces that trouble our era."

"They were notable for their specifically modern subjects, the frequent attempts to replace studio conditions with direct, natural lighting, and generally their lightened palette of pure colors. Later, these features developed into the qualities now usually considered to define Impressionism in the strict sense: the attempt to render a pure, momentary experience rather than to create a formal and finished composition; and the use of painting to analyze how light and color were perceived, so as to reconstruct and extend visual experience itself." [17]

Rejecting the objectivity of realism, they had selected one element from reality – light – to interpret all of nature. By applying their paint in perceptible strokes, they had succeeded in blurring the outlines of objects and merging them with the surroundings. The topic of plein air painting was one of the subjects most discussed by Manet and his friends at their meetings at the Café Guerbois. In 1873, Manet, still trying to catch the effects of natural light, could be found at the riverbank. He carried his canvases to the same riverbank that Monet had been painting so prolifically and following Monet's lead, he replaced the somber colors and sharp contrasts of so many of his earlier canvases with a lighter palette of blues, yellows, and ochers, which he added to his canvas in strokes of pure, unmixed color. As a tribute he painted *Claude Monet and his Wife on his Floating Studio*.

Manet continued to submit his works to the Salon and while it still upheld its usual retrograde standards, two of Manet's submissions, *Repose* (one of his portraits of Berthe Morisot) and *le Bon Bock*, his painting of an old man in a bar, contentedly puffing at his pipe over a glass of beer were accepted in 1873. *Le Bon Bock* represented the engraver Bellot sitting at a table in the Café Guerbois. When the Salon jurors met, according to custom, at the close of the day in the garden of the Palais de l'Industrie to exchange their first impressions of the paintings submitted to the exhibition, the favorable verdict of *le Bon Bock* was generally confirmed. The press at once made known the judgment of the experts, and the public accepted it. *Le Bon Bock* became one of the most popular pictures of the year.

The public conceded that Manet had at last corrected his "former errors and had produced a work, which was worthy of the fullest praise." It was a portrait of a life-sized engraver Belot, one of the habitués of the Café Guerbois. The big, jovial fellow was captivating and seemed to return the publics cordially warm welcome. Duret claimed, "The unexpected success gave the public and the press an opportunity of adopting a more conciliatory attitude toward Manet. Full of self-congratulations; they claimed that long ago they had expressed their opinion that all the objectionable features of Manet's paintings – his violence, his 'patchwork,' his choice of extraordinary subjects – simply proceeded from the insolence of youth, from a desire to force himself into notoriety, and that sooner or later he would adopt the ordinary, conventional rules like everybody else. In *Le Bon Bock* they detected the signs of the change, which they had predicted, and the picture pleased them all the more in that it bore witness to their own sagacity." [18] Manet was able to obtain his first great success since 1861. *Le Bon Bock* became virtually inescapable - through actual photographs, caricatures in newspapers and a club called "le Bon Bock" founded by Bellot.

Manet, however, shifted from overconfidence to bleak despair, characteristic of cyclothymic oscillation or mood swings. This form of neurosyphilis from which Manet suffered develops ten to twenty years after the onset of infection. In the pre-penicillin era, tabes dorsalis, which affects the limbs rather than the brain, accounted for one-third of the patients with neurosyphilis. Despite Manet's illness, he continued to be Morisot's mentor, a model, a man she loved to the end of his life, and possibly the end of her own. To Manet, Berthe Morisot's appearance was understandably dazzling. She was unlike any woman of her society that he had known. While Berthe's dream of being a serious painter would scare off most men who merely wanted a wife, to Manet she was a breathe of fresh air even though his illness in 1873 was causing him grave concern.

It was also in 1873, after a series of rejections of her work by the Paris Salon, that Cassatt learned that one of her Spanish paintings, a large canvas *Offrant le panal au torero* (*Offering the Panal to the Bullfighter*) influenced by both travel to Spain and the paintings of Édouard Manet, had been accepted. Cassatt continued to study Degas' paintings in exhibitions, galleries, and shop windows and was eager to absorb whatever she could from them. "I had already recognized who were my true masters, I admired Manet, Courbet, and Degas… the first sight of Degas' pictures was the turning point in my artistic life." [19]

Monet began a new round of attempts to borrow money from his friends – all received desperate pleas for help. He wrote a note to Zola "If I haven't been paid by tomorrow night, Tuesday, the sum of six hundred francs, our furniture and all I own will be sold and we'll be out on the street. I haven't a single sou of this amount. None of the transactions on which I had counted can be concluded for the moment. It would pain me deeply to reveal the situation to my poor wife. I am making a last attempt and am turning to you in the hope that you may possibly lend me 200 francs. This would be an installment, which may help me obtain a delay. I don't dare to come myself; I would be incapable of seeing you without daring to tell you the real purpose of my visit. Please send me word, and in any case, don't speak about this, for it is always a fault to be in need." [20]

Despite his financial laments, Monet's rate of sales went on increasing. In addition to Durand-Ruel, other dealers and collectors (some of them rich commercial bankers) had already begun to buy his work. He was determined to capitalize on his success, and was still convinced that a group exhibition would maximize all the painters' chances in the market.

Early in 1873 Degas sailed back from America to France. In the autumn he was deeply affected by the burning of the Paris Opera, which deprived him of one of his favorite objects of study. But soon as the dancing classes were installed in new, temporary quarters, he began again to paint the petite rats, the musicians and the ballet master. The world of the theater formed an essential part of Degas' life and oeuvre.

It was also around this time that Degas had lost the sight of his right eye. For the rest of his long life he suffered from myopia, blurred vision and intolerance of bright light and lived with the constant threat of blindness. He had impaired central vision and suffered "the torment that it was to draw, when he could only see around the spot at which he was looking, and never the spot itself." In 1873, "I shall remain in the ranks of the infirm until I pass into the ranks of the blind." He wore special blue glasses that embarrassed him very much. As his vision deteriorated, he switched from oils to pastels, which did not require mixing of pigments, drying time or varnishing.

In 1873, Cézanne painted three or four carefully executed portraits of M. Chocquet, which took an important place in his work: one was the head exhibited in the Impressionist exhibition of 1877. Another, a half-length, with the figure in white standing out against a background of green plants, was painted in the open air in Normandy in 1885. Between the seclusion of 1870 and the distinction of 1873, Cézanne's world turned. By the end of the decade he had found himself sufficiently to feel that he understood what it was to be an artist. Almost imperceptibly, he would become the most extraordinary artist of his generation. He did not know it yet, and neither did the public. Pissarro was the one who had the earliest insight into that phenomenon, and the deepest understanding of it. Monet, too, for he owned fourteen Cézanne's – three hung in his bedroom - *Château Noir*, a *View of L'Estaque*, and a Bathers. In 1899 Cézanne was paid 6,750 francs at auction for *Snow Melting at Fontainebleau* (1879-80).

Cézanne went to live at Auvers-sur-Oise, there he would see Pissarro and Vignon, both of whom for a long time had been painting in the open air. In 1872, at the age of 33, Paul began to follow their example, and painted landscapes, with the bright color effects, which play over a countryside bathed in light immediately before his eyes. Hitherto he had seldom gone out of the studio even his landscapes were far from the actual scene they represented. When he began to paint systematically in the open air at Auvers, he had now been working for a long period of time; he had a sure command over the methods of his art. When he came into direct contact with nature and with the intense coloration of the open air, the originality of his genius found its full expansion. "He developed a range of color - strong, unexpected, and absolutely individual."

It was in spring of 1873 that Paul Alexia, a friend of Cézanne's, made public the proposal for an independent exhibition in *L'Avenir National*. Evidently his article drew upon talks amongst the Batignolles circle in the Café Guerbois. Monet replying on behalf of the circle promised that one was in preparation. Alexis published Monet's letter on 12 May, adding the information that a number of important artists were already behind Monet.

Eventually a charter was drawn up and dated 27 December 1873 for a joint stock company with shares, articles of partnership and other routine provisions. Each member was to contribute sixty francs a year at the rate of five francs a month. It was known as the *Societe Anonyme Cooperative des Artistes, Peintres…* The initial group, the core group of six impressionists, signed the founding charter, with a plan to enlist more.

The persistent rejection from the Salon prompted Renoir, Monet, Sisley, Pissarro, Degas, Cézanne, and others to form a group. Like Monet, they viewed the charter as a potential business opportunity. Degas' friends had been surprised by his readiness to be involved, but since he had already exhibited six times at the Salon, he did not see why exhibiting independently should compromise his reputation. Unlike Manet, moreover, he hated the Salon's reward system and had no desire for medals or rosettes. He saw the independent exhibition as an opportunity for greater exposure.

Chapter Twelve: Independent Exhibitions

As Mary noted, "the first sight of Degas' pictures was the turning point in my artistic life" and it seemed like such a short time ago when Mary discovered Degas' paintings. She was walking along Boulevard Haussmann in Paris, when she was drawn to a picture in a storefront window. With her nose flattened to the glass, Mary, for the first time, gazed upon a painting by Degas one of the members of *La Societe Anonyme des Artistes* – now, better known as the Impressionists. From that brief encounter – her life and her work changed entirely. When she said it changed her life, she was by no means exaggerating. It changed her life because it changed her work. An entirely new way of seeing and painting for which she was to become famous, began then.

This new hero Degas, whom she met in 1874, inspired Mary Cassatt. Having seen some of her work, Degas had asked a friend to arrange an introduction. When she first met Degas, she spoke quite differently of him. In spite of her deep admiration for his work, her comment to a friend was, "Degas is a pessimist and dissolves one so that you feel after being with him, 'Oh, why try, since nothing can be done.' " [1] There were significant differences, "He was a pessimist; she was optimist. Degas painted horses; Cassatt rode them. He hated automobiles; she loved them and was a pioneer of motoring. His art grew more satiric, hers more sentimental." [2]

Mary and Degas, however, had a lot in common: strong family ties, a background of power and wealth, and an almost fanatical dedication to their work. They grew fond of each other, and Degas began to accompany her and Lydia (her sister and chaperone) to fashionable soirees and salons, galleries and the Louvre. Cassatt and Degas saw each other socially and had dinners, visited museums and galleries, shopped together for her clothes and hats, and worked together in their studios. He bought her a dog and admired her "horsewoman's passion." He portrayed her several times and suggested the maternal theme that became dominant in her art. The friendship between Cassatt and Degas would last for forty years. However, the details of their relationship have never fully been revealed. To finalize any probing, close to the end of her life, Cassatt burned many of their letters to one another.

Degas soon realized that Mary would be a definite asset to the group. They came to her studio and after an hour's conversation, Degas asked her to join the Impressionists, making her the first and only American among the group. She would also be one of only two women. The other was the French painter, Berthe Morisot. "I accepted with joy," Cassatt wrote. "Finally I could work with absolute independence without concern for the eventual opinion of the jury ... I detested conventional art and I began to live." [3] They all loved her, especially Caillebotte and Renoir, who were amused by her accent. She even seemed to understand Cézanne who she agreed made a startling first impression. But she could see that beneath the surface he was very sensitive, even childlike. "When I first saw him, he looked like a cut-throat, with large red eyeballs standing out from his head in the most ferocious manner, a rather fierce-looking pointed beard ... he soon revealed the gentlest nature possible ...."

Now, a wonderfully different Impressionistic palette of colors embraced Mary's paintings, which included no black.. She began preparing paintings for the Impressionist show. The core members of the Impressionists participating in the show were Degas, Monet, Renoir, Cézanne, Pissarro, Sisley and Berthe Morisot, who became Cassatt's friend and colleague.

An admirer of Degas and other Impressionists, Mary herself began collecting Impressionist paintings, and helped several friends from America acquire French Impressionist art for their collections. Among those she convinced to collect Impressionists was her brother, Alexander. Her motives were genuine and generous. She was convinced that these works by Degas, Manet and Monet would increase in value. She did not grow up in the midst of her stockbroker father's values without some of them rubbing off on her.

While Degas and Cassatt were discussing the first Impressionist show, Degas's father had taken ill; he had subsequently moved to Naples and died there in February 1874. After his death, the family bank was found to be in serious difficulties. Degas' father had made his son René a large unsecured loan for his wine importing business in New Orleans, which he was unable to repay. Details are relatively obscure, but in addition other loans were outstanding. The situation was rendered more complicated because of the falling prices of cotton, and general financial crisis that had caused bankruptcies in many countries. Then, too, small banks were struggling against the new growth of larger banks, such as the Rothschild Bank. Degas as the oldest son felt that such obligations were his to meet, in accordance with his Victorian family principles. Degas felt obliged to help liquidate the business debts by seeking all means of selling his work, a painful procedure for a proud man.

The 1874 failed fortunes of the family gave Degas a sense of embitterment. In an attempt to maintain his sense of eliticism, Degas constructed an art devoted to all people who served or entertained the well to do - ballet dancers and masters, laundresses, jockeys, journalists, musicians, cabaret performers, and milliners. Although relatively impoverished, Degas was still able to live more or less as he liked. He made various trips to Naples not for pleasure but for matters of family business.

Degas also suffered public humiliation from his brothers' outrageous behavior. In August 1875, his brother Achille was involved in a fracas with an engineer called Victor-Georges Legrand. Achille had been married in Louisiana but had a mistress in Paris whose husband had challenged him to a duel. His brother Achille shot and wounded his former mistress' husband twice when the man had assaulted him at the Paris Stock Exchange. The judges would find him guilty and he was sentenced to six months in prison, later commuted to one month, and a fine of fifty francs. Another scandal, but this one must have proved more wounding for Degas; on 13 April 1878, his brother René abandoned his blind wife Estelle and her children. Degas was a survivor like his grandfather and despite these family hardships and his perennial eye trouble, he was determined to continue to paint and to carry out his various artistic experiments in a variety of media. Degas' financial difficulties, however disagreeable, may have stimulated him to work more and to extend his painting repertoire.

Like Degas, Monet's personal life was a disaster. Monet was constantly short of money and endured his family's disapproval of both his career and mistress. His place for escapism from these daily woes would be Argenteuil. In 1874 Manet, Monet, and Renoir went there to paint. These three formed a close friendship, which seemed to bind them together through bad as well as happy days. Manet, in spite of all his difficulties, remained superbly indifferent to success engendered by *le Bon Bock* and showed himself to be solely preoccupied with his art.

The artists, however, were also beginning to feel the pressure of time. After all, Pissarro would soon be forty - even the youngest, Morisot and Renoir, were both nearly thirty. They decided they would rent a large studio together, where they could exhibit as much of their work as they wished. Only Manet made it clear that he did not wish to be involved. He had no intention of being diverted from the Salon.

It took some time for the young artists to realize that the process of educating a new audience was one that needed to take place outside the walls of the Salon. Now they realized that to succeed, they needed to display their works independently; a course of action that Théodore Duret strongly advised - against. But slowly the others recognized that this should be their next move. Duret advised Pissarro that if these independent exhibits came to pass, he should decline; the Salon was the only way for an artist to become publicly known and accepted by dealers and art lovers. Manet and Degas were of the same opinion, as was Renoir, who wrote to Durand-Ruel that there were at best "in Paris scarcely fifteen art-lovers capable of liking a painter without Salon approval."

The plans went forward for an independent exhibition; at first conceived to be only a stage on the way to the Salon, not a substitute for it. Nonetheless, the real importance of the independent exhibitions was captured by the critic Armand Silvestre who wrote the catalogue for the first of the exhibitions. The painters were submitting their work, he said, "… directly to the public, to the public that makes reputations even when it seems only to submit to them, and which will not fail to turn away, some day, from those who are content to follow its taste toward those who make an effort to guide it." [4]

In the initial stages of the exhibitions there was considerable unity of spirit and purpose through informal meetings at the Café Guerbois. Surprisingly, Degas believed, that "he was destined to play a predominate role in the organization of the first exhibition: he even saw himself as being very much in command of the enterprise." Degas argued, "The realist movement no longer needs to fight with the others, it already is, it exists, it must show itself as something distinct, there must be a Salon of realists." [5] Another of Degas's strong beliefs was that the members of the group ought not to send their paintings to the Salon and to exhibit just with the Independents. At this point in time that may have been easier for Degas, but the poorer members of the group, Renoir, Monet and Sisley, needed to place their pictures wherever they could for simple economic reasons. Degas was highly intolerant of human weakness or indeed necessities in this respect.

The idea for an exhibition separate from dealers and official exhibition societies was endorsed by most of the Impressionists with Monet being the most enthusiastic one. Monet, who was constantly in need of money, pursued it with a dogged sense of determination. Because of the current state of affairs, the exhibition was a risky thing for the Impressionists to do. "Collectors would have refused to hang a work of the Impressionists in their houses, even if it had been given to them, they would have considered that in doing so they were ruining both their collections and their reputations as men of taste. Durand-Ruel, the only dealer who had yet bought such discredited works, ran counter to the popular taste to such an extent that he was unable to sell them at any price." [6] Despite all this, credit should be given to M. Durand-Ruel for he was one of the first to anticipate the Impressionist school and to buy the first works of these painters, who were treated as madmen and charlatans.

Degas, who up until now, was unknown or at best ignored by the public. He only exhibited at the Salon during the early years of his career; his works were mainly shown at private exhibitions or through some art dealers. Degas alone had derived a true benefit from the private exhibitions of the Impressionists; and the reason for this must be sought in his talent. He was never one of those persecuted by the official Salon. He was accepted, since his artistic temperament is a delicate one, since he did not have an impressive power, the crowd passed before his pictures without seeing them. He eventually joined Manet in his thesis that the battle for recognition ought to be fought at the Salon.

For now, Degas was among the most faithful contributors of the Independent Exhibits. Until about 1874, unlike the others, he had lived a life of relative ease and sold few works, openly expressing his disdain for the art market. He never shocked the viewing public with his dazzling colors for then he restricted himself to neutral grays with quiet harmonies. A friend explained Degas' motives: "[He} used to exhibit at the Salon. He stopped doing so because his work was badly hung, and in his opinion, the public did not pay enough attention to it, although the artists gave him the appreciation he deserved." [7] The increasing difficulty of getting his work accepted at the salons, together with the development of the peculiarities of his style, led Renoir to join with his friends Monet and Sisley in holding independent exhibitions of their paintings.

The first exhibition was to be held in the studios of photographer Feliz Tournachon (known as Nadar). Nadar had recently renovated the space, putting in large floor-to-ceiling windows that were visible from the street and permitted a wealth of natural light. The show was kept open from ten to six and from eight to ten and charged only one franc for admission. They received more than a dozen notices in Paris newspapers even before the show opened and they attracted a commendable number of visitors during the show's run - 3,500 - a respectable number. Some of the reviews were rather negative, "the paintings were quite simply the negation of the most elemental rules of drawing and painting" announced Emile Cardon in the conservative daily, *Le Presse*. Despite what one might think, Monet's *Impression, Sunrise* did not attract much attention other than being singled out by Louis Leroy.

"Degas' friend, the American artist James Whistler, had developed a new way of showing paintings—on the eye line, rather than salon style, and the works were arranged in alphabetical order. Working in London, Whistler had revolutionized gallery installation by creating, first, an upscale interior setting, the kind that might be found in the home of an art collector and second, a total work of art. The entire *décor* was color-coordinated with the paintings on view, from the color of the walls, to the upholstery on the chairs, to the color of the servants' livery. The artists were, in fact, showing the buyers how to hang their purchases, utilizing the display techniques of the department store: entice and educate." [8]

Another innovation of the exhibition was the refusal of the artists to accept the traditional frames for paintings with their Baroque carving and gaudy gilding. These innovations, which we take for granted today were, in fact, rebukes to the Salon system. First, by showing the paintings on one line, the Impressionists eliminated the hierarchy of judgment where the least favored entries were "skied," or hung too high to be viewed. Second, the frames were plain, simple and often white, drawing attention to the elements inside the frame and on the canvas itself." [9] Degas and Pissarro were known as the leaders in frame innovation. Pissarro thought the gilt frames "stank of the *bourgeois*." "White frames quickly became associated with Impressionism. The Salon, the dominant institution in French art at the time, made conservative stipulations about how works should be presented and in this context, white frames were a radical departure." [10]

Monet, Morisot, Renoir, Degas, Cézanne, Pissarro and Sisley were the contributors. Degas thought Berthe's talent and social standing would lend prestige to the show, and hoped she might be able to persuade the reluctant Manet to join the group. In some contentious years, Morisot served as a mollifying force. As she modestly observed: "This project is very much up in the air, Degas' perversity makes it almost impossible for realization; there are clashes of vanity in this little group that make any understanding difficult. It seems to me that I am about the only one without any pettiness of character; this makes up for my inferiority as painter." [11]

Morisot exhibited *The Cradle,* which would become her most famous painting and is based on Edma and her baby, Blanche. Edma is seated in profile and wears a characteristic black dress with a deep ruffled neckline. One hand rests reflectively on her chin, the other on the cradle. The paintings Degas exhibited were modern portraits of modern women — milliners, laundresses and ballet dancers — painted from radical perspectives.

Over the course of the next twelve years, the group staged eight such Impressionist exhibitions, and Degas exhibited at all of them. His most famous paintings during these years were *The Dancing Class* (1871), *The Dance Class* (1874), *Woman Ironing* (1873) and *Dancers Practicing at the Bar* (1877). While Degas' paintings are not overtly political, they do reflect France's changing social and economic environment. His paintings portray the growth of the bourgeoisie, the emergence of a service economy and the widespread entrance of women into the workplace.

Renoir was represented by five paintings in oil and one in pastel. Two works, which he said to be among his best, were *La danseuse* and *La Loge*. *La danseuse* is a young girl, life-sized, standing up, wearing a short tulle ballet skirt. *La loge* represents a woman sitting in a box in the theater and near her a young man in evening dress. These two works, which now all the world admires, in 1874 simply provoked jeers and laughter.

Critics were dismayed to see simple oil sketches presented as completed works. Two years later his painting *Nude in the Sun* (also known as *Woman's Torso in the Sunlight*) was badly received. Critic Albert Wolff claimed he wanted to "*Try to explain to M Renoir that a woman's torso is not a mass of decomposing flesh."*

"The crowds pressed down the rue des Capucines, two hundred arrived on the first day and about a hundred every day there after. The faint of heart Parisians, screamed with horror and alerted their friends who were also aghast. The reaction of the audience was a repeat performance of the 1863 Salon des Refusés. Why would anyone want to pay good money to look at pictures of laundresses, the Opera's *petits rats* or a ploughed field?" While audiences mocked Monet, Degas, Renoir, Pissarro, Cezanne and even Berthe Morisot, Meissonier quietly sold *Charge of the Cuirassiers* for 300,000 francs. [12]

"Although their canvases shocked their contemporaries as being brazen, they represented in fact the true continuation of the endeavors and theories of their predecessors. Thus the new phase in the history of art inaugurated by the Impressionist exhibition of 1874 was not a sudden outbreak of iconoclastic tendencies: it was the culmination of a slow and consistent evolution." [13] The critics and press, however, followed the same previous trajectory and once again were in perfect agreement … "unfinished, slovenly, anarchist and subversive" … "a national disgrace" … "try to tell M. Pissarro that trees are not purple or the sky the colour of butter; that the things he paints cannot actually be seen anywhere in nature. …" Try telling M. Degas to see reason; tell him about drawing, colour, execution, purpose…" [14]

In *Le Figaro* Albert Wolff wrote of the Impressionist's First Exhibition: "The impression the Impressionists convey is of a cat trampling on the keys of a piano, or an ape that has got hold of a box of paints." … There is a woman in the group, as is the case with all famous gangs. Her name is Berthe Morisot, and she is interesting to behold. In her, feminine grace is preserved amidst the frenzy of a mind in delirium." [15] Another detractor called her a "whore" - Pissarro chivalrously defended her by punching the critic in the face.

Critics noted that every rule of composition was broken: pictures with no recognizable perspective, uniformly bright, and with emphatic color highlights, pictures that trampled on the traditional sense of near and far. They commented on how sloppily the paint had been applied and noted that the brushwork ought not to draw attention to itself. One variation of the criticisms was that the Impressionist were now being compared to the rebellious Communards. If the situation had been only a little more sensitive their paintings would have been burnt," wrote Gustave Geoffroy, a friend of the Impressionists.

"Cézanne's paintings represented the triumph of "ugliness" and were the universal target of ridicule. He had submitted three Pontoise works: an Auvers landscape, *The House of the Hanged Man at Auvers*, and *A Modern Olympia*. Even open-minded critics who welcomed Impressionist art as 'lively, captivating, full of vitality' noted that Cezanne's work 'gave them pause.' " [16] George Riviere's response in *L'Impressioniste* to the scathing assault on Cézanne was: "Of all these painters, M. Cézanne has suffered the most attacks and abuse over the past fifteen years. He has been the butt of every conceivable kind of defamation. His work is laughed at and will continue to be laughed at … for my own part I know of no painter's work that makes me laugh less. His work might prompt one to compare M. Cézanne with an Ancient Greek. His paintings emanate the same peaceful, heroic serenity as the pictures and terracottas of antiquity. The ignorant people who laugh at a picture like his Bathers remind me of barbarians criticizing the Parthenon." [17]

The critics unabashedly crucified him, " M. Cézanne gives the impression, of being a species of lunatic, painting with delirium tremens." Paul responded, "So be it! I shall go on hurling paintings of this kind at them for all eternity." But the criticisms were talking their toll and Cezanne who seemed to lack interest in his work once it was finished. His disinterest, bordering on the careless, led him to shed paintings whenever they had served their purpose, "casting them off like old clothes." A consolation to the rejection and his subsequent indifference was his son Paul. Paul truly was special to Cézanne and he doted on him when they were together. Cézanne continued to make every effort to conceal his family from his father and continued to fear his disapproval and no doubt disinheritance.

Zola, years later, described the novel atmosphere of the first exhibition resounding with the guffaws of curiosity-seekers: "These laughs were no longer smothered by the handkerchiefs of the ladies, and the men distended their bellies the better to give vent to them. It was the contagious mirth of a crowd which had come for entertainment, was becoming excited by degrees, exploded apropos of nothing, and was enlivened as much by beautiful things as by execrable ones … They nudged each other, they doubled up… every canvas had its appreciation, people called each other over to point out a good one, witty remarks were constantly being passed from mouth to mouth … expressing the sum total of asininity, of absurd commentary, of bad and stupid ridicule that an original work can evoke from bourgeois imbecility." [18]

After the exhibition, "having named Renoir president of the meeting, they listened to the treasurer's report and learned that, after paying all external debts, and the liabilities of the association their debt was 3,713 francs (money advanced by members), whereas only 277.99 francs remained in the till. Thus every member owed 184.50 francs for the payment of internal debts and in order to reestablish the operating fund. In view of these conditions, it appeared urgent to liquidate the society."[19]

"Manet's disappointments at the 1874 Salon led him to a kind of show of solidarity with his fellow outcasts, the Impressionists and in particular with Claude Monet. Manet and Monet had come a long way since 1865, they got to know one another sometime in the 1860s when Manet invited the younger painter to the Café Guerbois 'at which point,' Monet later recalled, 'we immediately became firm friends.' Monet was to look back on these evenings in Manet's company at the Café Guerbois as vital to his artistic development. 'Nothing could have been more interesting than our discussions with their constant clashes of opinion. They kept our wits sharpened, encouraged us to press forward with out own experiments, and gave us the enthusiasm to work for weeks on end.' In 1872 (or 1873), Monet painted *Impression: Sunrise* (*Impression: soleil levant*) depicting a Le Havre landscape. It hung in the First Impressionist exhibition in 1874 and is now displayed in the Musée Marmottan-Monet, Paris. Despite all the criticisms the group received, there was one thing the *première exposition* gave to the group – their name.[20]

While his contemporary friends were engaged in their First Exhibit, Manet was drawing a fashionable couple engaging in a leisure activity - *Boating on the Seine*. Both the subject matter and the palette of this later picture are more closely tied to Impressionism, while the flattened picture plane refers back to the Japanese prints that so intrigued him. *Boating* was painted in Argenteuil during the summer of 1874, when Manet frequently worked side by side with Monet and Renoir.

Mary Cassatt also did not exhibit in the first independent show. Her work was going well and her name was becoming known in art circles in both Paris and New York. She listed herself now as Mary Cassatt. A portrait of hers, *Madam Cortier*, had been hung in the Salon. The summer of 1874 Mary spent back at Villiers-le-Bel working with Thomas Couture. That fall she rented a studio in Paris and, with sister Lydia, moved into a small nearby apartment on the rue de Laval at the foot of Montmartre. The course of her life was set. If becoming a professional artist – never "a woman who paints" meant giving up marriage and family of her own, so be it. She was adamant, at times even abrasive, on the matter.

Mary was in Paris with her mother and two sisters, and nineteen-year-old Louisine Havemeyer who was most eager to see and learn as much as possible. Louisine was enthralled by all that Mary had seen and accomplished, the places she had been, and wondered how she had ever summoned the courage to go off to Italy and Spain by herself. Mary took her to the opera and theater and engaged in long talks about Correggio and Velázquez. "I felt that Miss Cassatt was the most intelligent woman I had ever met and I cherished every word she uttered…" These first encounters between Louisine and Mary marked the beginning of fifty-year-long friendship of far-reaching consequences.

For her friend Emily Sartain, Mary's strong-willed, occasionally dictatorial ways became too much. There was a dispute over some unknown matter and bitter feelings resulted. "Miss Cassatt is a tremendous talker and very touchy and selfish, so if you hear her talking of me at home, as she has done lately in Paris, you will know the origin of it all. I shall never become intimate with her again…" [21] Emily went home to Philadelphia to teach at the School of Design for Women, where she would have a long and distinguished career.

The First Exhibition was now over and the only result appeared to be an increase in the public's contempt for the painters, which rendered their works un-saleable. In March 1875, they held a sale of their work. Seventy pictures by Monet, Sisley, Renoir, Morisot were put up to auction at the Hotel Drouot. Because of unprecedented violence, the auctioneer was obliged to summon the police to prevent the altercations from degenerating into fistfights. Hecklers howled at each bid. The paintings sold for practically nothing, barely covering the cost of the frame. One of the newspapers, *The Paris Journal*, reported the event: "We had good fun with the purple landscapes, red flowers, black rivers, yellow and green women, and blue children which the pontiffs of the new school presented to the admiration of the public." [22]

The total of the sale amounted to only 10,346 francs. With a hostile crowd and few buyers Renoir sold twenty canvases for 2,000 francs compared to the 300,000 francs a respected Salon artist such as Meissonier could earn from one painting alone. Early on Renoir depended on friends to purchase paintings and received support from Édouard Manet, Victor Chocquet and others. Chocquet, who was a government employee at the Ministry of Finance, was at the auction. Renoir was reported to have said of him, "What a charming crackpot … He scraped up the means to buy paintings from his salary … and never gave a thought to whether or not the art would appreciate in value." Chocquet had the spirit of a true collector preferring to make his own discoveries by himself wholly uninterested in what others did or thought. Renoir said, "He paid me all sorts of compliments on my painting, and asked me if I would consent to do a portrait of Mme Chocquet."

[23] Great as Chocquet's real admiration for Monet and Renoir, his enthusiasm was for Cézanne who painted several portraits of him. Meeting Chocquet was the only benefit the friends drew from their sale in 1875.

The Second Exhibition was held in 1876. The exhibitions allowed Degas to introduce his pastels to the public – it would be difficult to imagine women at their toilette being accepted at the Salon. Degas introduced Caillebotte to the other Impressionists and in 1876 he was invited by Renoir and Henri Rouart to show in the Second Impressionist Exhibition, which was held at the Durand-Ruel gallery in the rue Le Peletier. He emerged as one of the prime organizers of the Third Exhibition in 1877 as the Durand-Ruel gallery was not available. Callilbotte was a keen buyer of Degas' works at this time. But 1876 was not a great year, the dealers were overstocked with Impressionist works and the entire clan of painters was in distress. Manet speaks of watching his expenses and giving up his studio. The wealthy Caillebotte provided financial security for some of the artists. In fact, it was largely due to Caillebotte's untiring enthusiasm and tenacity that the third exhibition of the group was organized in the spring of 1877.

As to the reviews for the second exhibition, the art critic held in high repute Albert Wolff wrote, "The rue Peletier is unfortunate. Following upon the burning of the Opera House, a new disaster has fallen upon the quarter. There has just been opened at M. Durand-Ruel's an exhibition of what is said to be painting. The innocent passer-by enters, and a cruel spectacle meets his terrified gaze. Here five or six lunatics, of whom one is a woman, have chosen to exhibit their works. There are people who burst out into laughter in front of these objects. Personally I am saddened by them. These so-called artists style themselves Intransigents, Impressionists. They take paint, brushes, and canvases; they throw a few colours on to the canvas at random, and then they sign the lot. In the same way the inmates of a madhouse pick up the stones on the road and believe they have found diamonds." [24]

Abandoning their original title of Societe Anonyme, they decided to appropriate the name of Impressionists. The adoption of the word Impressionist led to the withdrawal of those less daring artists, painting in a modified scale of color, who had been associated with them in their first exhibition. Only eighteen painters took part in the exhibition of 1877. However, more than two hundred and thirty works were put on exhibit with each of the Impressionists contributing a larger number than before. After 1874, however, Cézanne exhibited in only one other Impressionist show, the third, which was held in 1877 and to which he submitted sixteen paintings.

Degas exhibited *The Absinthe Drinker*, a rather depressive scene of a simply dressed woman in a café, who is sitting in front of her absinthe-filled glass. "The man to the right is smoking a pipe and is looking out of the picture, without paying any attention to his companion at his side. The sad expressions on their faces, the bleakness of the café interior, and the lack of any distraction make this a compelling image of the misery of the lower classes, who hope to find some relief from their daily burden in a glass of alcohol." [25]

An even greater uproar was caused by Degas' painting *Terrace of a Cafe in the Evening* when it was shown at the Third Impressionist exhibition. Degas had dared to depict prostitutes chatting at a boulevard café; a subject, which through certainly not uncommon to encounter in the streets of the city, shocked men visitors of the show because of its frank portrayal of the subject and its acute observations of human behavior. Degas also showed his *L'Etoile*, among other dance scenes, and the young critic George Riviere expressed his enthusiasm: "After having seen these pastels, you will never have to go to the Opera again."

With a few exceptions, the press, in the days that followed, rivaled each other in stupid attacks and facile jokes, a monotonous repetition of its former comments. Cézanne's works especially excited general hilarity. No one was more outraged by the attitude of the public than Victor Chocquet. He vociferously challenged the laughers; made them ashamed of their jokes and lashed them with ironical remarks. Zola also wrote a review of the show. He called Monet the outstanding personality among the exhibitors "Next I wish to name M. Paul Cézanne who is certainly the greatest colorist of the group. There are, in the exhibition, some Provencal landscapes of his, which have a splendid character." [26] The general consensus summed up by a critic writing of the Impressionist works for *La Chroniques des Arts*: "They provoke laugher, and yet they are lamentable. They display the profoundest ignorance of drawing, of composition and of colour. When children amuse themselves with a box of colours and a piece of paper, they do better." [27]

At the Café Guerbois, Degas and Caillebotte were talking over their plans for a fourth independent exhibition for the summer of 1879. This time Degas was adamant about the name, they were not going to call themselves Impressionists any longer. It was a red flag to a bull; Caillebotte thought the opposite. The Compromise: "*Exposition faite par un groupe d'artistes independents, realists et impressionists.*" The relations between Degas and Caillibotte were deteriorating and before the opening of the Fourth Impressionist Exhibition in 1879, Caillebotte wrote to Monet: "Don't think, for instance, that Degas sent his twenty-seven or thirty pictures. This morning there were only eight canvases by him. He is very trying, but we have to admit that he has great talent." "Degas' relations with his other colleagues hardly presented him in a favorable light. Besides being selfish and showing little understanding of their financial situations, one might say, he used the exhibitions as a means of bringing in his own friends, not least the Italians, or those of Italian extraction who were in Paris – Zandomeneghi, Giuseppe de Nittis, and J.F. Raffaelli. Caillebotte, who had helped to finance the exhibition, took the not unreasonable line that shows should consist only of those painters who "have contributed real interest to the subject." [28]

The Fifth Exhibition was a startling one for Degas. Joris-Karl Huysmans' review of Degas' pictures at the exhibition read as follows: "When your eyes are trained on these leaping figures, the illusion becomes so complete that they all come to life and gasp for breath, and you can almost hear the shouts of the dancing mistress piercing the shrill din of the violin –'Heels forward, hips back, hold up your wrist, now crack your joints' – while at that final command, the grand développé gets under way, and uplifted legs, lifting puffed tutus with them, come to rest, strained, on the highest bar." [29]

During the Sixth Impressionist exhibition of 1881, which did not include Renoir, Monet and Sisley, one critic claimed that the two women were the only interesting artists: "Morisot and Cassatt were the obvious standard bearers of the new style … and for the first time in recorded history women artists were singled out as the undisputed leaders of avant-garde painting." "Morisot's sitters (like herself) seemed softer and more tender than the rather stiff, seemingly

Puritanical characters portrayed by Cassatt," claimed Gauguin. He thought Cassatt was the greater artist.

Stimulated by his sculptor friend Paul Albert Barholome, Degas produced numerous wax and clay models of dancers and horses. He valued wax for its mutability, and sometimes friends visiting his studio would happen upon a sculpture returned to a state of a ball of wax, as if the result had not been satisfactory. With the exception of *The Little Dancer Aged Fourteen*, he never exhibited any of them. An important variation of the theme of dance this famous work exists in several casts and shows the young Belgian ballerina, Marie van Goethem, who was then a pupil of the Opera. Her mother was a laundress and oldest sister a prostitute and thief.

Hyuysmans, the most brilliant and penetrating art critic of Degas' time ignored the banal reactions and recognized his revolutionary achievement. He called the statue of The Little Dancer "the only really modern attempt that I know in sculpture … All the ideas about sculpture, about cold, lifeless whiteness, about those memorable formulas copied again and again for centuries are demolished. … M. Degas has knocked over the traditions of sculpture, just as he has for a long time been shaking up the conventions of painting." [30]

She was presented at the sixth exhibition in 1881. The work was unanimously considered to be an extraordinary creation, "a truly modern effort, and essay in realism in sculpture," according to the critic Charles Ephrussi. The original wax sculpture was dressed in a real bodice, tutu, stockings and ballet shoes, on her head was a wig with a pigtail tied with a leek-green ribbon, and she wore a similar ribbon around her neck. The wax was tinted to simulate flesh.

The combination of artificial and natural materials – wax, cloth, and hair – was unique combination and the most remarkable aspect of the statue. It blurred the boundaries between reality and artifice. The sculpture was posthumously cast in bronze in 1921. During the later years, Degas modeled a number of small wax sculptures to study the effects of movements of dancers. Although originally not meant to be cast in bronze, they can be found today in a number of museums.

By the eighth and last Impressionist exhibition in 1886, the painters had established their reputations. They were then able to move to prominent dealers like Paul Durand-Ruel, who now had international connections and provided greater visibility, publicity, sales, and prestige. The final Impressionist exhibition was held on the first floor of the famous Maison Doree, on the corner of the rue Laffitte and the Boulevard des Italiens. Degas who as usual organized the event, exhibited a series of seven pastels of female nudes bathing, washing or doing their hair, all seen from an absolutely original angle, as if observed "through a keyhole." "Up until now," explained the artist, "the nude has always been shown in poses which implied a viewer, but these women of mine are simple folk … I show them unconscious of their appearance." [31] The public was deeply shocked.

Of the original Impressionists only Degas, Morisot and Pissarro participated in the eighth exhibition. Degas only hung ten of the fifteen works he had listed in the catalogue, but those ten won critical acclaim. However, the "series of female nudes bathing, washing, drying themselves, wiping themselves off, combing their hair or having their hair combed" created more of a stir than Seurat's *Afternoon on the Island of La Grande Jatte*, now considered the showpiece of the 1886 exhibition.

Monet told Georges de Bellio a Romanian aristocrat who purchased several Impressionist paintings that he was too depressed to consider exhibiting with the rest of the group. "I am absolutely sickened with and demoralized by this life I've been leading for so long. When you get to my age, there is nothing more to look forward to. ... I'm ruling out the possibility of participating in it, as I just don't have anything worth showing." [32]

But, the Eight Exhibition attracted nearly sixteen thousand paying visitors, all expenses were met, and each painter made a profit of 439 francs instead of the usual loss.

Chapter Thirteen: Public Sales

Renoir, in order to study his Montmartre models *in situ*, moved up the hill, renting a dilapidated stable-block in the garden of a 17th century house at 12, rue Cortot. The house consisted of the ground floor, an old stable, which would serve as studio, and from the two rooms above there was a view out to the garden. Renoir painted a great many canvases in the garden - 1876 was a prodigious year in his work, hardly equaled afterward.

While renting his stable, Renoir was to paint several masterpieces, one of which was *La Balancoire* (The swing). He also, in 1875, began to work on his most ambitious and original painting up to that time, *The Ball at the Moulin del la Galette,* which has since become an icon of the Impressionist movement. This painting is doubtless Renoir's most important work of the mid 1870's. Though some of his friends appear in the picture, Renoir's main aim was to convey the vivacious and joyful atmosphere of this popular dance garden on the Butte Montmartre. However, it was painted primarily in the garden of his studio with friends posing for him. It was shown in the Third Impressionist exhibition in 1877 and while it won some acclaim, the overall result of the entire show was again disappointing as far as sales go.

A new model entered Renoir's life in 1875, Margot Legrand. She became his favorite model for the next four years. In 1879 she died of smallpox; Dr. Gachet was unable to save her. Renoir's grief at her death seemed to indicate that their relationship had been more intimate. Even prior to her death, Renoir had some dark periods mainly due to the abuse he received from the critics and, in consequence, the difficulty he experienced in selling his pictures. From the onset of his career, Renoir had known the lack of money and had suffered the extreme of poverty; he had never really freed himself from these difficulties and after taking part in the exhibitions of the Impressionists he found himself in greater financial embarrassment.

Renoir had tried to increase his resources by selling his pictures by auction. He combined with Monet, Sisley, and Morisot in holding the first public sale of Impressionist paintings in March 1875 and with Pissarro, Sisley and Caillebotte in May 1877. The twenty canvases put up to auction in 1875 sold for 2,150 francs. Among them were some of his most important works: *Avant le bain* (a young woman, bare to the waist, with arms raised to undo her hair), which realized no more than 140 francs. After the failure of these two public sales, Renoir did not attempt to repeat the experiment. His works, moreover, were held in such low esteem on account of the sentence of condemnation, which had gone forth against them, that he was also unable to sell them privately at reasonable prices.

Funds were not sufficient to enable him to live, so Renoir turned to portrait painting. He painted portraits, which were to rank as important works both in respect of their size and of their composition. He was able to obtain sufficient support from people of wealth and people of intelligence to enable him to free himself from the extreme financial embarrassment in which he had hitherto lived. As it happened, in 1875 Zola's publisher Georges Charpentier was walking through the streets of Montmartre when he noticed a small canvas signed by an unknown painter

Auguste Renoir. Charpentier had recently inherited his publishing business from his father and was a man of discriminating taste. Charpentier, who had recognized the greatness of the Impressionists, even when they were universally decried, was the first to commission Renoir to paint portraits. Renoir temporarily deserted the plein-air when he accepted the major commission from Charpentier that of painting a large portrait of Mme Charpentier and her children in her small, so-called Japanese salon.

In the same year he met two wealthy society people M. and Mme. Bérard a retired banker and diplomat and developed a close friendship which lasted until Berard's death in 1905. They admired the charm of *La Danseuse* and commissioned Renoir to paint a portrait of their eldest daughter, Marthe. The picture was a great success and they had come to look upon Renoir as a friend. Renoir was frequently invited to their spacious chateau at Wargemont in Normandy. For now portraits were important to Renoir, they became less and less important after his career had been firmly established. In his later years most of his portraits were of his family and some close friends.

For those Impressionists who did not have the patronage that Renoir had just found, Caillebotte, with an annual private income of fifty thousand livres, was able to provide constant support to his other Impressionist friends. In 1875, at an auction at the Hotel Drouot, he made the extremely timely purchase of seventy-five paintings, including works by Monet, Renoir, Sisley, and Morisot. It was he who financed the 1877 exhibition at rue Le Peletier. He also regularly rented studios and accommodations for Monet; helped the ever-needed Pissarro, and flew to the assistance of Renoir.

Despite Caillebotte buying works done by Monet, he, time and again, was obliged to borrow money from various friends and acquaintances. On several occasions Monet asked Manet for help, writing in June, "It's getting more and more difficult. Since day before yesterday, not a cent left and no more credit, neither at the butcher or baker. Although I have faith in the future, you see that the present is very painful. Could you possibly send me by return mail a 20-franc note? That would help me for the moment." [1] His urgent appeals went out to others.

Monet began to focus his time on the Tuileries and parc Monceau. He concentrated on the world of the garden as he had done at Argenteuil. Later that year, he moved to Montgeron at the request of his patrons Ernest and Alice Hoschedé. The Hoschedés had commissioned him to paint four large decorative pictures for their dining room of their chateau. He worked in this lavish setting for six months from July to December 1876 and produced four huge canvases and also painted numerous views of the Yerres River, which ran near the Hoschedé property. With money in his pocket again, Monet returned to Argenteuil – determined to live like a gentlemen in a newly rented pink house with green shutters in the rue Saint-Denis. He resumed the lavish life of a bourgeois hiring gardeners, maids, and cooks - the problem was that none of these people were being paid.

It was also in 1876 that Degas seems to have given up the greater part of his fortune to ease the financial predicament of one of his brothers, who supposedly lost everything by imprudent speculation in American securities. Degas would never speak of such private affairs, yet it is known that he began from then on to depend on occasional sales. He did not have much trouble in finding buyers and obtaining reasonably high prices, but he was now obliged to part with his works.

Cézanne spent part of the year 1877 with Pissarro at Pontoise, where they painted again side by side. He wrote to Zola, "It appears that profound desolation reigns in the Impressionist camp. Gold is not exactly flowing into their pockets and the pictures are rotting on the spot. We are living in very trouble times and I do not know when an unhappy painting will regain some of its luster." [2] Cézanne decided he was disgusted with both Renoir and Monet and disillusioned with Paris. For the time being, he retreated to Provence seeking refuge and tranquility in L'Estaque where he was secretly hiding Hortense and Paul.

Cézanne was leaving Paris after the humiliation of the Third Impressionist exhibition. His old friend Zola, however, was celebrating his first major triumph, the novel *L'Assomoir* 1877. The novel was set amongst the Parisian working classes and described a family destroyed by alcohol and poverty with unremitting frankness and exactness of observation. The novel and a stage adaptation made Zola famous and filled his pockets. The success of *L'Assommoir*, however, had turned Zola into something of a recluse. He had purchased a large, ungainly house just south of Giverny, at Medan. Cézanne and Zola had drifted apart as their lives diverged and for some time had had very little to do with each other.

Cézanne was also drifting apart from the Café Guerbois group and worked in increasing isolation at his home in Aix. Perhaps there are several reasons for his recluse behavior but one may have been the direction that his art was taking, which further separated him from the style and technique of the other Impressionists. And, second, the debilitating abuse he and his work received from the Salon, critics, and public. In fact, after the Third Independent exhibition, Cézanne did not show his works publicly for almost twenty years.

Monet also remembered the reviews, particularly of the First Exhibition with one critic declaring that these artists had to clean their glasses. "Poor blind idiots!" he said to Renoir. "They want to see everything clearly, even through fog!" This had given him an idea: he would paint fog. One day he announced to Renoir, "I've got it! The Gare Saint-Lazare! I'll show it just as the trains are starting, with smoke from the engines so thick you can hardly see a thing. It's a fascinating sight, a dream world." [3] In reality, Monet, may have been readying for 1877 Third Exhibition. He must have realized that he needed some new modern-life pictures for this show, which undoubtedly motivated him to consider the train as a subject.

He did not, of course, intend to paint it from memory. He would paint it *in situ* so as to capture the play of sunlight on the steam rising from the locomotives. "I'll get them to delay the train for Rouen half an hour. The light will be better then," he told Renoir who then told him he was crazy. He went to the Director of the Western Railway, who knew nothing about painting, but was reluctant to show his ignorance; he knew that some painters were celebrities. Monet announced the purpose of his visit: "I have decided to paint either the Gare du Nord or Gare Saint-Lazare, but … yours has more character." The Gare Saint-Lazare was a vivid symbol for the origins and explosive growth of one of the nations most important assets as well as one of the country's primary sources of change and advancement. Permission was granted.

The Gare Saint-Lazare: Arrival of a Train, 1877 (oil on canvas), Monet, Claude (1840-1926) / Fogg Art Museum, Harvard University Art Museums, USA / Bequest from the Collection of Maurice Wertheim, Class 1906 / The Bridgeman Art Library

The astonished director instructed the train driver to make steam. All the trains were halted; the platforms were cleared; the engines were crammed with coal so as to give out all the smoke Monet could possibly want, while Monet sat and painted. He finally left carrying a dozen or so new paintings. The entire personnel with the Director at the head, walked him out. Renoir finished the story by saying, "I wouldn't have dared to paint even the front of the corner grocer!" Monet painted his last pictures of Paris, including the famous seven paintings of the Gare Saint-Lazare. He moved to Vetheuil in 1878 and never again painted Paris or its near suburbs.

Monet always lived on the banks of the Seine, in order to be near the water; in 1878 he left Argenteuil and went lower down the river to Vetheuil. It was around this time that Monet's affair with Alice Hoschedé, wife of the rich but incompetent financier, was thought to have begun. Alice, who was one of the Impressionists' best patrons, was the original owner of *Impression –*

Sunrise.

Mme Hoschedé, who had been living in a well furnished house, left her husband during the summer of 1878 – shortly before or after the disastrous sale of his collection – and with her six children joined Monet at Vetheuil. Mme Hoschedé was able to take care of the painter's wife whose weak condition had failed to improve after her recent delivery of Michel on 17 March, 1878. Vetheuil, off the beaten track and inaccessible by rail, promised the obvious advantage of reducing the Monets' cost of living. The disadvantage to living in Vetheuil was that the journey to Paris took the best part of the day; Monet would effectively be cut off from life in Paris. Despite reducing expenses, by the end of the year Monet found himself again without money, too poor to buy canvas or paints. He terminated his lease on his Paris apartment and moved his studios from the rue Moncey to a small, ground floor apartment in the name of Caillebotte, who paid the rent.

Vetheuil was a picturesque village when Monet moved there in 1878. It was here that Monet would work for the next three years. The place appeared to agree with him. Over the time he was there, he produced nearly three hundred paintings – one every four days. Remarkable output, surpassing the number of pictures he completed during his seven years at Argenteuil by a large margin. His work was different from those earlier works, as Monet now sought out spaces in and around this rural village that revealed its quiet secrets – the backwaters of the Seine, as in *Seine at Vetheuil*, the orchards that dotted the surrounding hills and the well-trodden dirt paths of the little town of Lavancourt just across the river.

The scene at home was not as bucolic as the small villages Monet painted. When Camille gave birth to her second son Michel, her health rapidly deteriorated. Camille was experiencing continued loss of strength and soon had to be confined to bed. The illness, probably cancer, began to affect her entire system. According to Monet's letters, she suffered terribly during that summer. On 5 September 1879, mercifully, she died; she was 32 years old. Monet painted an extraordinary portrait of her on her death bed. But besides having to deal with her loss and with becoming a single parent for his two young children aged twelve and one, Monet had to deal with the fact that Camille had not died simply in the bosom of her own family. The house in Vertheuil had also been home to Alice Hoschedé, her five daughters and newly born son. In 1892, Monet and Alice married, a year after Ernest Hoschedé's death. All these changes coincided with the artist's virtual abandonment of figure painting. After 1878, except for a few paintings of family and friends, large-scale figures disappear from his easel.

Charles-François Daubigny died 19 February 1878 and a sale of his effects was announced to take place in May of that year. The sale showed the contempt in which Monet's work was held. According to Duret, in 1873 Daubigny bought one of Monet's views of Holland, *Canal a Saardam* from M. Durand-Ruel for 500 francs. Duret admired this painting and went to the sale hoping to make a successful bid. The painting was not among his effects. "I supposed that the Daubigny's did not want to part with it. A fortnight later, I happened to be visiting the Hotel Drouot, when I came across a room full of unfinished sketches and old canvases. *Canal a saardam* was among them. I had come across the scourings of Daubigny's studio. Apparently, Daubigny's heirs had put Monet's picture there because it would have disgraced the official sale of Daubigny's effects. I obtained it for 80 francs." In 1894 circumstances led Duret to sell his collection; *Canal* was secured for the sum of 5500 francs from Durand-Ruel. He resold it to M. Decap, who, when he was putting a part of his collection up to action in 1901, withdrew it at 80,00 francs. [4]

After 1878, Cézanne spent much of the rest of his life painting in Provence. Relatively isolated from the Paris art scene, Cézanne pursued his own artistic path. While the Impressionists depicted changing light and atmospheric effects, he was more interested in studying the underlying structure of the landscapes he painted. He said, "I wanted to make of Impressionism something solid and enduring like the art in museums."

In autumn of 1879 Manet was seized with acute pains and weakness of the limbs, resulting in his fall upon leaving his studio. Paralysis of a nervous centre, ataxy, had set in, and was pronounced incurable. Walking became so difficult that he was almost entirely confined to his chair. The paralysis remained local; it never affected his mind nor did it diminish his power as a painter. Manet was at the height of his career.

There were gradual indications that the critics were beginning to understand what the Impressionists were aiming for – glimpses of the modern world in action, contemporary scenes viewed with the immediacy of real life. These changing views were quite apparent with Manet who had arrived at a particular kind of renown, which adhered to him throughout the rest of his life. He was now one of the most prominent men in Paris; everybody knew who he was. For most of his life, however, he was never really understood either by the world at large or by the smaller world of Parisian society. He was always regarded simply as a violent and extravagant artist, who lacked the qualities of a true master. There was always, however, a select circle of writers, artists, connoisseurs, distinguished women, and a small band of disciples that gathered around him.

Monet constantly cried poverty, throughout the 1870s, which has led most biographers to claim he was in dire straights. But in most years, he actually was making more money than doctors and lawyers in Paris. His solicitations, therefore, were provoked not by his paltry earnings but by his extravagant habits and lack of fiscal restraint. They also may have been a way to drum up sympathy. Renoir observed that "Monet was penniless and he wore shirts with lace cuffs."

Toward the end of 1877, Monet became so weary of the struggle that he began to lose faith in the future. He asked Chocquet "to be good enough to take one or two daubs which I'll let you have at any price you may make: 50 francs, 40 francs, whatever you are able to pay, because I can't wait any longer." [5] It was then that Manet conceived a plan for rescuing him: "I went to see Monet yesterday," he wrote Duret, "I found him quite broken down and in despair. He asked me to find him someone who would take ten or twenty of his pictures at 100 francs each, the purchaser to choose which he liked. Shall we arrange the matter between us, say 500 francs each? Of course nobody, he least of all, must know that the offer comes from us. I had thought of some dealer or collector, but I foresaw the possibility of a refusal. It is unhappily necessary to be as well informed as we are in order to bring it off – in spite of the repugnance we may feel – an excellent business transaction, and at the same time, to do a good turn to a man of talent." [6]

As one closes in on the end of the 1970s, the influence of photography was beginning to be felt. The instantaneousness of the photograph; its ability to capture a moment in time, and its arbitrary framing of scenes were all qualities that the Impressionist painters sought in their art – particularly Degas. The subjects of his paintings – dancers and horses, for example, reflected the immediate world around him. Paintings captured the rehearsal room atmosphere, full of movement and activity, chattering dancers adjusting their costumes and yawning and scratching while the teacher watches a dancer go through her steps. Degas' work appears to mimic the snapshot effect of photography.

Credit: Apples and Oranges, 1895-1900 (oil on canvas), Cezanne, Paul (1839-1906) / Musee d'Orsay, Paris, France / Giraudon / The Bridgeman Art Library

The group began to split apart in the late 1870s, but despite their differences of opinion, their friendships remained firm. Monet was among the first to threaten desertion. He was becoming cynical about the effect of the group identity on his prospect and told the other members that he had no intention of exhibiting with them again. The first member to actually defect was Renoir. He could see that his portrait of Madam Charpentier and her children was obvious Salon material. Two little golden-haired children dressed alike in blue satin and white chiffon posing with their mother in the luxurious drawing room, with lavish drapes and rugs, arrangements of flowers and a bowl of grapes glistening on a side table.

Cézanne moved into his late phase. Now he concentrated on a few basic subjects: still lifes of studio objects built around such recurring elements as apples, statuary, and tablecloths; studies of bathers, based upon the male model and drawing upon a combination of memory, earlier studies, and sources in the art of the past; and successive views of the Mont Sainte-Victoire, a nearby landmark, painted from his studio looking across the intervening valley.

Cézanne reminiscing with Joachim Gasquet, noted, " I too was an Impressionist, I won't hide it. Pissarro had an enormous influence on me. ... all of us perhaps come out of Pissarro." Already in 1865 he had eliminated black, bitumen, sienna and the ochers from his palette. Cézanne now painted only with the three primary colors and their immediate derivatives. [7]

Historically, it was not until the 17th century that still life came to be taken seriously. And it was in his still lifes that Cézanne's outstanding qualities as a painter were first recognized. The still life was welcomed as heralding a new realism in painting, alongside the landscape revival. Still lifes and landscapes gave the artist his first practice in disciplining his "temperament" and in improving and controlling his technique and composition. And it was in his still lifes that Cézanne's outstanding qualities as a painter were first recognized. His landscapes and figural works could strike even well disposed critics as too distorted and "primitive," but his still lifes prompted acknowledgment from almost every connoisseur of art.

Joris-Karl Huysmans, a familiar in Zola's Medan circle, wrote of Cézanne's still lifes: "There, in full light, in china fruit-bowls or on white table-cloths, are his pears and apples, set down quickly in crude strokes and smudged with a thumb: seen from close to, they are a wild mess of bright red and yellow, green and blue. Seen from the correct distance they are choice, juicy fruits that set the mouth watering. And suddenly one becomes aware of altogether new truth, unfamiliar yet real shades, patches of colour with a character all their own, shadows falling from the far side of fruits across a white table cloth, with a hint of blue that makes them quite magical if one compares with ordinary still lifes done in senseless asphalt colours." [8]

To Cézanne, the starting point of still lifes were fruits. "I decided against flowers. They wither on the instant. Fruits are more loyal. It is as if they were begging forgiveness for losing their colour. ... They come to you laden with scents, tell you of the fields they have left behind, the rain that nourished them, the dawns they have seen. When you translate the skin of a beautiful peach in opulent strokes, or the melancholy of an old apple, you sense their mutual reflections, the same mild shadows of relinquishment, the same loving sun, the same recollections of dew ..." [9]

In his seclusion, Cézanne spoke to only one man in these terms. His name was Joachim Gasquet, a young poet, the son of a friend of Cézanne's youth, Henri Gasquet, a baker. Joachim would accompany Cézanne on his daily expeditions to paint *sur le motif*. The young poet was extremely enthusiastic about Cézanne and his art. Initially Cézanne was put off by this enthusiasm, but the young man's patent sincerity led him to accept it. On their joint wanderings through the dearly beloved countryside of Provence, Cézanne began to confide in this new friend; though the age gap was considerable, they shared their love of Provence, with Mont Sainte Victoire at its heart.

"Look at Sainte-Victoire," said Cezanne to Gasquet. "What a sweep! What a commanding thirst for sunshine! And what melancholy in the evening when all that heaviness settles upon it. Those blocks were fire. The fire is still in them. The shadow, the day, seems to recoil from them in awe, to be afraid of them. Plato's cave is up there; when great clouds pass over, you will notice that their shadows tremble on the crags as if scorched, as if they were being quaffed by the fiery mouth at the same time." [10]

The history of mountain's name goes back to bloody battles fought between Roman legions under their general Marius and the tribe of the Cimbri. The name certainly points back to pre-historic cultic rituals that were celebrated in the caves on the mountain and in the vicinity. Provence is one of the most ancient inhabited parts of the world. The grotto of the hermit St. Ser, which had a Romanesque church built over it, was still used for pilgrimages in Cézanne's time, by girls in quest of husbands and mothers whose children were sick.

Cézanne put Impressionism behind him, and separated from the Impressionists. He had to go his own way, far from the controversies and mockery of the Parisian avant-garde. He needed the solitude of Provence. But more than likely it was that modernity of Paris from which Cézanne was escaping. He did not need the inspiration of life in Paris, as Renoir and Degas did. The motifs of his home parts: near Jas de Bouffan, on walks near his brother-in-law's house, or in the woods of Chateau noir, up to the Bibemus quarry were enough for him.

Cézanne's financial position was far from easy; not daring to confess to his father the circumstances of his private life, he was obliged to subsist on his bachelor's allowance. Fortunately Dr. Gachet helped him with occasional purchases. Cézanne was not valued highly either as an artist or as a human being. In the parental home he was spied on and kept tied to the apron strings. His despotic father treated him with condescension and suspicion. His elder sister Marie looked after him to the point of smothering him in care, but did not understand his art or approve of it. Good society, which Zola valued so highly, was not open to Cézanne. It was a vicious cycle; the more he was excluded, the more he opted out of society. So what Cézanne was looking for in contact with Nature, and in tracing the structures of Nature, was some fixed stability. [11]

In 1879 Degas and Pissarro invited Cassatt to contribute to a new journal, *Le Jour et la Nuit*, in which they planned to publish original prints that could experiment with the effects of light and shadow. Maybe Degas thought that he was returning a favor because Cassatt had arranged for Havemeyers to buy Degas' painting, *Collector of Prints* (1866) for $1,000. Degas, as usual wanted to keep the picture and retouch it. After two years, when he felt it was ready, he declared that the value of his work had increased and demanded three thousand francs. Havemeyer was not only deprived of the picture during this time, but had to pay the 300 percent increase. Cassatt was outraged and, for a long time, severed relations with Degas.

Chapter Fourteen: Hors Concours

It had now been twenty years since their youthful encounters at the studios of Gleyre and Suisse. The oldest was Pissarro now fifty; they all had experimented with plein-air painting; Degas had expanded his artistic repertoire to include sculpting. Monet had abandoned paintings of Paris. Cézanne moved further away from the ephemeral Impressionist style. Their mistresses were now their wives and their surviving children were growing. Manet at forty-eight was still regarded by the public as the leading force of the movement. Paris itself had also gone through dynamic changes in the past twenty years. She shed her medieval garb and changed into an elegant and prosperous City of Light. Paris had altered her environs to suit the futuristic visions of Haussmann and to capture the imperial grandeur sought by Napoleon III. The confines of Paris had broadened as railway lines now connected the city with riverside villages and towns.

Monet decided to break with his prior practice of trying to show and sell his work through the independent exhibitions. His decision caused a lot of grumbling among the core Impressionists. Pissarro was particularly irate, so much so that he resisted the idea of allowing Monet to rejoin the Impressionists' show the following year. "One should suffer just punishment for mistakes committed," he told Caillebotte, who was an advocate for Monet. Monet's decision to go his separate ways was announced in the press as a mock funeral notice that appeared in *Le Gaulouis* in late January 1880. The notice read: "The Impressionist school has the honor of informing you of the grievous loss it has suffered in the person of M. Claude Monet, one of its revered masters. The funeral for M. Claude Monet will take place on 1 May next, at ten o'clock in the morning – the day after the opening at the church of the Palais de l'Industrie – in M. Cabanel's gallery. You are requested not to attend." It was signed "De Profunsis!" and was followed by a footnote saying the invitation had been sent "on behalf of M. Degas, head of the school; M Raffeilli, successor to the deceased; Miss Cassatt, M. Caillebotte, M. Pissarro, M. Louis Forain, M. Bracquemond, M. Rouard [sic] etc… his ex-friends, ex-students, and ex-supporters." [1]

Monet's return to the Salon marked the end of his exclusive reliance upon the good offices of Durand-Ruel who had supported him since the dealer's first purchases in early 1872. From 1880 onwards, Monet explored a variety of marketing strategies – exhibitions in elite settings such as the offices of the newspaper *La Vie Moderne* and galleries of Durand-Ruel's primary rival Georges Petit, often playing one dealer against the other. He developed a much broader repertoire appealing to a wider range of prospective clients. His favorite site during the 1880s was the Normandy coast; it was in his blood from his childhood in Le Havre and Saint-Adresse and was easily accessible from Vetheuil and later from Giverny. His most frequented spots – Pourville, Varengeville, Étretat and Dieppe and out of 400 landscapes he completed during the first half of this decade, over one third depicted these spots.

After several difficult months following the death of Camille on 5 September 1879, a grief-stricken Monet (resolving never to be mired in poverty again) began in earnest to create some of his best paintings of the 19th century. During the early 1880s Monet painted several groups of landscapes and seascapes in what he considered to be campaigns to document the French countryside. His extensive campaigns would evolve into his series paintings.

The disintegration of the Impressionist group was further underlined by Monet, who in answer to the partial refusal that the jury returned to him, organized in June 1880, an important one-man show at La Vie Moderne where Manet had had an exhibition in April. When he was asked if he had ceased to be an Impressionist he replied, "Not at all. I am still and I always intend to be an Impressionist … but I see only very rarely the men and women who are my colleagues. The little clique has become a great club which opens its doors to the first-come dauber." [2] Monet may have been referring to Degas' friends Raffaelli or Gauguin.

Beginning in 1881 Monet left his studio and family for concentrated periods of several weeks, sometimes months. Alice and the children joined him for the summer of 1882 at Pourville, but usually he went by himself. For the better part of each year, he painted the landscape of Giverny and its environs. Giverny served as a settled base for his outlying campaigns of tours along the Channel. Furthermore, Monet reached forty at the beginning of 1880, an age when many artists begin to reorient their work.

The events of the years following 1886 added emphasis to the fact that the Impressionists movement had finally broken up. Monet's growing quest was to make Naturalism more intellectually rigorous and he spent a good part of the 1880s period in experimentation. He traveled widely from Norwegian snowscapes to the southern French coast and came to depend closely on Japanese prints for inspiration. The 1880s were the decade of Monet's rise to great fame and considerable fortune, and his letters reveal his success in manipulating his market. It is no accident that all the sites Monet painted along the French coast were tourist spots whose fame preceded their appearance in his dealers' Parisian showrooms. As the decade progressed Monet's prices rose dramatically and so did his reputation and influence. He passed from the status of young rebel to a recognized living master.

After the 1870s, Cézanne's oppressive visual themes of his early work were replaced by calm, "natural motifs." He now learned a good deal from the "school of nature" and from Pissarro. Cézanne recalled Pissarro as his first advocate in Paris, his paternal friend and adviser. However, as noted by Duret, Cézanne's art was still misunderstood by the novice-viewing public but people of literary culture did not at once either understand or appreciate Cézanne's art: "In the opinion of those who only understand drawing under the form of an arrangement of fixed and precise lines, Cézanne did not draw at all. For those who demanded that a picture shall present a historical or anecdotal subject, his pictures, which presented nothing of the kind, were simply not pictures at all. To those who desired surfaces uniformly worked over, his execution, which in some places left the canvas bare and in others loaded it with paint, appeared to be that of an incompetent bungler. His method of juxtaposing or superimposing uniform touches of color, in order to obtain great density, seemed to be coarse, barbaric, and monstrous." [3]

In Duret's view, Cézanne's strengths lay in "the value of the pigment in and for itself, the strength and harmony of the colour. Cézanne's pictures offer a range of color of great intensity and of extreme luminosity. From this the picture derives a strength independent of the subject; so much so that a still life, a few apples and a napkin on a table, assume a kind of grandeur, in the same degree as a human head or a landscape with the sea." [4]

Among his Café Guerbois painters, he was an object of fascination and admiration. His peers were his earliest collectors; Pissarro owned twenty-one. Gauguin used to take one of his favorite Cézannes to a nearby restaurant and hold forth on its amazing qualities. Renoir said, "He has only to put two strokes of color on the canvas and it's already something."

Cézanne and his family rented lodgings in Gardanne, so that he did not have to travel the twenty kilometers every day. Gardanne is a commune in the Bouches-du-Rhône department in southern France. He described his new sense of motivation in a letter to Chocquet on 11 May 1886, " … this area is full of treasures. There has not yet been anyone whose paintings were worthy of the riches that lie dormant here." Above all, Cézanne could see Mont Sainte-Victoire from Gardanne, a subject also "full of treasures" that he was to concentrate on in increasing measure. "Working on the motif of the mountain gave Cézanne new hope and strength. The landscapes he painted there expressed a new self-confidence "I am beginning to paint again," he wrote to Zola at the end of August, "now that I have so little to worry about. In the 1880s, the mountain occupied Cézanne regularly and took a central position in his work." [5]

Cézanne continued to turn to Zola, as if the gesture were imprinted, until well into his forties. "Zola was his friend and confessor, mentor, and motivator, and goad, storm lantern, trusted intermediary, and lender of last resort. He bared more of himself to Zola than to any living thing." *Nana*, Émile Zola's newest literary undertaking, was completed in 1880. *Nana* is the ninth installment in the 20-volume *Les Rougon-Macquart* series, the object of which was to tell "The Natural and Social History of a Family under the Second Empire," the subtitle of the series.

In the early 1880s, after the death of Lydia, her sister and frequent model, Cassatt was further drawn to painting children. She portrayed their ever-changing activities: "sleeping, dozing, talking, nursing, eating … always quiet and well behaved." A sense of security pervaded Cassatt's work. "In the 1880s, Cassatt also began to experiment with drypoint (engraving on copper) as Degas had tried pastels and sculpture. Her finest drypoints all reveal Japanese characteristics, and the female subjects look faintly Japanese in features and skin color." [6]

Manet's health continued to deteriorate. He consented to grueling hydrotherapy treatments intended to stimulate his dysfunctional nerves, dilate his blood vessels and restore his ability to walk. He endured five-hour sessions of ice-cold showers and intense massages at a medical clinic in Bellevue, on the Seine, west of Paris. In June 1880 he wrote to a friend, "I'm doing my penance, my dear Mery, as never before in all my life. Still, if the end result is good, there'll be no regrets. I find the water treatment here absolute torture." His illness was officially attributed to poor circulation in his legs. But it was really locomotor ataxia a degenerative disease of the spinal cord that led to a classic triad of symptoms: lightning pain; failure of muscular coordination, paralysis in the legs, difficult urination, incontinence of the bladder and sexual impotence.

Manet spent another summer close to Paris, at Rueil, too ill to engage in any absorbing work. He did watercolors, wrote charming letters to many of his elegant lady friends, but winter brought no improvement. Early in 1883 his strength visibly abandoned him and he was forced to stay in bed. In April he was operated upon, but the amputation failed to save him.   He was given massive doses of ergot, a drug derived from the fungus on rye plants, which contracts the blood vessels and smoothes the muscle tissue. Ergot is still used to induce contractions in childbirth and relieve migraines. But it is highly toxic when taken in large quantities, as Manet rashly did, in hopes of a cure.

Manet now worked in a less physically demanding medium of pastels rather than painting at an easel. His thoughts often turned to relishing the sweetness of youth and the lively conversations with his Impressionist friends that took place nightly as Café Guerbois. But Manet continued to submit paintings at the Salon. In May of 1881, Manet exhibited his *Portrait of M. Pertuiset* and the *Portrait of Henri Rochefort*. In issuing awards, Duret related the process: "It was the customary for the jury first to pass through the galleries, and in front of the pictures themselves to draw up a preliminary list of artist's names who were to receive distinction. When the jury arrived in front of the *Portrait de Pertuiset*, a heated discussion took place between the members who wished to include it among the pictures qualified for a medal and those who were determined to exclude it. Cabanel, the President of the Jury, noted, 'Gentlemen, there are not, perhaps, four among us here who could paint a head like that.' "[7] Manet had taken special pains to make the head stand out and to give it the impression of fitting solid into the hat. The painting was awarded a second-class medal.

At the age of 38, Renoir met Aline Charigot, a 22-year-old woman from Essoyes in Burgundy. She did the laundry for a seamstress, and also for Renoir and Monet. Soon she became one of Renoir's models and eventually his wife. He loved her looks: a pretty girl with red hair, a retrousse nose, and healthy appetite. But more than that it was her naturalness – her wholesomeness. Aline and Renoir were spending their summer afternoons at the hotel Fournaise. Renoir did not marry Aline until 1890 when their eldest son was five years old, ten years after their first meeting. The Renoirs had three sons, one of whom, Jean, became a filmmaker of note and another, Pierre, became a stage and film actor; Claude was involved in film productions. The first painting for which Aline modeled was the ambitious *Luncheon of the Boating Party* painted 1880-1.

Luncheon of the Boating Party is of the terrace of this hotel on Ile de Chatou, a little island in the Seine River near Ile de Croissy. The scene depicted is well known: we view the crowd relaxing after eating their lunch; the tables are strewn with bottles. It is a wonderful explosion of color and conversation. Aline sits in the foreground, a small griffon dog on her lap. The hotel Fournaise was a short train ride from Renoir's studio in the center of Paris. The owner, Alphonse Fournaise, had built a landing platform for Parisians who wished to swim and rent boats on the river, and he began to serve refreshments on the platform. Renoir recalled the place "where life was a perpetual holiday and the world knew how to laugh in those days."

"In January 1881 Durand-Ruel had begun purchasing far greater numbers of Renoir's paintings than previously and that year he spent 16,000 francs on them. This offered Renoir an unprecedented degree of financial security and, at this point in time, Renoir did not have a family to support, which left him free to spend the money on foreign travel. His first two trips were to Italy and North Africa, destinations common for nineteenth-century artists."[8]   Renoir will be completely conquered by Italy especially by Venice that he will paint it in several canvases. Like Degas in New Orleans, he was hardly able to paint there was so much to look at. He wrote to Durand-Ruel explaining his need for this temporary exile revealing that his loyalty to his friends was a deep concern. This period of his life is known as his "dry period," or "Ingresque Period" after the French painter Jean Ingres due to the fact that he focused on drawing spending much of his time emphasizing figure outlines.

In Renoir's words, "I had wrung Impressionism dry, and I finally came to the conclusion that I neither knew how to paint nor draw. In a word, Impressionism was a blind alley." He moved away from his previous Impressionist style - the contours of his characters become more precise. He drew shapes with more required line; colors became colder. His transition would be progressive because Renoir was in perpetual search of an absolute pictorial art. In 1881, he wrote to Durand-Ruel, "I am again in the illness of research. I am not happy and I erase, I erase again."

Renoir became a devoted follower of the art of Raphael, the great Italian painter of the High Renaissance. He became interested in the methods of Renaissance artists and he criticized the modern teaching methods that had replaced the apprenticeship system. *The Blond Bather,* 1887 was painted at the height of his dry period. The formal figure, most likely Aline, poses against a classical landscape. Renoir no longer will paint the "modern" women of Paris but will paint timeless beauties removed from their real setting and placed in some Eden-like landscape in a golden age full of innocence.

If the trip to Algeria was in a sense a confirmation of his earlier work, then the Italian journey was to be influential for Renoir's art through the remainder of the 1880s, the most experimental and troublesome decade of his career. Much of the work produced in the 1880s is groping and experimental in nature. In the light of changes in his artistic process Renoir would now opt for the Salon as the natural venue for his paintings, rather than the independent exhibition. In 1882, when Durand-Ruel was desperate to present a seemingly united band of Impressionists at exhibition in what has to be the seventh group show, Renoir was still in the south with Cézanne. Renoir made it clear that he "mistrusted the combination of Pissarro and Gauguin and that to be associated with Gauguin at an exhibition would cause his canvases to fall by 50% in value. Renoir's rupture with the group and with the style was complete – he did not exhibit at the eighth and final show in 1886." [9]

Luncheon of a Boating Party, which he finished in the summer of 1881 was his second large-scale masterpiece. Two years later, Renoir executed three of his most stunning paintings: *Dance in the City, Dance in the Country*, and *Dance at Bougival*. The two paintings *City* and *Country* were painted as a pair; the "elegant restraint of city dancers and the cool background contrasts with the more rural atmosphere of a country dance in the open air." The open-air cafés of suburban Bougival, on the Seine outside Paris, were popular recreation spots for city dwellers, including the Impressionist painters. The woman's face, framed by her red bonnet, is the focus of attention, both ours and her companion's. [10]

In this same year the state abandoned its traditional authority over the Salon. The Salon was finally released from the exclusive control of the Ministry of Fine Arts and placed under the government of the Société des Artistes Français. The first result of this change was to eliminate from the juries those members nominated by the administration of Fine Arts. Artists also wished to abolish the restricted suffrage by which the elected members of the jury were chosen. Accordingly, by the new regulations, "the jury was henceforth to be composed solely of members elected by the suffrage of all the exhibitors without distinction. The jury was selected on this basis and was of an entirely different character from any that had gone before. The younger and more independent men, who had hitherto scarcely ever been represented, now found themselves in strong force." [11] For Manet, this was a major breakthrough since it meant that he might be awarded the *Legion d'honneur*.

Manet would occasionally spend his evenings at the Folies-Bergère. Manet loved looking at the elaborate layout of the place, with its mezzanine levels, complex lighting and mirror reflections and brilliant chandeliers. Folies-Bergère was a long-running spectacle. It was one of the most elaborate variety-show venues in Paris, showcasing circus aerial acts, acrobats, dancers, men on the prowl, and barmaids, who were assumed by many contemporary observers to be available as clandestine prostitutes. The poet Maupassant said the barmaids were "vendors of drink and of love."

Here Manet could shut out the sound of his fears; he could mingle with the crowds and not betray his infirmity. One day he asked Suzon, a fresh-faced young woman who actually worked there but had none of the expected vulgarity, if she would pose for him. Suzon was a young blonde and dressed in her black décolleté dress seemed to cast a spell on all her customers. Manet asked her to come to his studio in uniform, a lace-trimmed, square-necked fight fitting velvet bodice over a long skirt. He set up a marble-top counter to serve as one of the many bars on the cabarets' galleries where patrons gravitated.

In the center of the picture Suzon is seen full face. Manet had painted her with the vacant eye and placid expression, which he always gave to this type of woman. A mirror behind her shows that she is talking to a man who is seen only in reflection. The mirror is also reflecting the various figures and objects in the room, which made people declare that the composition was incomprehensible.

The picture was *Un bar aux Folies Bergère*. And on the frame of this picture was the inscription, the infallible guarantee of respectability – *Hors Concours* – loosely translated, "standout." Evidently this altered the attitude of the public towards Manet. It was no longer possible to ridicule him as light-heartedly as in former days. But though the public ceased to denounce Manet's works openly, it was still far from their really understanding or enjoying them. When large masses of people have formed a certain opinion, it biases their judgment indefinitely. "So if at the Salon 1882 the public no longer displayed the same contempt for Manet, they scarcely showed any more real appreciation of his pictures than formerly; they were altogether unable to understand the meaning of the principal picture that he sent that year." [12]

When an artist had attained the rank of *Hors Concours,* it was the rule for the French Government to confer the decoration of *Legion d'honneur*. Manet's case was the exception; "He was still the subject of such contentious disputes that his decoration appeared an audacious proceeding, and

A Bar at the Folies-Bergere, 1881-82 (oil on canvas), Manet, Edouard (1832-83) / © Samuel Courtauld Trust, The Courtauld Gallery, London, UK / The Bridgeman Art Library

once more provoked the bitter indignation of the party of tradition." He was denied the *Legion d'honneur*.

In the same year, his neighbor and fellow painter, Alphonse Hirsch, brought a friend to the studio. Manet was out of sight though not out of hearing when a female voice exclaimed "But that's very good! As Proust relates the scene, "Manet wept with joy." [13] The woman was Mery Laurent, her natural charm and taste soon attracted a coterie of eminent men in all the arts many of them friends of Manet's. Mery Laurent was the model for the first part of Zola's *Nana*. The tall, powerfully built daughter of a laundress, born in 1848, as Anne Rose Louviot. She ran away, while still very young, from her husband a grocer in Nancy, and became a nude dancer and unsuccessful actress on the Paris stage. She had stately good looks, was statuesque, buxom features, luxuriant blonde hair, and a perfect complexion. [14]

From Mery's first meeting with Manet, she gained a permanent place in his life. They may have had a brief fling that ripened into an uncomplicated, utterly devoted friendship or they may have remained occasional lovers until Manet's health gave out. Manet was hooked; Suzanne turned a blind eye to it.

In 1883, near the end of life, Manet was too ill to paint elaborate compositions; he occupied himself with a series of small flower pictures. When Mary Laurent arrived with more blossoms, Manet asked her to sit for him and he began a pastel portrait, which was found on his easel, unfinished, after his death on 30 April 1883. Manet's official cause of death was syphilis -.the scourge of the 19th century. "Of all the contagious diseases that can affect the human species, and that can cause the greatest harm in society, there is none more serious, more dangerous and more to be feared than syphilis." [15]

Manet's final will designated "Suzanne Leenhoff, my legal wife, as my sole legatee. She shall bequeath by testament everything I have left her to Leon Koella, known as Leenhoff, who has given me the most devoted care, and I believe my brothers will find these dispositions entirely natural." [16] He then stipulated an outright bequest of fifty thousand francs to Leon the only bequest in the will (outside of a painting to be chosen by Théodore Duret, who was to arrange for the posthumous sale of his works.) With a widowed mother to whom he owed a lot of money, two brothers, a niece, and any number of needy friends, it might seem curious that Leon was Manet's sole beneficiary, after Suzanne.

Manet certainly saw beyond his own time to a future in which he felt confident in his posterity to the point of telling Albert Wolff that he would rather see in his lifetime the laudatory article he was sure Wolff would write after his death. On the death of Manet, Pissarro wrote, "Manet, great painter that he was, had a petty side, he craved recognition by the duly constituted authorities, he believed in official recognition, he longed for honors. He died without achieving them." [17] The Café Guerbois was draped in black crepe; its patrons silently saluted a man who belonged to Impressionism through his modernity and comprehension of character.

"It is inconceivable that the juries of the Salons failed to understand him. They waxed indignant over his subjects which offer only a restricted interest, and they did not see the altogether classic quality of this technique without bitumen, without glazing, without tricks; of this vibrating color, of his rich paint; of this passionate design so suitable for expressing movement and the gestures true to life." [18]

"Manet fought through all his life; few artists' lives have been nobler. His has been an example of untiring energy; he employed it as much in working, as in making a stand against prejudices. Rejected, accepted, rejected again, he delivered with enormous courage and faith his attack upon a jury, which represented routine. This great painter, one of those who did most honor to the French soul, had the genius to create by himself an Impressionism of his own which will always remain his own." [19]

After Manet's death, Morisot, Monet, his brothers and wife conceived the idea of holding an exhibition of his works. In his will Manet had appointed Duret his executor, who decided to apply for permission to exhibit his works in the École des Beaux-Arts. The space available was sufficient for the assembling of a large collection of his works. The prestige attaching to the École des Beaux-Arts would give the exhibition the character of a kind of posthumous triumph, which was precisely what they desired. In 1884, Manet's worth was recognized only by an intelligent minority of artists, men of letters, and connoisseurs.

The attitude of the public was still hostile, while in official circles and among the directors of the École and the national galleries the opposition was as persistent as ever. The director of the École des Beaux-Arts, M. Kaempfen, refused the first request. Monet then went to the Minister of Public Instruction, M. Jules Ferry, who had control over the administration of the Beaux-Arts; permission was granted. The exhibition took place in January 1884 displaying a collection of comprised works of every description, including *Le Buveur d'absinthe*, *Le Dejeuner l'Herbe* and *Olympia* – those that excited the bitterest hostility.

The exhibition was followed by sale at the hotel Drouet on the 4th and 5th of February. There was a great deal of uncertainty. However, all the works were sold and among the buyers were many new collectors, whose interest in Manet had not previously been suspected. *Le Bar aux Folies-Bergere* sold for 5,800 francs, *Le Balcon*, three thousand francs, *Olympia* was withdrawn at ten thousand francs and the *Argenteuil* at twelve thousand francs. The total realized was 116,637; the success for the sale left Manet in a far higher position in the publics' estimation than before.

Olympia attracted special attention of a certain collector, who contemplated buying it. Duret claimed, "It would be deplorable to lose to artists and the public if the picture, instead of taking its place in a gallery where all the world would see it, were to be buried in a private collection." [20] Twenty thousand francs was raised by subscription; the sum was to be paid over to Mme. Manet as the price of the picture. The painting was offered to Musée du Luxembourg.

Raising the money required an intense-letter-writing campaign, but Monet also had to overcome the government's resistance. The Musée did not relish the idea of having to accept the one canvas, with its blatant nudity, and crude application of paint, that so clearly represented the avant-garde's successful assault on the country's heralded artistic traditions. They would have taken any one of Manet's works they judged reasonable, such as the *Guitarero* of the Salon of 1861 or *the Bon Bock* of the Salon of 1873 but *Olympia* they rejected categorically. They still considered it as pernicious as when it aroused general indignation in the Salon of 1865.

That Monet devoted twelve months of his life to this project speaks about his affection for Manet and his widow who needed the money and his rightful recognition of the painting's value and stature. It suggests Monet's generosity, while underscoring the financial position he enjoyed. Few, if any, of his colleagues could afford to take that much time off. Monet finally received word that the picture would be accepted *san engagement* and would be hung in the Musée du Luxembourg before eventually moving to the Louvre. The victory prompted more invectives from the ever-vociferous conservatives. Monet did not go to the official opening ceremonies, demonstrating his continued disdain for such functions, but he could not resist visiting the museum a little while later. Nor could he resist from telling Berthe Morisot that the painting, "Never looked better."

In France pictures do not receive final sanction until they have been promoted from the Luxembourg to the Louvre. There, "they take their place under the masters who have stood the test of time, and if they can sustain the comparison, the question of their greatness is settled forever. According to the traditional rule, no work can be admitted to the Louvre until ten years after the artist's death. When, in 1893, ten years had passed since Manet's death, his friends repeatedly expressed their desire to see the *Olympia* transferred from the Luxembourg to the Louvre. Opposition was encountered at every step." [21]

The directors of École des Beaux-Arts and the authorities, who controlled the admission of new works to the Louvre, turned a deaf ear and remained unresponsive to the representations that were made to them. When M. Clemenceau, an old friend of Manet's, became Prime Minister, Claude Monet, who had been instrumental in securing for the *Olympia* a place in the Luxembourg set to accomplish its promotion to the Louvre. In 1907 Georges Clemenceau had it quietly moved to the Louvre. It was not actually displayed for another ten years. The *Olympia* now hangs in the Musée d'Orsay, Paris.

Is one's posterity in the hands of Divine Providence? "Meissonier was the most famous master alive. In 1890, the year before his death, one of his works was purchased for 850,000 francs - a sum which was 50,000 francs more than the annual budget of the Paris Opéra, which maintained an eighty-piece orchestra, seventy dancers and sixty choristers. Manet, on the other hand, only began to receive a little public recognition at the very end of his life. ... There is a statue that exists of Meissonier carved in 1895 by Antonin Mercie - Meissonier sits in his concrete armchair and gazes glumly at a modern world that rushes heedless past his stern marble stare. The monument is, more than anything else, an image of acquiescence and defeat, of an artist grimly accepting his unhappy encounter with posterity." [22] More than a century after their deaths, Manet endures in glory, flooded with light and fame; while Meissonier gathers dust in museum storerooms.

Chapter Fifteen: Impressionism de la tour Eiffel à La statue de la Liberté

The Impressionists slowly gained recognition after 1880, when the public began to recognize the value of their works. Maybe this was why Cézanne, who had ceased in 1877 to exhibit, made one exception. In 1882 the desire to force his way into the official exhibition again took hold of him, and accordingly he sent *Portrait of Louis-Auguste Cézanne, Father of the Artist, Reading l'Evénement*, 1866 (National Gallery of Art, Washington, D.C.), to the Salon of 1882. Guillemet, one of his friends of student days in Paris, was then a member of the jury, and secured its acceptance. The Salon of 1882 was the only one to which a work of Cézanne's was ever admitted and it was his last. Twenty years had elapsed during which the public remained either ignorant or contemptuous of him and with the public must be included writers, collectors, dealers, all those who make the reputation of an artist and assign him the reward of his labor. Only the small group of Café Guerbois friends - Pissarro, Monet, Renoir appreciated Cézanne.

Many of the Impressionists moved to Poissy, which Monet hated. From the doorway of the little train between Vernon and Gasny, Monet discovered Giverny. In April 1883, the Monets moved to Vernon, then to a rented house in Giverny, Eure, in Upper Normandy. The house was situated on two acres and was near the main road between the towns of Vernon and Gasny at Giverny, in Haute-Normandie. There was a barn that doubled as a painting studio, orchards and a small garden. The house was close enough to the local schools for the children to attend and the surrounding landscape offered an endless array of suitable motifs for Monet's work. The family worked and built up the gardens. As Monet's fortunes began to change for the better as his dealer Paul Durand-Ruel had increasing success in selling his paintings, by November 1890, Monet was prosperous enough to buy the house, the surrounding buildings and the land for his gardens. Within a few years by 1899 Monet built a greenhouse and a second studio, a spacious building, well lit with skylights. He filled his house in Giverny with his sizable collection of Japanese prints and he transformed a large portion of his property there into the magnificent water lily garden that became the focus of his attention for the last twenty-six years of his life.

But for the other Impressionists, 1883 was another crisis year. The problems within the group were doubtless the main cause. They no longer pulled together as they once had. Many of the artists were going their own ways; some were beset with doubts. Pissarro thought his own work too tame, insipid and flat. Renoir was plunged into a profound crisis and destroyed his own paintings. Monet, despite his new rented home, was dissatisfied with his own work. He reworked many of his paintings and destroyed others.

Renoir claimed, in his wretched state of mind, "Around 1883 a sort of break occurred in my work. I had gone to the end of Impressionism and I was reaching the conclusion that I didn't know how either to paint or to draw. In a word, I was at a dead end." [1] He destroyed a number of canvases and set out with determination to acquire the draftsmanship, which he thought he lacked. He applied himself to simplifying forms at the expense of color. "Searching at times for a sober, at times for an elegant line, he tried imprison breathing forms in strict contours but did not always completely escape the danger of rigidness and dryness. He began to realize that while working in the open he had been too preoccupied with the phenomena of light to devote enough attention to other problems. 'While painting directly from nature,' he stated, 'the artist reaches the point where he looks only for the effects of light, where he no longer composes and he quickly descends to monotony.' " [2] It was in 1883 Renoir had his first one-man show, at the gallery of Durand-Ruel with limited success. Only with the help of faithful friends, was Renoir able to continue his work.

In 1883 Monet and Renoir traveled to the Cote d'Azur in quest of new inspiration All the old Impressionists were trying to rid themselves of the constrictions of the group; they were after new subjects, new approaches, a new techniques. It was the first time since his military service in Algiers that Renoir had been so far from home and the first time he had ever experienced the Riviera. Monet undoubtedly had been convinced by Renoir, who had recently come back from Italy by way of Provence that there were wonderful things awaiting them there. He was not disappointed. The two artists spent almost two weeks traveling from Marseille to Genoa and Monet was thrilled by what he saw.

Mary Cassatt was looking for a retreat from her work now and in her later years. In 1884 Cassatt purchased a chateau, Mesnil-Beaufresne, in the French countryside. Mary was able to maintain her health well into her sixties. Though Cassatt had no husband or children, she was responsible for her elderly parents and invalid Lydia, and their health problems stole precious time from her work. She wrote to Pissarro, "I am at my wits' end with my Mother not well & my sister incapable of helping anyone." Lydia, Mary's favorite sibling, suffered from the incurable Bright's disease, which affects the kidneys, and during the final months of her life "was treated with doses of arsenic, morphine, and the blood of animals drunk fresh at the abattoit." After this ghastly treatment, Lydia died, at the age of 45, in November 1882. Family deaths drew Cassatt into the spiritualist movement that came into fashion in France nearing the turn of the century. She became fascinated by various aspects of the occult that attempted to communicate with the spirits of the dead.

As he approached 50, Degas became acutely aware of his increasing loneliness. Aging made him feel somehow inauthentic. During earlier times, Monet noted Degas' brilliant talk in the Café Guerbois, which was in sharp contrast to the fierce image of ferocity and isolation that he now displayed. But Degas didn't know how to be agreeable in society, at his most bearish, he responded thus to Monet's dinner invitation, "But listen: will you have a special dish without butter prepared for me? Mind you, no flowers on the table, and you must have dinner at half past seven sharp. I know you don't have your cat around and please don't allow anybody to bring a dog. And if there are to be women, I hope they don't come reeking of perfume. How horrible all those odors are when there are so many things that really smell good, like toast or even manure! Ah." He hesitated, "and very few lights. My eyes, you know, my poor eyes!" When all the preparations had been properly made and the dinner had punctually begun, a nervous little boy (warned, no doubt, about the fearsome guest) nervously started to tap his plate with a knife. Degas roughly cried out - 'What's that racket!' - which so frightened the lad that he immediately turned pale and vomited all over the table." [3]

When Degas turned fifty, he shared his morose thoughts with his friends. "There is something artificial even about this heart of mine. The dancers have sewn it into a pink satin bag, a slightly faded satin, like their ballet slippers." [4] In his correspondence Degas periodically lapsed into disillusionment that surfaced in comments about growing old, his impending death, loneliness, illness, money problems, and the gradual loss of old friends. By the mid-1880s Degas appeared to have exhausted the receptiveness of the public, which showed signs of tiring of the artist's obsessive use of dance subjects as his principal form of expression.

One bright spot in Degas' life was Julie, Morisot's daughter, and she responded in kind. Moreover, the money that he made from his paintings allowed him to indulge in travel and collecting art. His purchased paintings were truly amazing: two major El Grecos, works by Goya and numerous Daumiers, he owned 20 paintings and ninety drawings by Ingres, 13 paintings and 190 drawings by Delacroix, 2 works by Morisot, 12 by Cassatt, 30 by Manet and many other pictures by Pissarro, Sisley, Cézanne, and Renoir. His collection would have filled a substantial museum, instead it was dispersed in five massive sales, after his death. But despite his pessimistic thoughts, a distinguishing feature of Degas' genius lay in his ability to excel in different media; coupled by his desire for constant experimenting to improve his work, which led him to embark on fresh ventures.

In 1885, Renoir's first son Pierre was born followed by the eventual marriage to Aline in 1890. The new family moved from the cramped lodgings to a more spacious apartment still in Montmartre with four rooms and a large kitchen. The role as head of a family occupied Renoir relatively late in his life, but he turned out to be a caring father for his children. Renoir's interests began to shift from the subjects of urban society to that of nature, family life, and motherhood.

Probably the most significant event of this year, was the 1886 publication of the novel *L'Oeuvre* by Zola. *L'Oeuvre* was a thinly disguised account of a failed painter. Zola drew on his memories of his acquaintances at Café Guerbois to compose his main character, a painter name Claude Lantier, from three contemporaries – Manet, Cezanne, and Monet. The self-doubts of Cezanne predominate but elements of Manet's character and career are also present – the hostile public reaction to early pictures, with their subject bound to shock the bourgeoisie and his surprise and hurt when he was not accepted by them. Lantier is a man so devoted to his own dreams that he is destined to lose himself in a world of fantasy. His character is summed up in the ending: Lantier's suicide in front of a picture that he cannot finish. Cézanne took this presentation as a critical denunciation of his own career and was bitterly hurt.

Zola was reworking a story by Balzac, "The Unknown Masterpiece." Zola's theme was not a new one in the nineteenth century. His *L'Oeuvre, The Work*, or in English, *The Masterpiece,* enraged many of the Impressionists. All of the Café Guerbois group discovered themselves in the book of an artist reaching for the stars and squandering his genius. Cézanne thanked Zola for the gift of the book and signed off on a formal and sad note: "In memory of the days that are gone. 4 April 1886." [5] They were never to meet again. Zola did indeed lament Cézanne's inability to mature the powers within him.

While the painters were busily preparing their eighth group exhibition, Durand-Ruel was assembling the three hundred canvases, which he intended to take to *Amérique*. The works of the

Impressionists owed their introduction to the United States to M. Durand-Ruel. He organized an exhibition in New York in 1886, which was held first at the American Art Association, and afterwards transferred to the Academy of Design. It included 14 pictures by Manet, 22 by Degas, 41 by Pissarro, 50 by Monet 12 by Sisley, 36 by Renoir, 8 by Morisot, 7 by Guillaumin. He followed this up by exhibiting a fresh collection at the American Art Association in 1887. Increasingly more American money was invested in Impressionist paintings. The exhibition in New York in 1886 was a watershed event.

"On 10 April, collectors, dealers and an intrigued American public arrived in Madison Square for the exhibition of *Works in Oil and Pastel by the Impressionists of Paris*. For the first time Americans saw the works of the Impressionists: all members of the original group spanned five large rooms Galleries A to E. Unlike Parisian audiences twenty years earlier, the New York viewers were not here to laugh or sneer. They looked with open minds at works of art that were unusual, even perhaps rebellious. They saw pictures painted with talent and passion."[6] *The New York Tribune* praised works of beauty surpassing anything by Rousseau or Corot. There was none of the ferocious uproar the Impressionists had initially aroused in their own country. The luxurious rooms in Madison Square were quiet, as viewers looked thoughtfully at the paintings and pastels, which represented two and a half decades of dedication and struggle.

Manet's *le Buveur de l'absinthe*, the painting rejected two decades earlier by the Salon when it had sparked rumors that the artist of such dissolute subjects must himself be a greasy-haired, good-for-nothing bohemian. When journalists had tracked him down, they discovered him in a lavish studio in which the rich and famous in top hats and Worth dresses had gathered to watch the artist at work. Berthe Morisot's works included *Peasant Hanging the Washing* 1881, one of her early paintings of the *banlieues* (suburbs) of Paris. Degas paintings of dancers alone and in groups, in the wings and on stage, included *Chorus d'Opera* and *Behind the Wings*.

Among the 38 paintings by Auguste Renoir was the *Portrait de Mlle Savaray* an actress who had modeled for him in Montmartre, *A Box at the Opera*, and *Au Cirque* his depiction of the troupe, which came to perform in Montmartre. These paintings with their vibrant colors and dappled sunlight and glimpses of trees in full leaf celebrated joy and cheerfulness of the people of Montmartre were some of Renoir's greatest subjects. Of all the works exhibited by Durand-Ruel in America, those that received the most attention were the 48 works by Claude Monet including *Poppies in Bloom* of the poppy fields of Vetheuil, *The Setting Sun,* and his *Impression: Sunrise*, which had shocked Paris when it was first exhibited there in 1874. None of Cassatt's own works were exhibited in New York. In the three years following Lydia's death, Mary had found it difficult to concentrate on her painting. She distracted herself with domestic tasks; Cézanne, was also unrepresented in New York.

There were some, naturally, whose comments showed little difference from those in the French papers. *The Sun* 11 April 1886, spoke of "the lumpy and obnoxious creations of Renoir, the degenerate and debased pupil of so wholesome, honest, and well-inspired man as Gleyre." *The Critic*, 17 April 1886, also stated that Degas "draws badly" that Pissarro's landscapes are "fantastic and amusing; sometimes he is serious but without intending apparently to be so."[7]

All works had to be shipped back to France. It was for this reason that in 1888 Durand-Ruel returned to New York and opened an apartment at 2997 Fifth Avenue, the first Durand-Ruel gallery in America. He kept his two galleries in Paris, and for the next few years traveled back and forth across the Atlantic, setting up his New York operation.

Degas would sell pictures from time to time to Durand-Ruel and now and again he would request money, "You have put off coming to see the pastel, so I am sending it to you he wrote in 1886. You'll be getting another (of horses) and a little racetrack scene (in oils) with a background of mountains. Kindly send me some money *this afternoon*." [8]

In 1886 Paul Cézanne, artiste-peintre, and Hortense Fiquet, sans profession, were married in the Town Hall in Aix. Cezanne's father and mother were present; both signed their names effortlessly. Hortense's father was recorded as "absent but consenting." The next day the marriage was solemnized at the Church of Saint-Jean-Baptiste, the parish church of the Jas de Bouffan. The death of his father at the end of 1886 had suddenly improved his financial situation. His share of the inheritance ran to 40,000 francs a year, and a further 25 thousand for Hortense and Paul. Cézanne and Hortense had now married under pressure from his family, but they were no closer – quite the contrary – in fact. Hortense spent most of her time in Paris with their son, fascinated by the sophisticated luxury of the capital. Cézanne kept to his former lifestyle. He lived at Jas de Bouffan, where his mother and sister Marie ran the household and felt lonelier and more misunderstood than ever. After his breach with Zola, Cézanne completely avoided contact with the old Impressionists. Cézanne left Aix and its environs less and less.

In 1887 Renoir exhibited his new paintings at the Georges Petit Gallery. They were exhibited alongside paintings by Monet, Pissarro, Morisot and James Whistler and caused something of a stir because of Renoir's departure from Impressionists. Painter Camille Pissarro, wrote to his son "Durand has been to Petits; he has seen the Renoirs and doesn't like his new style – he doesn't like it at all." [9]

Renoir was open about his fascination with women; to the artist they were objects to be observed and depicted – "the quality of the skin was compared to a fruit that must respond well to the light, and the arrangement of the facial features must be in harmony with almond-shaped eyes that should be halfway between the top of the head and the tip of the chin." [10] Some critics think that this is why his models appeared to be without spirit – they are painted as if they were fruit or flowers. Renoir's depiction of the female form is without lust. Renoir had been in the south early in 1888 and had paid a visit to Cézanne at the Jas de Bouffan, occasionally working at his side. He traveled quite a bit but toward the end of the year he suddenly began to suffer from severe neuralgia: part of his head was paralyzed and he had to undergo electrical treatment.

It was also in 1888 that Monet noticed that the local farmers stored their wheat in large rounded stacks in the cleared fields. After reaping a harvest, farmers built fifteen- to twenty-foot-high stacks of grain that remained outdoors for some months before being threshed. These forms, which appeared somewhat mysterious in Monet's paintings, were ordinary elements of northern France's agricultural landscape, and carried certain symbolic associations with sustenance and abundance.

Monet set up his easel and began to observe the action of the sun on the hill-like grain stacks at different times of the day. Over the course of the next two years, he returned to the same location each season and -- equipped with several canvases -- switched from one to another as the light changed. In a letter to friend and writer Gustave Geffroy, Monet admitted that he sought to render the impossible -- the instant and ever-changing effect of light. What renders them enigmatic is the extraordinary atmosphere surrounding them—the "envelope," as the artist described it, "of pulsating, colored light that both defines and alters forms."

In the fall of 1890 Monet arranged to have the grainstacks near his home left out over the winter. By the following summer he had painted them at least thirty times, at different times throughout the seasons though the fading of fall into the snows of winter 1891. He painted both in the field, where he worked at several easels simultaneously, often carried by a trailing band of children, and in the studio, where he refined pictorial harmonies.

It was an arduous undertaking. The pioneer of the instant glance, the quick look, came to realize that he needed to work much more slowly, more deliberately, in order to capture the moment. As he wrote to Gustave Geffroy in October 1890: "I have become so slow in my work that I am exasperated, but the further I go, the more I see that one has to work a lot in order to express what I am looking for: 'instantaneity,' especially the atmosphere, the same light diffused everywhere, and more than ever I am disgusted by easy things that come at once." [11]

By the end of the 1880s, Degas had virtually fulfilled his wish "to be illustrious and unknown." He was worldly and influential, so constantly in contact with a large number of artists; he exhibited his works only in a few selected public places, which called him to the attention of the influential art journals in Paris. Degas was conscious of commercial pressures and seems to have distinguished between a market-oriented production – his fabricated "articles" as he called them and the rest of his art. Works of the first category are primarily characterized by their degree of finish, the latter ones distinctly more avant-garde. Several of these found their way to the gallery of Theo van Gogh – Vincent's brother.

Chapter Sixteen: Later Years

Criticized, misunderstood, Renoir, little by little, would leave his "dry" period and, once again, capture the magnificence of his talents in delicacy, form, color, light and sensuality. The scene of his new painting recalls an eighteenth-century bourgeois scene of domestic life; it is Renoir's *Two Young Girls at the Piano*. Renoir sought to paint an ideal world, peopled with graceful young girls with an elegant, comfortably furnished interior. Renoir lavished extraordinary care and continually refined this composition for he knew the scrutiny to which this painting would be subjected. Refining the composition would result in a series of five canvases. His extensive labors were due to the French government's request for Renoir to execute a painting for the new museum in Paris, Musée du Luxembourg. The Musée would be dedicated to living artists. One of the pictures in this series will be submitted to the Salon.

It had been seven years since Renoir exhibited at the Salon; 1890 would mark his last submission. It was the double portrait of the daughters of Catulle Mendès at the piano, *Young Girls at the Piano* and was purchased by the French State. His second submission was a large group portrait of *The Artists Family*. It is an informal study in the garden of the Château des Brouillards in Montmartre, in which the Renoirs lived starting in the fall of 1890. Madame Renoir, a vast matriarchal figure, presides over the group, resplendent in her magnificent bonnet. Her eldest son, eleven-year-old Pierre, hangs on her arm, dressed in a fashionable sailor's suit. In the foreground, Gabrielle Renard, without a hat and wearing an apron, is very much in the role of family servant, attending to the toddler Jean in a long gown and with a sumptuous bonnet like his mother's. The third child is the daughter of the writer Paul Alexis. The work appears to affirm the Renoir's arrival into bourgeois.

Renoir's maturity was marred by ill health; unfortunately around 1892, Renoir developed rheumatoid arthritis. A fall from his bicycle in the summer of 1897 left him with a broken right arm, which exacerbated his arthritis. But despite these health setbacks, during the 1890s Renoir began a series of foreign travels, often to see the great museums of the world. In 1892 he went to Madrid and admired the work of Velázquez in the Prado. Later he visited Dresden, England and Netherlands where he saw a large Rembrandt exhibition in Amsterdam. In France he continued to live in Paris, but the family bought a house in Essoyes in 1895.

It was also around this time that Renoir had met the picture dealer Ambroise Vollard. He would become one of the most important people in Renoir's life. Vollard became one of the chief buyers of Renoir's pictures, would host exhibitions and would influence both Renoir's choice of subject matter and medium. He also wrote one of the most widely read monographs of original lithographs and "artists' books." He was also the author of monographs on Cézanne, Degas and Renoir, not to mention the account of his memories. He controlled a large cache of Renoir's work after his death, ensuring his posthumous reputation. His enlightened investments now seem incredibly far-sighted.

In 1890 Monet was content to paint various subjects around Giverny that suggested the bounties of the soil and the poetry of rural light. Monet was exceptionally fond of painting controlled nature: his own gardens in Giverny, with its water lilies, pond, and bridge. Monet was not interested in

Young Girls at the Piano, 1892 (oil on canvas), Renoir, Pierre Auguste (1841-1919) / Musee d'Orsay, Paris, France / The Bridgeman Art Library

painting nature in a descriptive manner, he said that he wanted to be true to his "sensation of nature," that is, to what he perceived in nature. After nearly 30 years of painting in the open air, he had become extraordinarily sensitive to the fact that, when light changed, his whole perception of a landscape changed.

He also painted up and down the banks of the Seine. He was enjoying his new house and had expanded the garden into a beautifully landscaped park with what will become his immortalized lily pond. While he painted many landscapes, his water lily pond became the favorite subject of his paintings. Monet bought extra land and expensive plants to employ gardeners and to enlarge a pond to accommodate a Japanese-inspired water lily garden. For the last decades of his life, apart from a group of paintings of London exhibited in 1904, Monet spent his time at the pond and its glorious flowers became the principal focus of his art.

The poet Guy de Maupassant watched Monet and later remembered, "I often followed Claude Monet in his search of impressions. He was no longer a painter, in truth, but a hunter. He proceeded, followed by children (his own and Mme Hoschedé's) who carried his canvases, five or six canvases representing the same subject at different times of day and with different effects. He took them up and put them aside in turn, according to the changes in the sky. Before his subject, the painter lay in wait for the sun and shadows capturing in a few brush strokes the ray that fell or the cloud that passed … " [1]

At sunrise, he is said to take with him some twenty canvases, which he changed from hour to hour, taking them up again the next day. He noted, "from nine to ten the most subtle effects of sunlight upon the hay stack and follows the step by step modification of the atmosphere until nightfall. He has painted a haystack in a field twenty times over, and the twenty haystacks are all different." [2]

Monet's series paintings, beginning in the 1880s and 1890s, would continue until the end of his life in 1926. The "series" paintings involved capturing a subject as it changed according to the varying light and weather conditions. His first series exhibited as such was of grain stacks. Fifteen of the paintings were exhibited at the gallery of Durand-Ruel in 1891. He later produced several series of paintings including: Rouen Cathedral, Poplars, the Houses of Parliament, Mornings on the Seine, and the Water Lilies on his property at Giverny.

Why was Monet so drawn to the serial idea? "To begin with even before 1890 he had often returned to certain motifs, such as cliffs, bridges, fields and rivers. Moreover, since light in nature is constantly changing, painting the movement of light was a form of realism. Most important, in serial images Monet could deepen Impressionism's resistance to Academie painting, with its linear precision and fixed structure, and reinforce his argument for the primacy of shifting and timeless nature." [3]

Monet chose his subjects, especially those that he repeated in series, with an awareness of their underlying significance. Grain stacks were formerly and scholars now believe incorrectly called "Haystacks." Because very few artists and art historians were also farmers, many of the so-called "haystacks" in western art actually depict stacks of wheat or other grain crops. Grainstacks, in any event, were making as a statement about the fecundity of the French soil. In discussing the

"Poplars," which suggest natural organ pipes or a triumphant march, also represent "trees of liberty" and were used as a symbol of the French republic from its inception. The Cathedral of Rouen, the subject of the most intellectually challenging series, was a symbol of a Gothic architecture and a past when France - or so it seemed in the late 19th century - had been united by spiritual purpose, a sense of community and pride in craft." [4]

In Monet's series paintings, everything seems "soft and flowing, and there is no beginning, middle and end. When Monet was able to fix on his canvas a fleeting moment, he also found a slice of eternity. Series paintings have precedents in oriental art of which Monet was keenly aware. Japanese landscape prints were often issued in series - such as views of the provinces, famous views around Japan's major cities and of Mount Fuji. The Japanese people revered Mount Fuji as a sacred site of deep spiritual significance. The idea of devoting a series to a single motif such as Mount Fuji — presenting different aspects according to the season, the weather, the time of day and the artist's viewpoint — may have been an inspiration for Monet's series." [5]

The Creuse Valley paintings are considered Monet's first true series, having been conceived, executed, and exhibited solely as one ensemble. Monet spent three months in the Creuse Valley in central France to capture the brilliancy and hues of color apparent in the valley; each canvas is modified showing the variance of light and mood. After three months, Monet returned to his home at Giverny to continue his work on his grain stacks series, which would become his first public success. For centuries before the hay-baler and combine-harvester dropped bales of similar dimensions in hayfields and wheat-fields, haymaking and harvesting created very different landscapes. In many parts of the world they still do. Monet's haystacks are relatively few, always done in the dappled light of summer, and to be even more precise, they are haycocks, small, shaggy, temporary heaps of hay, soon to be carted off to the farmsteads of Giverny. The grain stacks have a typical conical form and appear more solid.

Monet's "series" met with tremendous success. All his haystack pictures were sold within three days after the opening of his exhibition at prices ranging between three and four thousand francs. His Café Guerbois comrades witnessed Monet's series with a certain sadness that his career as an Impressionist was ending in technical prowess. Degas' contention that Monet's art "was that of a skillful but not profound decorator." [6]

Upon completion of his grain stack series, Monet began to paint along the Epte River, which was quite close to his home. He became quite confident about his new series approach and started painting the poplars along the river before receiving word on how his grainstack paintings were being received. One may think of Italy and its Cypress trees or sycamore trees of Provence but along the highways or entrances to historic chateaus throughout France, one finds poplar trees. Poplars are slender and stately. Perhaps the most famous in this series, however, were his paintings of the Rouen Cathedral, which was built between the 12th and the 16th centuries. It encapsulated the entire medieval era while bearing witness to the changes the Gothic style experienced.

Monet painted more than thirty views – different times, different angles, varied weather conditions - of the Cathedral to capture the elusive point when light and mood seems to be just changing.

Monet was at the mercy of a fleeting cloud or an early morning fog. These radiant colorist cathedrals are even more of a tour de force of his talent. They consist of seventeen studies of the Rouen Cathedral. Monet's paintings in which "the towers fill the whole of the picture, grey stone, worn by time and blackened by centuries find means of making the most dazzling atmospheric harmonies sparkle upon the stone ... Pale and rosy at sunrise, purple at midday, glowing in the evening under the rays of the setting sun, standing out from the crimson and gold, scarcely visible in the midst." [7]

To execute these paintings, Monet rented a room opposite of the Rouen Cathedral that offered the most all-encompassing view of the west portal. After painting the view of the cathedral several times, he changed rooms so as to slightly shift his angle of view. After painting his new view, he moved again, and again after more pictures. In all, he seems to have changed his viewing angle five times, searching for the new highlights and shadows as the sunlight fell across the front of the building.

The cathedral, however, haunted Monet, who wrote to Hoschedé, "I spent the night having nightmares. The cathedral was falling on top of me, it seemed blue or pink or yellow." [8] But Monet was not a man who surrendered easily, "More than ever I detest the things in which I have success at the first attempt," he wrote while working on the grain stacks series. Monet was even forced to finish several canvases of the Cathedral in his own workshop, entrusting the success of the series to his wonderful visual memory. Two years later, in 1894, the mission was fulfilled.

After creating a coherent ensemble, Monet selected twenty paintings that he considered "complete" and "perfect," for an exhibition at Durand-Ruel's Paris gallery in May 1895. Pissarro and Cézanne visited and praised the series, and patrons quickly purchased eight paintings from the group. Camille Mauclair, in a review of the Cathedral's exhibition, said Monet "goes a little too far" in his use of color. Mauclair was a member of a school of critics who dismissed Impressionism in its early days and was finally forced, some twenty years after it burst upon the art world, to at least grudgingly admit that Monet's work was singularly important. He goes on, somewhat surprisingly, to state that the exhibition was "the capital event of this month…so eagerly awaited."

Camille Pissarro felt so strongly about the exhibition that he sent numerous letters to his sons in London and France that they should abandon what they were doing to come to Paris before the exhibition closed. "His Cathedrals are going to be scattered one side and another, and it is particularly as a whole that they must be seen." The French statesman Georges Clemenceau also felt that the paintings must be viewed together to appreciate their true significance. Collectors at the time failed to take this advice to heart; only one collector, Camondo a Jewish financier and philanthropist, bought five, which were subsequently given to the Louvre. No other museum currently owns more than two, excepting the Musée d'Orsay's owning six, thanks to Clemenceau's purchase in 1894.

Degas was still overwhelmed by family debts but paradoxically was able to move, in 1890, into a three-story apartment, which he now needed to accommodate his burgeoning collection of masters both old and new: Ingres, Delacroix, Gauguin, and Cézanne. Degas also lost contact with his colleagues. He seems not to have attended the "Impressionist dinners" held monthly between

1890 and 1894 but for the most part led a hermit's life in the center of Paris, steadily complaining about failing eyesight.

He did not even feel the urge to show his works any more; after 1886 he appeared only once before the public with a series of landscape pastels, exhibited at Durand-Ruel's in 1892. These very delicate sketches were supposedly executed in his studio and were not really typical of his work at that time. He was, however, striving as a sculptor to give form to the instantaneous seeking mass in movement when age dimmed his eyesight to the point where he had to give up brush and pencil altogether, he devoted himself exclusively to modeling. In kneading clay or wax as he did with his fingers what he could no longer do with his eyes.

Morisot became a widow in 1892; when Eugene died her health rapidly deteriorated. She subsequently left her home and moved with her daughter Julie to a smaller home where she continued to paint. That same year, Cassatt accepted an offer of three thousand francs to join other women artists and paint a mural for the Woman's Building designed to exhibit the products of female skills and handicraft in the World's Columbian Exposition in Chicago. She explained that "I took for the subject of the central and largest composition young women plucking the fruits of knowledge or science and that enabled me to place my figures out of doors and allowed brilliancy of color. I have tried to make the general effect as bright, as gay, as amusing as possible." [9]

In order to paint the top of the fourteen by fifty-eight foot mural, "Modern Woman," without using a ladder, she had a 60' long by 6' deep trench dug on her country estate and lowered the canvas into it. Knowing that Cassatt's talents were not suited to massive paintings, Degas was strongly against her doing the Chicago mural. Cassatt misjudged the requirements of mural. "When the massive work was hoisted aloft and seen from below," wrote Nancy Mathews, "the theme that had seemed so logical became indecipherable to the average viewer, and the style that had seemed so sunny and realistic became a jarring pattern of bright colors that was out of sync with the rest of he building." Cassatt went to Europe and escaped the humiliating public rejection of her work, which was stored away and later disappeared.

February 21, 1894 marked the death of Gustave Caillebotte, a naval architect by profession who painted in his spare time and had built up a prodigious collection of Impressionist works, which on his death were bequeathed to the French State. Caillebotte's Collection gift put the old Impressionists back at the center of attention. He had named Renoir, as one of its executors and Renoir required a great deal of tenacity in order to see his friend's wishes upheld. The bequest comprised sixty-seven pictures – including both drawings and paintings: eight works by Renoir including *The Swing* and *Ball at the Moulin de la Galette*, five by Cézanne, four by Manet, seven by Degas, eighteen by Pissarro, nine Sisley's and sixteen Monet's.

Renoir had to face repeated opposition on the part of Henri Roujon, Director of the École des Beaux-Arts to Caillebotte's bequest of these Impressionist works. Roujon did not want them in the Musée du Luxembourg. Several official artists threatened to resign from the École and Jean-Léon Gérôme summed up the position of the Institute with the words; "I do not know these gentlemen, and of this bequest I know only the title. Does it not contain paintings by M. Monet, by M. Pissarro and others? For the Government to accept such filth, they would have to be great moral slackening."[10] The uproar of protest from politicians, academicians, and critics, equaled and even surpassed the insults heaped upon the painters at the occasion of their first group exhibitions.

After two years of wrangling, the State finally accepted thirty-eight of the canvases, including *Le Ball du Moulin del la Galette*. As Renoir later explained: "It was the only one of my paintings he [Henri Roujon] unquestioningly accepted .. because [Henri] Gervex was in it."[11] In 1896 the government announced it would accept two by Manet and Cézanne, six by Renoir and Sisley, seven by Pissarro and Degas, and eight by Monet. They were hung in a new addition to the Luxembourg that was inaugurated in early 1897. But no sooner had the doors opened than the conservatives renewed their condemnations that these new additions would "pollute" the masterpieces in the Luxembourg's collections and would be the "ruin of the French nation."

In 1895 Monet visited Jacques Hoschedé who had married a Norwegian widow and had moved to Christiania (present day Oslo) where he plied his trade as a shipbuilder. His trip was prompted primarily by Jacques' lack of communication with his mother and family and by Alice's desire to know if he was ever returning to Giverny. As his recently legalized stepfather, Monet may have shared Alice's concern. While there Monet painted a few pictures but the most important of these was Mount Kolsaas, which rose like Cézanne's Mont Sainte-Victoire from the flattened plains on the outskirts of the town through a ring of conifer trees to an impressive though gradually assumed height.

In the summer of 1890, Cézanne went to Switzerland and stayed with Hortense and their son for a period of about five months. During that time, the family went to Neuchâtel, Bern, Fribourg, Lausanne, and Geneva. Cézanne was not happy about these trips. But, by November he was back in Aix and Hortense returned to Paris. Cézanne was now beginning to suffer from diabetes, which made him extremely irritable.

Cézanne's new emphasis in 1890 was the spiritual and it's especially apparent in the portraits. His attitude was determined not only by personal fears and doubts but also by a general shift in French culture at the time. "Time and again in that period Cézanne contemplated the nothingness of life; skills that appeared in some of his works were evidently symbols of that nothingness. But so too was the melancholy visible in the poses in which his sitters were shown. Cézanne's religious leanings towards the end of his life (his medieval phase) were prompted less by fear of death itself than by fear of not being able to see his great artistic aims achieved."[12]

Cézanne met Ambroise Vollard, a man of taste who had instinctively foreseen the future that lay before the Impressionists. Having to choose a career, Vollard set up as a picture dealer. Just at this time the movement was growing in favor of the Impressionists – at least for some. As his connection grew larger and he was able to raise the price of his pictures, he accumulated capital, which he invested in the purchase of pictures by Cézanne. He acquired altogether some two hundred of them for the sum of 80,000 or 90,000 francs. To complete the undertaking, he took a shop in the rue Lafitte, where he showed the pictures keeping them prominently before the public, connoisseurs and the general public – this was an important event for Cézanne; it induced him to sell his works, which were now permanently brought before general public.

Vollard was also the first to organize a one-man exhibition devoted to Paul Cézanne, which would take place in November 1895. After having been absent from Paris exhibitions, Cézanne's works came as a great surprise. The pictures were shown unframed, and owing to space problems, which prevented Vollard from showing all of them simultaneously, the exhibition was changed midway. Vollard put three paintings in the window - the bathers scene from the Caillebotte gift, *Leda and the Swan*, and a further nude. The response of the critic's and public was unanimous. The *Journal des Artistes* typically demanded to known whether "the sight of these depressing monstrosities, which go beyond all legally permissible obscenity would not make the sensitive throw up." [13] But the most trenchant and unfeeling opposition originated in Zola's circles, where Cézanne had supposed he had allies who understood him.

The only ones who thought highly of his pictures, were the old Café Guerbois group. While the public was outraged and the critics judged his efforts with their customary ignorance and brutality, vanguard artists and Cézanne's former comrades greeted him as a master. "Vollard's Cézanne exhibition is truly magnificent. There are still lifes, utterly wonderful landscapes, and distinctly unusual, extraordinarily simple and carefully done bathing scenes." [14] Commenting on the show, Pissarro wrote his son: "My enthusiasm was nothing compared to Renoir's. Degas himself is seduced by the charm of this refined savage, Monet, all of us .. Are we mistaken? I don't think so. The only ones who are not subject to the charm of Cézanne are precisely those artists or collectors who have shown by their errors that their sensibilities are defective … Degas and Monet have bought some marvelous Cézannes, I exchanged a poor sketch of Louveciennes for an admirable small canvas of bathers and one of his self portraits." [15]

Yet, the recognition of the Impressionist artists could not console Cézanne in the face of this new wave of hostility and abuse. "I curse the Geffroys and the other smart-alecks who write articles for fifty francs a shot and attract attention to my person. My whole lifelong I have worked to earn my own living. But till now I believed that one could be a good painter without drawing attention to one's private life. Of course an artist wants to achieve as much – intellectually- as he can; but the man himself must remain in the dark," he wrote to Gasquet, 30 April 1896. [16]

Cézanne moved back to Montmartre in 1898, setting up house at the Villa des Arts, at 15, rue Hegesippe-Moreau. There, he painted several canvases, including a portrait of Ambroise Vollard. Vollard had been his dealer for three years, ever since organizing the first Parisian one-man show of Cézanne's works in his rue Laffitte gallery. It took no fewer than a hundred and fifteen sittings before the painter finished the portrait – almost finishing Vollard off in the process: "I'd been warned that Cézanne treated his models like slaves," confessed the unfortunate victim, whom the artist had installed on a rickety dais in order to prevent him moving. "I learned the full truth of this only too well … he treated his model like a still life … "Your posture should be that of an apple!" Cézanne would thunder, "Apples don't move, do they?" [17]

In his final period of Cézanne's life, from 1890 to 1905, an explosion of masterpieces followed – variations of Mont Ste. Victoire, still-life images (his beloved *Still life with Apples and Oranges*), and *Bathers*, a series of nudes. Matisse bought one of Cézanne's nudes, *Three Women Bathing*, and when giving this picture to the Musée du Petit Palais in Paris wrote, "I have had the picture for 37 years, and I hope I know it pretty well by now, albeit with some reservations; at critical moments in my own career as an artist it has restored my spirit; it has been the source of my belief and my endurance." [18]

Far more than in the bathing scenes, Cézanne achieved the harmony of nature and man with his drawing of portraits. Among his enduring masterpieces are *Lady in Blue* (1898/99), *Woman with a Coffee Pot* (1890/95) and *Two Card-Players* (1890/95). His delightful works of still-life art are from assembled motifs of apples and oranges and a few ordinary household items. It is his still-life paintings that bring first recognition and acknowledgement of his genius in technique and composition.

He would begin his work on landscape drawings at the crack of dawn, coming back in the evening to have supper with his mother at her house in the Cours Mirabeau. He organized outings for her by horse-drawn carriage; he would take her to sit in the sun at the Jas, or watch the world go by along the petite route to Le Tholonet. Their coachman, Baptistin Curnier, remembered Cézanne picking her up, delicately, carrying her from the house to the carriage, and from the carriage to her chair. He ministered to her with great patience, keeping her amused with a fund of little stories. She died on 25 October 1897.

Having lost his mother, Cézanne dedicated a room to her memory in his apartment, there he kept the bibelots that reminded him of her, and often shut himself away inside. One fine day, his jealous wife destroyed these mementos. Accustomed to his wife's foolishness, Cézanne came home, found everything gone, took off, and stayed away for several days in the countryside. His wife joyfully told a friend: "Do you know what! I burned everything. And what did he do? He went wandering in the countryside: he's an eccentric."

The Jas was sold at auction to Louis Granel, for seventy-five thousand francs. The disposal of his father's house (and with it his murals) was a traumatic experience. When the Jas de Bouffan was sold at the insistence of his brother-in-law who wanted the estate to be settled, Paul was very upset by the sale. "He removed the frames and burned all the canvases [stored there] a huge quantity, mostly early work, painted with the knife. Perhaps he burned them because he was afraid that he'd find them in the market selling for thirty sous, which had happened several times before with the sketches that his brother-in-law had first used to decorate his apartment, and then sold." [19]

From 1895 to 1899 Cézanne painted a number of pictures at the disused Bibemus quarry. They captured the chaos of bizarre, tumbled rocks, partly overgrown, in expressive and nicely unified visual terms. One of his most dramatic works of this period was Mont Sainte-Victoire as seen from Bibemus. Beyond the quarry in the middle distance, the crown of the mountain rears abruptly, seeming menacingly close; it takes up most of the upper third of the painting.

In a cycle of woodcuts of Mount Fuji, Hokusai expressed his reverence for the sacred mountain. He was considered to be a Japanese master and was most revered and often collected by French artists of the time. Like Monet's series paintings, Cézanne's approach to his mountain seems to have drawn upon similar sources in the imagination. The mountain's name, which translates as "Mountain of Holy Victory," was associated with a celebrated victory by Provence's ancient Roman inhabitants against an invading army. Cézanne painted more than sixty versions of what he called "his" mountain, yet none of the paintings look exactly the same.

But Cézanne's isolation in Aix began to lessen during the mid-1990s owing largely to the urging of Pissarro, Monet, and Renoir, and Ambroise Vollard. Thanks to their efforts public interest in his work slowly began to develop. In 1899, 1901, and 1902 the artist sent pictures to the annual Salon des Indépendants in Paris, and in 1904 he was given an entire room at the Salon d'Automne. Chocquet, who had been a great admirer of Cézanne from the very first, bequeathed his paintings to his wife. In July 1899, when Mme Cochquet died, there was an auction of thirty-one pictures by Cézanne.

The numerous portraits done in those years are eloquent of the distance Cézanne put between himself and the world. "The pictures of Hortense, in particular, are marked by indifference towards the figure and her setting. He transformed his son Paul into an alien creature – inspired perhaps by the Aix carnival. For reasons that remain obscure, Cézanne would break off relations to people he had always valued. Anyone who dared venture into his presence sensed the turmoil in him. His fear of contact stemmed from his fear of being dominated. He preferred solitude. The sole exception to this rule were his occasional visits to Monet's residence at Giverny, where Monet had recently begun his series of paintings of water lilies." [20]

Another exception may have been visits mostly from young artists of Gauguin's entourage who came to ask him for advice. "I think the young painters much more intelligent than the others," he wrote with unconcealed satisfaction to his son. "The young artists who came to visit Cézanne in Aix found a tall old man of almost exaggerated politeness, though he sometimes changed abruptly from cordiality to haughtiness. Interested in nothing but art, he liked to talk about painting yet could show some irritation if pressed to formulate theories." [21]

Cézanne habitually complained of "brain trouble" (*trouble du cerveau*) often linked to the heat of the day, which he found increasingly hard to bear. Disabling or at least disorientating, they interfered with his "sensations" especially the all-important sensations of colors and therefore interrupted his paintings. He could not bear to be touched. Once when he fell and a friend tried to help him: Cézanne shouted, "No one will touch me … no one will get his hooks into me. Never! Never!" Tenderness associated with diabetic nerve damage may itself have been a contributing factor.

Morisot continued to live a quiet productive life that focused on her work, her daughter and her travels of the south of France and abroad. She exhibited with the Impressionist until their last show in 1886. She participated in a successful show in Durand-Ruel gallery in New York and in 1894 sold *Young Woman in a Ball Dress* (1879) to the Musée du Luxembourg. It is highly ironic that Morisot, who'd always been anxiously concerned about Julie's health, at times suddenly canceling trips in Italy or taking her from Paris to a warmer climate, died of pneumonia from an infection she caught from her daughter. Morisot died at the age of 54 in 1895. She left a considerable amount of work of gardens, young girls, watercolors of refined taste, all of surprising energy and of a distinguishing coloring, as it is expected. Like the paternity of Leon Leenhoff, the liaison of Manet and Morisot is one of the puzzling mysteries of this Impressionist quartet.

In the spring of 1894 Mary Cassatt's personal fortune, the inheritance from her family and the sale of her increasingly valuable work enabled her to spend more time at her grand country estate Chateau de Beaufresne, in the village of Mesnil-Theribus, in the Oise Valley. It was near the cathedral town of Beauvais, about fifty miles northwest of Paris. The large, three-story, seventeenth century manor had forty-five acres of land, elegant gardens and a large pond. Cassatt was determined in old age to be as comfortable as possible and her modern innovations astonished the traditional villagers. "I have done more plumbing, another bath room. I hope I am now nearly up to the American standard. I need not say that I am so far beyond my French neighbors, that they think I am demented." [22]

Cassatt was given two one-woman shows at Durand-Ruel's gallery, in 1891 and 1893. In 1895 he organized a Cassatt exhibition in which she showed fifty-eight works. Unmarried and childless, she continued to please her public with paintings and etchings of mothers and children.

It was during this time, the mid-1890s, that an episode known as the Dreyfus Affair sharply divided French society. In 1894, Alfred Dreyfus, a young French artillery captain of Alsatian Jewish descent, was convicted of a treasonous act of communicating French military secrets to the German Embassy in Paris. He was sent to Devil's Island in French Guiana to be imprisoned and placed in solitary confinement for the rest of his life. Two years into his sentence, evidence was brought forth that proved Dreyfus's innocence: a French Army major named Ferdinand Walsin Esterhazy was the real culprit. This case now became a major political issue, dividing France into two camps, anti-Semites and royalists on the one hand and the anticlerical Dreyfusards. Rampant anti-Semitism kept him from being exonerated for another ten years.

With the country deeply divided between those in support of Dreyfus and those against him, Degas sided with those against Dreyfus and did not refrain from making anti-Semitic remarks. His stance against Dreyfus cost him many friends and much respect within the typically more tolerant avant-garde art circles.

Word of the military court's framing of Alfred Dreyfus and of an attendant cover-up began to spread, chiefly owing to *J'accuse*, a vehement open letter published in a Paris newspaper in January 1898 by the notable writer Émile Zola. Progressive activists put pressure on the government to reopen the case. Monet wrote to Zola, "Bravo and bravo again for the two beautiful articles. You alone have said what must be said and you have done it so well. I am happy to extend to you all of my compliments." Eventually, all the accusations against Alfred Dreyfus were demonstrated to be baseless. In 1906, Dreyfus was exonerated and reinstated as a major in the French Army. He served during the whole of World War I, ending his service with the rank of Lieutenant-Colonel.

Chapter Seventeen: Into History

During the Dreyfus turmoil, Monet could not pick up a paintbrush over the next fourteen months. Then in September 1899, he left his scandal-ridden homeland for a six-week stay in England. Unconcerned about expenses, Monet settled into a sixth floor suite in the fashionable Savoy Hotel, accompanied by Alice and Germaine Hoschedé. His room afforded spectacular views of the Thames and south London. He returned to the hotel for three months the following year and for the same period of time in 1901. The result of this extended effort, which did not end until he showed thirty-seven London pictures in 1904, was the largest series of paintings he had ever produced - nearly a hundred canvases depicting Charing Cross Bridge, Waterloo Bridge, and the Houses of Parliament with reflections of light in the river and fog. He even played tourist visiting the tower of London and watched Queen Victoria's funeral process, which he claimed was a unique spectacle. Monet summed up his sentiments of his visit to England, "Without the fog, London would not be a beautiful city."

In November and December 1900, Monet showed twelve of the Japanese Bridge pictures at Durand-Ruel's gallery. Later, in May, he unveiled twenty-six bridge pictures and ten views of the Houses of Parliament. He received the accolades he set out to receive. Georges Lecomte, French novelist and historian, believed that Monet had never "attained such a vaporous subtlety, such power of abstraction, and synthesis." Monet was now famous and quite rich, allowing him to partake in many personal luxuries. He could now indulge his passion for gardening, wearing fine clothes, and eating special foods. Monet "ordered twill suits from the fancy English outfitters Old England on the boulevard des Capucines; his ruffled cambric shirts came from the best shirt makers in Paris, and his boots were ordered from the same boot maker who outfitted the army regiment in Vernon." He loved foie gras, especially from Alsace; and frequently appeased his love for truffles from Perigord. His enthusiasm for food and drink caused him to gain several pounds.

French Statesman Georges Clemenceau was a staunch supporter of Monet. He ran a magazine entitled *La Justice*, which carried many favorable reviews of Monet's paintings as well as authoring flattering articles about Monet. He was instrumental in acquiring paintings by Monet for the State, especially after 1907, when he became prime minister of France. Between 1883 and 1908, Monet traveled to the Mediterranean, where he painted landmarks, landscapes, and seascapes, such as Bordighera. He painted an important series of paintings in Venice, Italy where he stayed for two months.

A *horrendum anno* occurred in 1911. Alice died and after more than thirty years together, the pain of her loss was simply excruciating for Monet. He grieved for months, unable to do anything else. "I am totally worn out," he told Bernheim-Jeune in August of that year. His oldest son Jean, who had married Alice's daughter Blanche, Monet's particular favorite, died in 1914. After Alice died, Blanche looked after and cared for Monet. It was during this time that Monet began to develop the first signs of cataracts. He underwent cataract surgery on both eyes, which was considered a partial success. But Monet's cataracts impacted his vision; his paintings had a general reddish tone.

Monet convalesced by spending most of his time in his gardens at Giverny.

~~~~~~~~~~

Cézanne was also spending a great deal of time at his newly purchased home. On 16 November 1901, he purchased a small rural property where he would spend most of his time. "His property was located within the bounds of Aix in the district called Les Capucins or Les Resquihado or the Hospital. The property consisted of an old building and some land laid out in orchards, olive trees and fruit trees. The property was on a hill north of the town, known as les lauves."[1] Perhaps, the best thing about this property is that Mont Ste Victoire could be seen from a hillside near his studio. In Cézanne's day, the property was quite rural.

There were several olive trees on his property but no doubt from his early explorative childhood years, his first love was for pine trees. To Cézanne, the pine itself brought back memories of his youth and the pleasant memories that he had stored away of his and Zola's adventures. At one point he wrote a reminiscent letter to Zola, "Do you remember the pine standing at the edge of the Arc Valley…?" Cézanne identified with the grandeur of the Pine as one can observe in *Mont Sainte Victoire With Large Pine* - it is more than a tree, it is a life – it is a vision. Even though he was melancholic, diabetic, depressed, dogmatic - nothing would stop him from painting.

In 1902 Zola died a horrible death of carbon monoxide poisoning, asphyxiated by the fumes of the coal fire in the bedroom of his Paris residence. When help arrived both Zola and Alexandrine were found unconscious - Alexandrine pulled through; Zola did not. The causes of his death swirled among widespread rumors that he had been assassinated by fanatical nationalists or had committed suicide for reasons unknown. While Cézanne had broken off his friendship with Zola in 1886 when the writer published *L'Oeuvre*, when he heard the news of Zola's death, Cézanne was racked with grief.

In 1927 an anti-Dreyfusard, made a deathbed confession, to the effect that Zola had been deliberately suffocated. According to the stove fitter's testimony, he and his men stopped up the chimney while doing repairs on the neighboring roof. Early the next morning they unstopped it. Their activities went completely unnoticed. The evidence is not conclusive but one thing is clear: "natural causes" can no longer be considered a safe verdict.

Cézanne vowed to die painting, and he did. While painting outdoors in the fall of 1906, he was overtaken by a storm and became ill. He died in Aix on 22 October 1906. At the Salon d'Automne of 1907 his achievement was honored with a large retrospective exhibition. Cézanne completed 954 paintings and over 100 still lifes of which about half featured apples. He painted at least 80 Bathers, almost equally divided between male and female; over 40 Mont Sainte-Victories, 645 watercolors and 1,400 drawings most of them from eighteen sketchbooks.

The sheer volume of his works underscores Cézanne's passion for art. In pursuing that passion, mistress/wife Marie Hortense Figuet and his son Paul, along with his friends, came in at distant seconds. He preferred to live and work in solitude as he painted every single day of his life. He was rarely satisfied with his work – most of which was unrecognized until the year before he died. From being virtually unknown, his paintings now demanded the attention they deserved. Young artists flocked to Aix to learn what they could from this great artist.

Cézanne, who had supported the long years of contempt very philosophically, did not even obtain some "official" measure of appreciation in his later years. In 1902, he let it be understood that, while he would not think of making any request, he would readily accept any decoration, which might be conferred upon him, as an official recognition of his merit. M. Roujon, the Director of the Beaux-Arts, was approached with a view of securing for Cézanne the *Légion d'honneur*. The request was met by a peremptory refusal.

The director declared himself ready to decorate any other of the Impressionists, especially Claude Monet, who was precisely the one who refused to be decorated. But to decorate Cézanne, Roujon regarded as tantamount to a repudiation of all the principles and laws, which it was his office to uphold. Cézanne, therefore, had to recognize that his appreciation by a minority of artists and connoisseurs did not prevent the fact, in the correct administrative mind, and in the spheres of official art, he was still regarded as an anarchist.

Cézanne kept trekking to the countryside to paint in good and in inclement weather. A few days after collapsing in a thunderstorm, Hortense and Paul, who were in Paris, were notified. His wife could have made it in time to Aix but, according to some historians, she was unwilling to cancel a fitting at her dressmaker. She had scant regard for Cézanne as a husband and as a painter. She certainly seemed to have regarded the paintings themselves as little more than "gambling chips, to be cashed in as the need arose." The feeling was apparently mutual if one judges Cézanne's family feelings from the portraits he painted of Hortense and Paul, which are void of any special tenderness. His family portraits were sold, sooner or later, like all the rest. His time will come but for now his friends are offered one more look at Cézanne's inspiration Mont Ste. Victoire – the mountain that reminded him of happy days with friends and of his desire to create art that was solid and enduring.

Of the old guard Impressionist only three remained Monet, vigorous hardworking conscious of his worldwide reputation surrounded by numerous admirers; Degas, threatened by total blindness and Renoir increasingly crippled by rheumatism yet joyfully painting in spite of extreme physical difficulties. He continued at best he could to put colors on canvas in order to amuse himself and merely stated "I believe that I deserve my little success since I have worked very hard."

~~~~~~~~~

Degas continued to explore new directions though his eyesight was deteriorating. In 1895 he bought a camera and began to take photographs of models and dancers and friends. Edgar Degas, however, had used photography in his early training years, when he made numerous copies of Italian old masters from photographs. But now he rediscovered incorporating photographs and began once again to explore the many possibilities of photography and painting. "These days, Degas abandons himself entirely to his new passion for photography," wrote an artist friend in autumn 1895. From that time forward Degas entered his most intense exploration of photography. "Most of his photographs were made in the evenings, when Degas transformed dinner parties into photographic soirees. He would requisition the living rooms at one of his friends, arrange oil lamps, and direct the poses of dinner guests enlisted as models. He went back and forth ... running from one end of the room to the other with an expression of infinite happiness," wrote Daniel Halévy, the son of Degas's close friends Ludovic and Louise Halévy. ... "At half-past eleven everybody left; Degas, surrounded by three laughing girls, carried his camera as proudly as a child carrying a rifle." [2]

Later in life, Degas found a new passion – poetry. He threw himself into poetry as passionately as he did to his art. Degas wrote twenty carefully crafted sonnets, limiting himself to this difficult and demanding form:

Tired and heavy, she sits on the edge of the bath
Washing her feet. You sit in the tub,
Breasts drooping, belly pleated as you stoop.
I scrub the smooth plane of your back,
Rub with a rough towel. A rosy warmth
follows my attention ...

But despite his poetry, sculpting in wax and clay, he was still leading a strange, solitary life, as he moved uncomplainingly to successively smaller apartments, until he was reduced to using his studio as his dressing room: The models were forced to pose in a dusty attic where he hung his own dressing gowns. "It was increasingly difficult for him to hear, and his eyes were of almost no use to him," was how Ambroise Vollard described Degas in 1912. "He's absorbed in solitude, cut off from emerging avant-garde movements, gradually going blind." Degas, increasingly removed himself from the world, but continued to linger on.

 He wrote to a friend, "You see my legs are good, I get around all right. But since I moved, I no longer work... I don't care; I'm letting everything go. It's astonishing, how indifferent you become in old age." But despite these pessimistic descriptions of his life, there didn't seem to be much of a change to his everyday routine. He worked at his studio until evening, then had a plain meal prepared by faithful maid Zoe Closier, unless friends like the Halévys had him over for dinner. He spent his summers with the Valpinçons and on rare occasions traveled to Switzerland, and made one trip to Naples in 1906.

Degas lived on well into the 20th century, and although he painted less during these years, he promoted his work tirelessly and became an avid art collector. Winters were especially hard for Degas; obliged to spend more and more time in bed. Degas had considered bequeathing his collection and studio contents to form a museum, but he was so disappointed by Musée National Gustave Moreau and was irritated by the museum men that he decided not to do so. He left everything to a brother, a nephew, "people without merit, unworthy of such a benefit," but "his people." To these people should be added his niece Mlle. Fevre, whose interests had been safe guarded by Mary Cassatt who arranged for a lawyer to act on her behalf. The Degas sales held in 1918 and 1919 were, in general, a considerable success. That London National Gallery and the Victoria and Albert Museum as well as the Louvre acquired works at this sale, which was yet another indication that Degas had become an Old Master of the modern movement.

Degas was never married although he did count several women, including the American painter Mary Cassatt, among his intimate friends. "Manet's passionate portraits expressed his love for Morisot; Degas' cool portraits, by contrast, revealed his constraints with Cassatt. He admired her breeding, culture, intellect, wit and conversation, her talent and dedication to her art. Mary was certainly different from the 'good little woman, simple, calm,'. She understood his 'whims,' believed passionately in his art and would never have called one of his pictures 'a pretty little thing.' Degas was too timid and reserved to express his feelings; and her reluctance to portray adult males, outside the family, suggests an estrangement from men and fear of intimacy. Despite their romantic yearnings, they both knew that their irascible characters were not cut out for domestic bliss. In the end their passion for work was greater than their desire for love or fear of a solitary old age." [3]

Degas passed away on 27 September 1917, at the age of 83.   Before Degas died Manet told Degas with obvious sincerity "We have all, in our minds, awarded you the medal of honor, along with many other things even more flattering."

"Degas is no more. We buried him on Saturday, [with] beautiful sunshine, a little crowd of friends and admirers, all very quiet and peaceful in the midst of this dreadful upheaval of which he was barely conscious. You can well understand what a satisfaction it was to me to know that he had been well care for and even tenderly nursed by his niece in his last days." Mary Cassatt [4]

~~~~~~~~~~

By 1911, Mary Cassatt had accumulated a fortune of 200 thousand francs, which, like Monet, allowed her to live quite luxuriously. She collected art, bought expensive clothes and antique jewelry not to mention her country chateau Beaufresne employing a maid, cook, coachman, three gardeners, and eight farmers. Mary also traveled and in February of that same year, took trips to North Africa, Vienna, Budapest, Sofia, and Constantinople. In Cairo, she took a cruise up the Nile with her younger brother, Gardner, and his family. "I wonder though if ever I can paint again … fancy going back to babies & women." The trip was interrupted when Gardner fell seriously ill with hives, dysentery, and Nile fever. The family managed to get back to Paris, but shortly thereafter, her brother died. After his death, Mary, like Cezanne, had been suffering from diabetes and like Renoir she was experiencing debilitating rheumatism. Mary suffered severe weight loss, which reduced her already thin body to less than one hundred pounds. Gardner's death, which filled her with grief and guilt, precipitated a major crisis. She became severely depressed, had a nervous breakdown, and was unable to work for the next two years.

Cassatt did have one romantic opportunity. James Stillman from Texas was six years her junior and a prominent business tycoon. Stillman was a cotton trader, President of the National City Bank of New York from 1891-1909 and thereafter Chairman of the Board. He was a close associate of the Rockefellers and Standard Oil. He collected Cassatt's work and asked her advice when buying art. Stillman described by his biographer as "loveable, whimsical person, violent in likes and dislikes, vehement and crotchety, quick tempered and soon over it … full of all sorts of fiery causes and beliefs." He saw that dogs were a way to her heart and bought pet-dog collars and feeding-bowls from Tiffany's. Cassatt graciously accepted the gifts but kept Stillman at a safe distance. Stillman made overtures, "I often think of you with very affectionate regards and hope you will find that happiness that you wish for." A few days later she conceded that he had touched her and "brought something into my life I had not had before." Undaunted, in 1911, Stillman proposed and was rejected.

After her trip to Egypt in 1912 Mary permanently moved to Beaufresne, and gradually began to work in the mornings and was able in the summer of 1913 to show Joseph Durand-Ruel, her long-time friend, buyer, adviser and gallery owner, a nearly completed pastel. Only four months later, he received seven more pastels. Her eyesight, like Monet's, continued to deteriorate due to inoperable cataracts. "I look forward with horror to utter darkness," Cassatt wrote in 1919, fearing that an operation on her left eye would be "as great a failure as the last one." It was, and she stopped painting.

While she was not able to draw due to almost complete blindness, she rallied to a new cause – women's suffrage. Mary believed in women's rights to vote, to obtain a good education, and to establish careers. She considered her art to be an expression of respect for women. Her earlier images reflected women of culture at the theater, reading newspapers, or engaged in quiet contemplation. Her later works show women and children experiencing "love and life."

Toward the end of her life the Impressionist group disbanded but Cassatt still had contact with some of the members, including Renoir, Monet, and Pissarro. Mary Cassatt stopped producing pictures almost entirely, and retired to the south of France during the First World War. She lived on in seclusion and virtual blindness, unable to work, until her death in 1926 at the Chateau de Beaufresne.

Did she love Degas? Did they have an affair? In later years one bold relative actually dared to ask her the question "Was Degas ever your lover?" Her reply was predictably indignant as well as surprisingly snobbish: "What, with that common little man; what a repulsive idea!" Apparently the idea itself did not bother her as much as the fact of his "commonness."

~~~~~~~~

The autumn Salon of 1904 was the occasion of a great triumph for Renoir. A large space was set apart for painters who had died or who were well advanced in their career. In the latter class Renoir held a distinguished place. Thus the public was able to see a representative collection of his pictures, drawn from all his various periods. The masterfulness, the variety, the charm of his work, seen retrospectively, aroused a universal chorus of praise. The press was unanimous in proclaiming its merit. The hour of justice, though long in coming, had at last arrived.

Like the other Impressionists, Renoir bought a house at Essoures, in Burgundy, Aline's native home. But because his arthritis was getting potentially worse, each winter he moved to the warm southern climate of Cagnes, in the mountains above Nice. He made it his permanent his home in 1903. Renoir had discovered an old farmhouse set in an olive grove, which he called "Les Collettes" and he lived out the rest of his days painting in the warm southern light. But despite the pain from his arthritis, he continued to paint; his hands were bandaged in order to hold a paintbrush - the brushes were placed between his bandaged figurers.

In 1911 Renoir turned seventy; his son Jean, who was to become a world-famous film director, gave this poignant description: "What struck outsiders coming into his presence for the first time were his eyes and hands. His eyes were light brown, verging on yellow. His eyesight was very keen… As for their expression, imagine a mixture of irony and tenderness, of joking and sensuality. They always looked as though they were laughing … perhaps it was also a mask. For Renoir was extremely modest and did not like to reveal the emotion that overwhelmed him while he was looking at flowers, women, or clouds in the sky, the way other men touch and caress." [5]

In the summer of 1913 Vollard suggested that Renoir attempt sculpture. Sculpting was not new to Renoir; it had always been the basis of many of his paintings. One of his first new adventures with sculpting, other than a mirror of sculpted flowers made for Mme Charpentier, was creating a few medallions of Coco (Renoir's youngest son, Claude) followed by a bust of the child in 1908. Vollard, however, continued to persuade Renoir to sculpt and when he hired a young Catalan man, Richard Guino, Renoir's sculpting became a reality. Renoir took up his sculpting projects with a passion and one of his finest is *Venus Victorious* by Renoir and Guino. The final version of the *Venus Victorious* is six feet in the height, slightly over life-size, but with a far greater sense of monumentality. The statue depicts the goddess Venus holding the golden apple, which she is awarded by Paris, a favorite mythological theme that preoccupied Renoir towards the end of his life.

In the final months of his own life, he told his son, "As a painter I am beginning to see more clearly how to work from nature … But I still can't do justice to the intensity unfolding before my eyes." Renoir died on 3 December 1919 in Cagnes, aged 78. His sickness was not the immediate cause of his death. He had a heart attack. His sons Jean and Claude were with him when he died. His estate, valued at five million francs, was bequeathed to his three sons. On the day he died he was still painting. He gave up his paintbrush with the words, "I think I am beginning to understand something about it." The world-renowned Renoir continued to paint until his death. He lived long enough to see one of his works bought by the Louvre in 1919, a tremendous honor for any artist.

~~~~~~~~~~

Despite Monet's aging body and deteriorating eyesight, the years following Renoir's death to about 1922 were watershed years for Monet. He had recently sold nineteen paintings to Durand-Ruel and his rivals the Bernheim-Jeune brothers during the course of the year for a total of 272 thousand francs an extraordinary amount of money, which added to his already substantial bank account. His works were receiving generous praise from the critics. He told Paul Signac that even though "the insidious critics of the first hour [of my career] have left me alone, I remain equally indifferent to the praises of imbeciles, snobs, and traffickers."

There were, of course, a few rather minor frustrations. In 1910, the Seine and the Epte surged over their banks and flooded both his Giverny gardens off and on for nearly two months. Waters were so high and turbulent that waves occasionally broke by the entrance to his house. Monet thought that surely his gardens - his life's passion - had been ruined. But by the end of summer the gardens were more radiant than ever because of the rich soil deposits let by the flooding waters.

As the seasonal waters returned to their beds, Monet gradually regained his strength and eventually he went back to painting his water lilies, spending six years on his water lily exhibition. One of the interesting things about Monet's work is his gradual shift from his depictions of modern life to the ageless depiction of nature itself. Here we see the wonderful mural-sized paintings of his lily pond at Giverny. And, to accommodate these rather immense paintings he built a spacious new studio with twelve large panels of approximately 2 meters high by 4.25 meters long, conveniently mounted on large, moveable easels. One suite of four canvases depicts two cropped willow trees with their foliage cascading in front of water lily clusters. Another triptych to the right of the willow panels concentrates on agapanthus; and a lone canvas to the left of the willow panels depicts irises.

Perhaps the most remarkable works in this group of new canvases actually constituted an entirely independent series that Monet began in 1918 and largely completed that year. There are ten paintings in the series, all of which depict one of two weeping willows that stood at the northern end of the water lily pond. So thick is the foliage that the sky is hardly visible. In 1923 Monet painted a series of Weeping Willow trees as homage to the French fallen soldiers of World War I.

Monet was quite bedridden now but was able to scrawl Paul Leon a letter in early October but also to inform him "I have regained my courage and despite my weakness am back at work," albeit he admitted "in very small doses." He invited Leon and the architect to the reconfigured Orangerie at Giverny for a preview.

Monet died of lung cancer on 5 December 1926; he had turned 86 three weeks earlier. He was the last of the core founders of Impressionism. Monet was buried in the Giverny church cemetery, alongside Alice, her first husband Ernest, their two daughters Suzanne and Marthe, and Monet's elder son Jean. He had insisted that the occasion be simple; thus about fifty people attended the ceremony, which was strictly non-religious as Monet had requested. There were no eulogies, no flowers, nothing to mark the tomb but a single shaft of wheat, a reminder of his undying love for his land.

The official opening of the Orangerie took place on Tuesday 17 May 1926. Not many people attended the official ceremony; and fewer still came to visit over the following weeks. Today, it seems like a mecca – visitors are transported in an ethereal way to the world of nature – just as Monet would have wanted. His remaining family and heirs bequeathed his Giverny home and gardens to the French Academy of Fine Arts in 1966 – just as Monet would have wanted.

~~~~~~~~~~

There are countless cafes in Paris but the Café Guerbois became the gathering center for the core group of artists who played a decisive role in challenging the accepted form of art. Art accepted, at the time, was deftly executed by Meissonier, one of the most treasured artists in all of France and beyond. It was at the Café, during the fledgling days of the Impressionist movement, that Manet, Monet, Degas, Renoir, Pissarro, Sisly, and Cezanne sat in the back corner around two tables, sipping their drinks while brainstorming their ideas that revolutionized art during their lifetimes. Monet's views of sun-dappled waters and flowering poppy fields, Renoir's views of boats, flowers, nudes, and portraits of families; Degas' dancers, Cezanne's explosions of color that made simple fruits come alive; Morisot and Cassatt's capturing young children alone and with their mothers, and Manet's café scenes that served as fascinating windows into the actuality of Parisian social life. All their art captured the fleeing impressions of "rippling shadows and shimmering lights" - and all their art grew out of endless nights of *débats sérieux* that took place among lasting friends at the artists' corner at the Café Guerbois …

"I can hear the glass door of the café grate on the sand as I open it. I can recall the smell of every hour. In the morning that of eggs frizzling in butter, the pungent cigarette, coffee and bad cognac; at five o'clock the fragrant odor of absinthe; and soon after the steaming soup ascends from the kitchen; and as the evening advances, the mingled smells of cigarettes, coffee and weak beer. The usual marble tables are there, and it is there we sat …"

Chapter Eighteen: Legacies

Each of the Impressionists, while choosing to dedicate their lives to art, had different techniques, subject matter, personalities, and ways of defining success. To Manet it was acceptance by the Salon, issuing medals culminating in the *Légion d'honneur*– while he never earned this coveted award, he did earn the respect, admiration and love of his peers. He provided the backbone for one of the most glorious chapters to the history of art. Yet he was a witty, charming, and a quintessential "flaneur." During his lifetime, the methods, subjects, indeed the whole system of aesthetics was revolutionized and Manet was the initiator who acted as a mentor to all who joined him in this discovery of unexplored territory. Manet painted life as it was. In his words, "A thing is beautiful because it is human. Forget all ideas about 'perfection' and the 'absolute.' A thing isn't beautiful because it's perfect according to certain physical and metaphysical precepts. A thing is beautiful because it lives." [1]

The antithesis to Manet's view of success was Degas; for him the markers of success were the freedom to paint and the freedom to continue to try to paint perfection. Degas wanted the joy of creating again and again, and the freedom to rework a painting until he reached perfection. To him critical opinions were worthless and wealth served only to satisfy his collecting of art. While Degas has always been recognized as one of the greatest Impressionist painters, his legacy has been mixed in the decades since his death. The misogynist overtones present in his sexualized portraits of women, as well as his intense anti-Semitism, have served to alienate Degas from some modern critics. Still, the sheer beauty of his early works and the distinctly modern self-conscious elusiveness of his later portraits ensure Degas a lasting legacy. One thing remains indisputable about Degas: His were among the most painstakingly polished and refined paintings in history. An obsessive and careful planner, Degas liked to joke that he was the least spontaneous artist alive. "If painting weren't difficult," he once remarked. "It wouldn't be so fun."

Morisot and Cassatt had the courage to choose a man's career, but needed to sell their work to validate that choice. Much of their creative energy went into dealing with the conflict between work and family life. What Mary Cassatt has done – establish a career when most women did not even dream of a life beyond home and hearth and to travel and live independently – says a great deal about her determination to reach her artist goal. Berthe and Mary worked diligently for immortality and the enduring nature of their lives and works suggest that it is theirs.

During the last few years of his life, Cézanne's art had begun to be shown and seen across Europe, and it became a fundamental influence on the Fauves, the cubists, and virtually all advanced art of the early 20th century. Cézanne's pictures of bathers were lauded for their combination of naturalness, spontaneity, and balanced composition. And the very clumsiness of his rendering of figures was taken as evidence of his unfeigned, genuine response. Paul did not produce a school but his work has been highly influential in the aesthetic development of many twentieth century artists – so much so that he is called the "Father of Modern Painting."

Renoir was a painter of women – all types of women from voluptuous nudes to Parisienne working girls at one of Montmartre balls. Renoir painted happy moments in life and he, in old age, even though he could not walk or even rise from a chair, kept his same good humor. That happiness is apparent in his works. His passion to draw never seemed to leave him. His art is timeless and worthy of comparison to the Old Masters – Raphael, Titian, and Rubens.

Monet was more the upstart provincial, devoid of irony and cynicism, determined to make his way by celebrating the landscapes of modern life. It is the life of their own day that has inspired their work. Monet was the last member of this unique and astonishing group. He died at a time when the ideas that he personified had become a reality. Monet was the first of the Impressionist painters to achieve success, and the only one of them to see it turn into a real triumph.

Théodore Duret phrased the legacy of this group as follows, "It is unlikely that any painters will ever again have to face the hostility which was manifested against The Impressionists. The repetition of such a phenomenon would be impossible. The case of the Impressionists, in which withering scorn yielded place to admiration, has put criticism on its guard. It will surely stand as a warning, and ought to prevent the recurrence of a similar outbursts of indignation against the innovators and independents whom time may yet bring forth." [2]

Endnotes Chapter One

[1] John W. Mollett, *Meissonier*, (New York: Scriber and Welford), 1882, p. 6.

[2] Ross King, *The Judgment of Paris: The Revolutionary Decade That Gave The World Impressionism*. (New York: Walker Publishing Company), 2006, p. 29.

[3] Richard Muther, *The History of Modern Painting*, vol. 2 (UK: Ulan Press), 2012, p. 106.

[4] Ross King, *Op. Cit.*, p. 3

[5] John W. Mollett, *Op. Cit.*, pp. 2-3

[6] Jean Louis Ernest Meissonier and Octave Gréard, *Meissonier, His Life and Art*, (New York: A.C. Armstrong & Son), 1897, p. 345

[7] *La Presse*, April 16, 1845.

[8] *Dictionary of Art Historians*

[9] J. E. de Goncourt, *Goncourt Journals*, (Paris: Manette Salomon), 1866, ch. v

[10] Ross King, *Op, Cit.*, p. 17

[11] Beth Archer Brombert, *Édouard Manet: Rebel in a Frock Coat*, (Boston: Little Brown), 1996, p. 67

[12] Sue Roe, *The Private Lives of the Impressionists*, (New York: HarperCollins), 2006, p. 9

[13] John Reward, *Op Cit.* p. 20

[14] Sue Roe., *Op. Cit.*, p. 7

[15] A. and W. Galignani, *Galignani's New Illustrated Paris Guide* (1860).

[16] Joanna Richardson, *The Bohemians,* (London: Macmillan and Co., Ltd.), 1969, p. 154.

[17] Cited in Myers, Nicole. "The Lure of Montmartre, 1880–1900". In *Heilbrunn Timeline*

of Art History. New York: The Metropolitan Museum of Art, 2000.

[18] Robert L. Herbert, *Impressionism: Art, Leisure, & Parisian Society,* (New Haven, CT: Yale University Press), 1988. p. 63

Endnotes Chapter Two

[1] Georges Bernier, *Paris Cafes: Their Role in the Birth of Modern Art* (New York: Wildenstein & Co. Inc.), 1985, pp.38-40

[2] Robert L. Herbert, *Impressionism: Art, Leisure, & Parisian Society,* (New Haven, CT: Yale University Press), 1988, p. 65

[3] Émile Zola, *The Masterpiece* (Gloucester: Alan Sutton Publishing Limited), 1986, p.74

[4] Sylvie Buisson and Christian Parisot, *Montmartre: A Mecca of Modern Art, 1860-1920*. (Boston: Museum of Fine Arts, David Godine, Publisher, Inc.) 1991, p.32

[5] George Moore, *Confessions of a Young Man,* (New York: Brentanos), 1901, p. 75

[6] Beth Archer Brombert, *Édouard Manet: Rebel in a Frock Coat*, (Boston: Little Brown), 1996, p. 119

[7] The Project Gutenberg eBook, *The French Impressionists (1860-1900),* by Camille Mauclair, Translated by P. G. Konady.

[8] Émile Zola, *Mon Salon*, (Paris: Garnier-Flammarion),1866.

[9] Sue Roe, *Op. Cit.,* p. 30

[10] Doris Lanier, *Absinthe: The Cocaine of the Nineteen Century*, (Jefferson, NC: McFarland & Company, Inc., Publishers), 1995, p.101

[11] Christian Philipp Müller, Sabeth Buchmann, Philipp Kaiser, Kerstin Stakemeier, Jacqueline Uhlmann, *Selection d'artistes*, vol. 12, (Ann Arbor, MI: University of Michigan), 2009, p. 29

[12] John Rewald, *The History of Impressionism,* (New York: Harry N. Abrams), 1990, p. 198

[13] Pamela Todd, *The Impressionists at Leisure*, (London: Thames & Hudson, Limited), 2007. p. 17

[14] John Rewald, *Op. Cit.,* p.48

[15] Ibid., p. 199

[16] Marion Harry Spielmann, *The Magazine of Art*, vol. 13, p. 423

[17] Theodore Reff and Edgar Degas, *The Notebooks of Edgar Degas: A Catalogue of the Thirty-Eight Notebooks in the Bibliotheque Nationale and Other Collections*, vols. 1 & 2. , (Cambridge: Cambridge University Press), 1977. *Notebook* 21

[18] John Reward, *Op Cit.,* p. 200

[19] Ibid., p. 42

[20] Edmond Bazire, *Manet* (Paris: A Quantin, 1884), p. 30.

[21] John Reward, *Op. Cit.*, p. 202

[22] Mariel Oberthur, *Cafes and Cabarets of Montmartre,* (Salt Lake City, UT: Peregrine Smith Books), 1984, p. 11-12

[23] W. Scott Haine, *The World of the Paris Café: Sociability among the French Working Class, 1789-1914* (Baltimore, MD The Johns Hopkins University Press), 1996, p. 7

[24] Muriel Oberthur, *Op Cit.,* p. 41.

[25] John Rewald, *Op. Cit.*, p. 198

[26] Ibid., p. 169

Endnotes Chapter Three

[1] Sir Alistair Horne, *Seven Ages of Paris*, (New York: Alfred A. Knopf), 2002, p. 52

[2] John Richardson, *Edouard Manet; Paintings and Drawings*, (London: Phaidon), 1958, p. 6

[3] Beth Archer Brombert, *Édouard Manet: Rebel in a Frock Coat*, (Boston: Little Brown), 1996, p. 7

[4] Jeffrey Meyers, *Impressionist Quartet: The Intimate Genius of Manet and Morisot, Degas and Cassatt*, (Orlando, FL: Harcourt), 2005, p. 3

[5] Ibid., p. 3

[6] Ibid., pp. 5-6

[7] Jeffrey Meyers, "Degas and Manet: A Study in Friendship." *Apollo*, February 1, 2005

[8] Edward Snow, *A Study of Vermeer*, (Berkeley, CA: University of California Press), 1994, p. 34

[9] Jeffrey Meyers, *Impressionist Quartet*, p. 153

[10] Roy McMullen, *Degas: His Life, Times, and Work*, (Boston, MA: Houghton), 1984, p. 332

[11] Ibid., p. 20

[12] Ibid., p. 23

[13] Ibid., 20, 23

[14] Jeffrey Meyers, *Op Cit.*, p. 133

[15] Ibid., p. 134

[16] Alex De Jonge, *Baudelaire, Prince of Clouds: A Biography*, (New York: Paddington Press), 1976, p. 21

[17] Jeffrey Meyers, *Op. Cit.*, p. 135

[18] Ibid., pp. 135-136

[19] Marilyn Brown and Edgar Degas, *Degas and the Business of Art: A Cotton Office in New Orleans*, (University Park, PA: Penn State Press), 1994, p. 37

[20] Jeffrey Meyers, *Op. Cit.*, p. 135

[21] Ibid., pp. 135-136

[22] Denys Sutton, *Edgar Degas: Life and Work*, (New York: Rizzoli), 1986, p. 31

Endnotes Chapter Four

[1] Denis Rouart, *Claude Monet*, (New York: Crown Publishers), 1972, p. 21

[2] Ibid., p. 22

[3] Douglas Skeggs, *River of Light: Monet's Impressions of the Seine*, (New York: Knopf), 1987, p. 11

[4] Sue Roe, *The Private Lives of the Impressionists*, (New York: HarperCollins), 2006, p 21.

[5] David Spence, *The Impressionists*, (Chicago: *TickTock* Books Ltd.,) 2010, p. 4

[6] Peter H. Feist, *Auguste Renoir: 1841-1919: A Dream of Harmony*, (New York: Taschen, 1987, p. 12

[7] Hajo Düchting, *Paul Cezanne, 1839-1906; Nature into Art*, (New York: Taschen), 2000. p. 11

[8] Ibid., p. 11

[9] Sue Roe, *Op. Cit.*, p. 16

[10] Alex Danchev, *Cezanne: A Life*, (New York: Random House), 2012, p. 53

[11] Cited in Alex Danchev, Ibid., p. 17

[12] Alex Danchev, *Op. Cit.*, p. 19

[13] Ibid., p. 20

[14] Ibid., p. 22

[15] Pierre Bonnard, *The Graphic Art. Exposición Metropolitan Museum of Art*, (New York: Metropolitan Museum of Art), 1989, p. 126

[16] Alex Danchev, Op. Cit., p. 44

[17] Ibid., p. 44

Endnotes Chapter Five

[1] Théodore Duret, *Manet and The French Impressionists*, Trans. By J.E. Crawford Flitch, (Philadelphia: J.B. Lippincott & Company), 1912, p. 53

[2] Ibid., p. 6

[3] Édouard Manet and Pierre Courthion, *Portrait of Manet by Himself and His Contemporaries*, (New York: Cassell), 1960, p. 39

[4] Beth Archer Brombert, *Édouard Manet: Rebel in a Frock Coat*, (Boston: Little Brown), 1996, p. 48

[5] Ibid., p. 49

[6] Camille Mauclair, *The French Impressionists* (1860-1900), (London: Duckworth & Co.), 1903, p. 95

[7] Theodore Reff, *Notebooks of Edgar Degas: Catalogue of the Thirty-eight Notebooks in the Bibliotheque Nationale and Other Collections*, (Cambridge: Cambridge University Press), 1977. *Notebook* 21.

[8] Jeffrey Meyers, *Impressionist Quartet: The Intimate Genius of Manet and Morisot, Degas and Cassatt*, (Orlando, FL: Harcourt), 2005, p. 17

[9] Susan Locke, *Manet and the Family Romance*, (Princeton, NJ: Princeton University Press), 2001. Cited in Jeffrey Meyers, Ibid., p. 18

[10] John Rewald, *The History of Impressionism,* (New York: Harry N. Abrams), 1990, p. 27

[11] Ibid., p. 38

[12] Ulrike Becks-Malorny, *Cezanne: Ediz Inglese*, (New York: Taschen) 2001, p. 4

[13] Théodore Duret, *Manet and The French Impressionists*, Trans. By J.E. Crawford Flitch, (Philadelphia: J.B. Lippincott & Company), 1912, p. 13

[14] Charles Baudelaire and Norman R. Shapiro, *Selected Poems from Les Fleurs du mal: A Bilingual Edition* (Chicago: University of Chicago Press), 2000

[15] Ross King, *The Judgment of Paris: The Revolutionary Decade That Gave The World Impressionism*, (New York: Walker & Company), 2006, p. 149

[16] Théodore Duret. *Op. Cit.,* p. 137

[17] John Rewald, *Op. Cit.*, p. 39

[18] Pierre Courthion, *Masters of Art: Manet*, (New York: Harry N. Abrams), 1984, p. 58

[19] Ibid., p. 58

[20] Alex Danchev, *Cezanne: A Life*, (New York: Random House), 2012, p. 67

[21] Camille Pissarro. (2013). *The Biography Channel website*. from http://www.biography.com/people/camille-pissarro-9441740.

[22] John Rewald, *Op. Cit.*, p. 61

Endnotes Chapter Six

[1] Ambroise Vollard, *Recollections of a Picture Dealer*, (Mineola, NY: Courier Dover Publications), 2011, p. 153

[2] Ross King, *The Judgment of Paris: The Revolutionary Decade That Gave The World Impressionism*, (New York: Walker & Company), 2006, p. 227

[3] Hajo Düchting, *Paul Cezanne, 1839-1906, Nature into Art*, (New York: Taschen), 2000, p. 32

[4] Sue Roe, *The Private Lives of the Impressionists*, (New York: HarperCollins), 2006, p. 3

[5] Théodore Duret, *Manet and The French Impressionists*, Trans. By J.E. Crawford Flitch, (Philadelphia: J.B. Lippincott & Company), 1912, p. 150

[6] Jeffery Meyers, "Degas and Manet: A Study in Friendship" *Apollo*, February 1, 2005

[7] Pierre Cabanne, *Edgar Degas* (Paris: Pierre Tisne, Pub.) 1958, p. 53

[8] Denys Sutton, *Edgar Degas: Life and Work*, (New York: Rizzoli), 1986, p. 279

[9] Jerrold Seigel, *Bohemian Paris: Culture, Politics, and the Boundaries of Bourgeois Life*, 1830-1930. (Baltimore: The Johns Hopkins University Press), 1986, p. 99

[10] Robert L. Herbert, *Impressionism: Art, Leisure, & Parisian Society,* (New Haven, CT: Yale University Press), 1988, p. 34

[11] Quoted in Albert Boime, "The Salon des Refuses and the Evolution of Modern Art," *The Art Quarterly,* 32, 1969, p. 414

[12] Beth Archer Brombert, *Édouard Manet: Rebel in a Frock Coat*, (Boston: Little Brown), 1996., p. 125

[13] cited in John Rewald. *Op. Cit.*, p. 86

[14] Ibid., p. 86

[15] www.laits.utex.edu

[16] Ibid.

[17] Beth Archer Brombert, *Op. Cit.,* p. 129

[18] Cited in Gary Tinterow, *Origins of Impressionism*, (New York: Metropolitan Museum

of Art). 1994, p. 453

Endnotes Chapter Seven

[1] Beth Archer Brombert, *Édouard Manet: Rebel in a Frock Coat*, (Boston: Little Brown), 1996, p. 131

[2] David McCullough, *The Greater Journey: Americans in Paris*, (New York: Simon Schuster), 2011, p. 341

[3] Anne Higonnet, *Berthe Morisot; Anne Higonnet*, (Berkeley, CA: University of California Press), 1995, p. 22

[4] The Project Gutenberg eBook, *The French Impressionists (1860-1900)*, by Camille Mauclair, Translated by P. G. Konady.

[5] Gerhard Gruitrooy, *Degas: Impressions of a Great Master*, (New York: Todtri Productions, Limited), 1994, p. 5

[6] Jeffrey Meyers, *Impressionist Quartet: The Intimate Genius of Manet and Morisot, Degas and Cassatt*, (Orlando, FL: Harcourt), 2005, p. 133

[7] Ross King, *The Judgment of Paris: the Revolutionary Decade That Gave The World Impressionism.* (New York: Walker Publishing Company), 2006, p 228.

[8] Frank Milner, *Monet*, (London: PRC Publishing Limited), 2001, p. 9

[9] Mary Mathews, *Monet and His Muse: Camille Monet in the Artist's Life*, (Chicago: University of Chicago Press), 2010, p. 22

[10] Timothy J. Clark, *The Painting of Modern Life: Paris in the Art of Manet and His Followers*, (New York: Knopf), 1985, p. 83

[11] John Rewald, *The History of Impressionism*, (New York: Harry N. Abrams),

1990, p. 123

[12] Ross King, *Op Cit.,* p. 153.

[13] Théodore Duret, *Manet and The French Impressionists*, Trans. By J.E. Crawford Flitch, (Philadelphia: J.B. Lippincott & Company), 1912, p. 26

[14] Beth Archer Brombert, *Op Cit.,* p. 63

[15] Ross King, *Op. Cit.,* p. 152.

[16] Charles Baudelaire, *The Poem and Prose Poems of Charles Baudelaire with an Introduction Preface by James Huneker*, (Hong Kong: Forgotten Books), 2012, p. xxxix

[17] Ross King, *Op. Cit.,.* p. 154

[18] Steven C. Hause and William S. Maltby, *Western Civilization: A History of European Society.* (Singapore: Cengage Learning,) 2004.

[19] Théodore Duret, *Op. Cit.*, p. 4

[20] Beth Archer Brombert, Op. Cit., p. 89

[21] Ibid., p. 79

Endnotes Chapter Eight

[1] Douglas Skeggs, *River of Light: Monet's Impressions of the Seine*, (New York: Knopf), 1987, p. 78

[2] John Rewald, *The History of Impressionism,* (New York: Harry N. Abrams), 1990, p. 122

[3] Claude Monet and Charles F. Stuckey, *Monet: A Retrospective*, (Paris: Beaux Arts Editions), 1985, p. 34

[4] Dover, *Spot the Differences Book 4: Art Masterpiece Mysteries, Book 4*

(Mineola, NY: Courier Dover Publications), 2013, p. 34

[5] Frank Milner, *Monet*, (London: PRC Publishing Limited), 2001, p. 11

[6] www.laits.utexas.edu/wettlaufer/painting/popups/manet.html

[7] Hajo Düchting, *Paul Cezanne, 1839-1906; Nature into Art*, (New York: Taschen), 2000, p. 40

[8] Jerrold Seigel, *Bohemian Paris: Culture, Politics, and the Boundaries of Bourgeois Life*, 1830-1930. (Baltimore: The Johns Hopkins University Press), 1986, p. 306

[9] Beth Archer Brombert, *Édouard Manet: Rebel in a Frock Coat*, (Boston: Little Brown), 1996, p. 93

[10] Wendy Beckett, *The Story of Painting*, (New York: Dorling Kindersley), 2000, p. 574.

[11] Alex Danchev, *Cezanne: A Life*, (New York: Random House), 2012, p. 92

[12] Ibid., p. 93

[13] Sue Roe, *The Private Lives of the Impressionists*, (New York: HarperCollins), 2006, p. 44

[14] Ibid., p. 48

[15] Théodore Duret, *Manet and The French Impressionists*, Trans. By J.E. Crawford Flitch, (Philadelphia: J.B. Lippincott & Company), 1912, p. 171

[16] Hajo Düchting, *Paul Cezanne, 1839-1906; Nature into Art*, (New York: Taschen), 2000, p. 32

[17] Ibid., p. 31

[18] Ibid., p. 38

[19] Théodore Duret, *Op. Cit.,* p. 49

[20] Édouard Manet, *Masters in Art: Manet*, (Boston, MA: Bates and Guild Company Publishers), vol. 9, 1909, p. 34

[21] John Rewald, *The History of Impressionism,* (New York: Harry N. Abrams), 1990, p. 184

[22] Camille Mauclair, *The French Impressionists (1860-1900),* (London: Duckworth & Co.), 1903, p. 33

[23] Ibid., p. 34

[24] Susan Roe, *Op. Cit.*, p. 61

Endnotes Chapter Nine

[1] David McCullough, *The Greater Journey: Americans in Paris*, (New York: Simon & Schuster), 2011, p. 25

[2] Ibid., p. 26

[3] Ibid., p. 26

[4] Juliet W. Bareau, *Manet and Monet and the Gare Saint-Lazare*, (New Haven, CT: Yale University Press), 1998, p. 19

[5] Robert L. Herbert, *Impressionism: Art, Leisure, & Parisian Society,* (New Haven, CT: Yale University Press), 1988, p. 141

[6] Gerhard Gruitrooy, *Degas: Impressions of a Great Master*, (New York: Todtri Productions, Limited), 1994, p. 57

[7] Beth Archer Brombert, *Édouard Manet: Rebel in a Frock Coat*, (Boston: Little Brown), 1996.

[8] Sue Roe, *The Private Lives of the Impressionists*, (New York: HarperCollins), 2006, p. 62

[9] Ross King, *The Judgment of Paris: The Revolutionary Decade That Gave The World Impressionism.* (New York: Walker Publishing Company),

2006, p. 262

[10] John Rewald, *The History of Impressionism,* (New York: Harry N. Abrams), 1990, p. 198

[11] Ross King, *Op. Cit.*, p. 65

[12] Ibid., p. 64

[13] David McCullough, *Op. Cit.,* p. 338

[14] Gerhard Gruitrooy, *Op. Cit.*, p. 21

[15] Berthe Morisot and Denis Rouart, *The correspondence of Berthe Morisot, with her family and friends: Manet, Puvis de Chavannes, Degas, Monet, Renoir and Mallarmé,* (Rochester, NY: Camden), 1986, p. 56

[16] Denys Sutton, *Edgar Degas: Life and Work,* (New York: Rizzoli), 1986, p. 90

[17] Karin Sagner- Düchting, *Monet, 1840-1926: A feast for the Eyes,* (Amsterdam: Lowe & B. Hould), 1990, p. 49

[18] Russell Ash, *The Impressionists and Their Art,* (Knollwood, NY: Orbis Publishing), 1980, p. 23

[19] Alex Danchev, *Cezanne: A Life*, (New York: Random House), 2012, p. 111

[20] E.B. Washburne, *Recollections of a Minister to France, 1869-1877* , vol. 11662, (New York: Charles Scribner's Sons), 1889, p. 324

[21] Beth Archer Brombert, *Op. Cit.,* p. 178

[22] David McCullough, *Op., Cit.*, p. 268

[23] Ibid., p. 269

[24] E.B. Washburne, *Op. Cit.*, p. 99

[25] Alfred Cobban, *A History of Modern France: 1799-1945*, (New York: Penguin Books), 1961, p. 204

[26] David McCullough, *Op. Cit.*, p. 305

Endnotes Chapter Ten

[1] David McCullough, *The Greater Journey: Americans in Paris*, (New York: Simon & Schuster), 2011, p. 308

[2] Sue Roe, *The Private Lives of the Impressionists*, (New York: HarperCollins), 2006, p. 90

[3] Berthe Morisot & Denis Rouart, *The correspondence of Berthe Morisot, with her family and friends: Manet, Puvis de Chavannes, Degas, Monet, Renoir and Mallarmé*, (Rochester, NY: Camden), 1986, p. 45

[4] Sue Roe, *Op. Cit.*, p. 84

[5] Ibid., p. 98

[6] Jerrold Seigel, *Bohemian Paris: Culture, Politics, and the Boundaries of Bourgeois Life*, 1830-1930. (Baltimore: The Johns Hopkins University Press), 1986, p. 306

[7] Théodore Duret, *Manet and The French Impressionists*, Trans. By J.E. Crawford Flitch, (Philadelphia: J.B. Lippincott & Company), 1912, p. 73

[8] Hajo Düchting, *Paul Cezanne, 1839-1906; Nature into Art*, (New York: Taschen), 2000, p. 56

[9] John Rewald, *The History of Impressionism*, (New York: Harry N. Abrams), 1990, p. 281

[10] Robert L. Herbert, *Impressionism: Art, Leisure, & Parisian Society*, (New Haven, CT: Yale University Press), 1988, p. 229

[11] Denys Sutton, *Edgar Degas: Life and Work*, (New York: Rizzoli), 1986, p. 94

[12] Susan Roe, *Op. Cit.*, p. 113

[13] David McCullough, *Op. Cit.*, p. 352

[14] Ibid., p. 358

[15] Ibid., p. 339

Endnotes Chapter Eleven

[1] Théodore Duret, *Manet and The French Impressionists*, Trans. By J.E. Crawford Flitch, (Philadelphia: J.B. Lippincott & Company), 1912, p. 93

[2] Ibid., p. 94

[3] Ibid., p. 119

[4] Susie Hodge, *How To Paint Like The Impressionists*, (New York: Harper Design), 2004, p. 22

[5] Cited in Steven Z. Levine and Claude Monet, *Monet, Naracissus, and Self-Reflection: The Modernist Myth*, (Chicago: University of Chicago Press). 1994, p. 69

[6] FranCois Mathey, *The Impressionists*, (New York: Henry Holt), 1961, p. 107

[7] Ross King, *The Judgment of Paris: The Revolutionary Decade That Gave The World Impressionism.* (New York: Walker Publishing Company), 2006, p. 52

[8] Susie Hodge, *Op. Cit.*, p. 16

[9] Nancy Mowll Matthews, *Mary Cassatt*, (New Haven, CT: Yale University Press), 1994, p. 137

[10] Ibid., p. 58

[11] John Rewald, *The History of Impressionism*, (New York: Harry N. Abrams), 1990, p. 228

[12] Roy McMullen, *Degas: His Life, Times, and Work*, (Boston, MA: Houghton), 1984, p. 224

[13] Jeffrey Meyers, *Impressionist Quartet: The Intimate Genius of Manet and Morisot,*

Degas and Cassatt, (Orlando, FL: Harcourt), 2005, p. 165

[14] Ibid, p. 174

[15] Ibid., p. 174

[16] George T. M. Shackelford and Edgar Degas, *Degas, The Dancers*, vol. 1984, part 2, (National Gallery of Art), 1984, p. 14

[17] Jerrold Seigel, *Bohemian Paris: Culture, Politics, and the Boundaries of Bourgeois Life*, 1830-1930. (Baltimore, MD: The Johns Hopkins University Press), 1986, p. 296

[18] Théodore Duret, *Op. Cit.*, p. 76

[19] Barbara E. White, *Impressionists Side by Side: Their Relationships, Rivalries And Artistic Exchanges*, (New York: Knopf Doubleday Publishing Group) 1996, p. 184

[20] John Rewald, *Op. Cit.*, p. 387

Endnotes Chapter Twelve

[1] Barbara E. White, *Impressionists Side by Side: Their Relationships, Rivalries, and Artistic Exchanges*, (New York: Knopf Doubleday Publishing Group), 1996, p. 186

[2] Jeffrey Meyers, *Impressionist Quartet: The Intimate Genius of Manet and Morisot, Degas and Cassatt*, (Orlando, FL: Harcourt), 2005, p.268

[3] David McCullough, *The Greater Journey: Americans in Paris*, (New York: Simon & Schuster), 2011, p. 352

[4] Jerrold Seigel, *Bohemian Paris: Culture, Politics, and the Boundaries of Bourgeois Life*, 1830-1930. (Baltimore, MD: The Johns Hopkins University Press),

1986, p. 307

[5] Denys Sutton, *Edgar Degas: Life and Work*, (New York: Rizzoli), 1986, p. 106

[6] Théodore Duret, *Op. Cit.*, p. 74

[7] Edgar Degas and Jean Sutherland Boggs, *Degas* [Exposition] (New York: Metropolitan Museum of Art), 1988, p. 80

[8] Dr. Jeanne S. M. Willette *Art History Unstuffed*.

[9] Ibid.

[10] Leo Carey, "Onward and Upward with the Arts, Frame Game," *The New Yorker*, March 27, 2006, p. 38

[11] Berthe Morisot & Denis Rouart, *The Correspondence of Berthe Morisot, with her Family and Friends: Manet, Puvis de Chavannes, Degas, Monet, Renoir and Mallarmé*, (Rochester, NY: Camden), 1986, p. 143

[12] Sue Roe, *The Private Lives of the Impressionists*, (New York: HarperCollins), 2006, p. 126

[13] John Rewald, *The History of Impressionism,* (New York: Harry N. Abrams), 1990, p. 8

[14] Ibid., p. 8

[15] Berthe Morisot & Denis Rouart, *The Correspondence of Berthe Morisot, with her Family and Friends: Manet, Puvis de Chavannes, Degas, Monet, Renoir and Mallarmé,* (Rochester, NY: Camden), 1986, p. 111

[16] Hajo Düchting, *Paul Cezanne, 1839-1906; Nature into Art*, (New York: Taschen), 2000, p. 80

[17] Ibid, p. 96

[18] John Rewald, *Cezanne: A Biography,* (New York: Harry N. Abrams), 1986, p. 105

[19] Ibid., p. 336

[20] Ross King, *The Judgment of Paris: The Revolutionary Decade That Gave*

The World Impressionism. (New York: Walker Publishing Company), 2006, p. 358

[21] David McCullough, *The Greater Journey: Americans in Paris*, (New York: Simon & Schuster), 2011, p. 341

[22] Russell Ash, *The Impressionists and their Art,* (Knollwood, NY: Orbis Publishing), 1980, p. 29

[23] Ambroise Vollard, *Renoir: An Intimate Record*, (New York: Dover Publications), 1925, p. 33

[24] Ibid., p. 33

[25] Gerhard Gruitrooy, *Degas: Impressions of a Great Master*, (New York: Todtri Productions, Limited), 1994, p. 57

[26] John Rewald, *Op. Cit*, p. 113

[27] Théodore Duret, *Manet and The French Impressionists*, Trans. By J.E. Crawford Flitch, (Philadelphia: J.B. Lippincott & Company), 1912, p. 116

[28] Denys Sutton, *Edgar Degas: Life and Work*, (New York: Rizzoli), 1986, p. 106

[29] Henri Loyrette, *Degas: The Man and His Art*, (New York: Harry N. Abrams, Inc, Publishers), 2001, p. 66

[30] George T. M. Shackelford and Edgar Degas, *Degas, The Dancers*, vol. 1984, part 2, (National Gallery of Art), 1984, p. 67

[31] Sylvie Buisson & Christian Pariso, *Paris Montmartre: A Mecca of Modern Art*, (Boston: Museum of Fine Arts, David Godine, Publisher, Inc.), 1991, p. 52

[32] Claude Monet and Richard Kendall, *Monet by Himself: Paintings, Drawings, Pastels, Letters,* (Martinez, CA: Knickerbocker), 1999, p. 29

Endnotes Chapter Thirteen

[1] John Rewald, *The History of Impressionism,* (New York: Harry N. Abrams), 1990, p. 291

[2] Ibid., p. 410

[3] Claude Monet and Charles F. Stuckey, *Monet: A Retrospective.* (Paris: Beaux Arts Editions), 1985, p. 64

[4] Théodore Duret, *Manet and The French Impressionists*, Trans. By J.E. Crawford Flitch, (Philadelphia: J.B. Lippincott & Company), 1912

[5] John Rewald, *Op. Cit.,* p. 412

[6] Ibid., p. 412

[7] Alex Danchev, *Cezanne: A Life*, (New York: Random House), 2012, p. 197

[8] Hajo Düchting, *Paul Cezanne, 1839-1906; Nature into Art*, (New York: Taschen), 2000, p. 171

[9] Ibid., p. 179

[10] Ibid., p. 204

[11] Ibid., p. 112

[12] Ibid., p. 112

Endnotes Chapter Fourteen

[1] Claude Monet and Charles F. Stuckey, *Monet: A Retrospective.* (Paris: Beaux Arts Editions), 1985, p. 69

[2] John Rewald, *The History of Impressionism,* (New York: Harry N. Abrams),

1990, p. 447

[3] Théodore Duret, *Manet and The French Impressionists*, Trans. By J.E. Crawford Flitch, (Philadelphia: J.B. Lippincott & Company), 1912, p. 182

[4] Ibid., p. 184

[5] Hajo Düchting, *Paul Cezanne, 1839-1906; Nature into Art*, (New York: Taschen), 2000, p. 112

[6] Jeffrey Meyers, *Impressionist Quartet: The Intimate Genius of Manet and Morisot, Degas and Cassatt*, (Orlando, FL: Harcourt), 2005, p. 290

[7] Théodore Duret, *Op. Cit*, p. 96

[8] Auguste Renoir Gallery, Biography of Pierre-Auguste Renoir.

[9] Ibid.

[10] *Dance At Bougival,* Museum of Fine Arts, Boston

[11] Théodore Duret, *Op. cit.*, p. 95

[12] Ibid., p. 99

[13] Ibid., p. 98

[14] Beth Archer Brombert, *Édouard Manet: Rebel in a Frock Coat*, (Boston: Little Brown), 1996, p. 374

[15] Ibid., p. 91

[16] Ibid., p. 82

[17] Alex Danchev, *Cezanne: A Life*, (New York: Random House), 2012, p. 146

[18] Édouard Manet, *Masters in Art: Manet,* (Boston, MA: Bates and Guild Company Publishers), vol. 9, 1909, p.33

[19] Ibid., p. 32

[20] Théodore Duret, *Op. Cit.,* p. 208

[21] Ibid, p. 198

[22] Ross King, *The Judgment of Paris: The Revolutionary Decade That Gave*

The World Impressionism. (New York: Walker Publishing Company), 2006, pp. 374-375

Endnotes Chapter Fifteen

[1] John Rewald, *The History of Impressionism,* (New York: Harry N. Abrams), 1990, p. 486

[2] Ibid., p. 486

[3] Ambroise Vollard, *Degas: An Intimate Portrait.* Trans. Randolph Weaver. (New York: Dover), 1986, p. 22

[4] Sue Roe, *The Private Lives of the Impressionists*, (New York: HarperCollins), 2006, p. 259

[5] Hajo Düchting, *Paul Cezanne, 1839-1906; Nature into Art*, (New York: Taschen), 2000, p. 126

[6] Sue Roe, *Op. Cit.*, p. 256

[7] John Rewald, *Op. Cit.*, p. 531

[8] Henri Loyrette, *Degas: The Man and His Art*, (New York: Harry N. Abrams, Inc, Publishers), 2001, p. 106

[9] Barbara E. White, *Impressionists Side by Side: Their Relationships, Rivalries And Artistic Exchanges*, (New York: Knopf Doubleday Publishing Group) 1996, p. 165

[10] David Spence, *Renoir: Color and Nature*, (Chicago: *TickTock* Books Ltd.,) 1998, p. 24

[11] Art Institute of Chicago, Andrew Forge, and Claude Monet, *Monet: Artists in Focus*, (Chicago: Art Institute of Chicago), 1995

Endnotes Chapter Sixteen

[1] Russell Ash, *The Impressionists and Their Art,* (Knollwood, NY: Orbis Publishing), 1980, p. 35

[2] Sir John Adams, *Exposition and Illustration in Teaching*, (New York: Macmillan) 1910. p. 337

[3] Michael Brenson, Monet's Complexity and Grandeur in His Series Paintings, *The New York Times*, February 7, 1990

[4] Paul Hayes Tucker, *Claude Monet: Life and Art*, (New Haven, CT: Yale University Press), 1995

[5] Charles F. Stuckey, "Claude Monet: Life and Work." book reviews, *Art in America, Nov, 1993*

[6] John Rewald, *The History of Impressionism,* (New York: Harry N. Abrams), 1990, p. 564

[7] Camille Mauclair, *The French Impressionists* (1860-1900), (London: Duckworth & Co.), 1903, p. 108

[8] Ginger Danto, "Rouen Renunites 17 Monet 'Cathedrals'," *The New York Times*, August 13, 1994

[9] Wendy Slatkin, *The Voices of Women Artists*, (Englewood Cliffs, NJ: Prentice-Hall), 1993, p. 138

[10] John Rewald, *Op.Cit.*, p. 570

[11] Sylvie Buisson & Christian Pariso, *Paris Montmartre: A Mecca of Modern Art*, (Boston: Museum of Fine Arts, David Godine, Publisher, Inc.), 1991, p. 101

[12] Hajo Düchting, *Paul Cezanne, 1839-1906; Nature into Art*, (New York: Taschen), 2000, p. 171

[13] Ibid., p. 199

[14] Ibid., p. 200

[15] John Rewald, *Op. Cit.*, p. 572

[16] Hajo Düchting, *Op. Cit.*, p. 200

[17] Ibid., p. 201

[18] Ibid., p. 153

[19] Alex Danchev, *Cezanne: A Life*, (New York: Random House), 2012, p. 322

[20] Hajo Düchting, *Op. Cit.*, p. p. 158

[21] John Rewald, Op. Cit., p. 578

[22] Nancy Mowll Matthews, *Mary Cassatt*, (New Haven, CT: Yale University Press), 1994, p. 274

Endnotes Chapter Seventeen

[1] Alex Danchev, *Cezanne: A Life*, (New York: Random House), 2012, p. 323

[2] Edgar Degas and Jean Sutherland Boggs, *Degas* [Exposition] (New York: Metropolitan Museum of Art), 1988, p. 32

[3] Jeffrey Meyers, *Impressionist Quartet: The Intimate Genius of Manet and Morisot, Degas and Cassatt*, (Orlando, FL: Harcourt), 2005, p. 224

[4] Ibid., p. 281

[5] Nancy Mowll Matthews, *Mary Cassatt*, (New Haven, CT: Yale University Press), 1994. P. 328

Endnotes Chapter Eighteen

[1] Édouard Manet and Pierre Courthion, *Portrait of Manet by Himself and*

His Contemporaries, (New York: Cassell), 1960, p. 164

[2] Théodore Duret, *Manet and The French Impressionists*, Trans. By J.E. Crawford Flitch, (Philadelphia: J.B. Lippincott & Company), 1912, p. 180

References

Adams, Sir John, *Exposition and Illustration in Teaching*, (New York: Macmillan) 1910.

Adams, Steven, *The Impressionists*, (Philadelphia: Quartro Publishing), 1991.

Ash, Russell, *The Impressionists and their Art*, (Knollwood, NY: Orbis Publishing), 1980.

Bareau, Juliet W., *Manet and Monet and the Gare Saint-Lazare*, (New Haven, CT: Yale University Press), 1998.

Bazire, Edmond, *Manet,* (Paris: A Quantin), 1884.

Beckett, Wendy, *The Story of Painting*, (New York: Dorling Kindersley), 2000.

Becks-Malorny, Ulrike, *Cezanne: Ediz Inglese*, (New York: Taschen) 2001.

Bernier, Georges, *Paris Cafes: Their Role in the Birth of Modern Art* (New York: Wildenstein & Co. Inc.) 1985.

Boardingham, Robert J., *Impressionist: Masterpieces in American Museums*, (New York: Hugh Lauter Levin Association), 1996.

Bockemuhl, Michael, *Turner: The World of Light and Color*, (New York: Taschen), 2000.

Bohm-Duchen, *The Private Life of a Masterpiece: Uncovering the Forgotten Secrets and Hidden Life Histories of Iconic works*. (Berkeley, CA: University of California Press), 2002.

Boime, Albert, "The Salon des Refuses and the Evolution of Modern Art," *The Art Quarterly,* 32, 1969

Bonnard, Pierre, The Graphic Art. *Exposición Metropolitan Museum of Art*, (New York: Metropolitan Museum of Art), 1989.

Brenson, Michael, Monet's Complexity and Grandeur in His Series Paintings, *The New York Times*, February 7, 1990.

Brombert, Beth Archer, *Édouard Manet: Rebel in a Frock Coat*, (Boston: Little Brown), 1996.

Brown, Marilyn and Edgar Degas, *Degas and the Business of Art: A Cotton Office in New Orleans,* (University Park, PA: Penn State Press,), 1994.

Buisson, Sylvie & Christian Pariso, *Paris Montmartre: A Mecca of Modern Art*, (Boston: Museum of Fine Arts, David Godine, Publisher, Inc.), 1991.

Clark, Timothy J., *The Painting of Modern Life: Paris in the Art of Manet and His Followers*, (New York: Knopf), 1985.

Courthion, Pierre, *Masters of Art: Manet*, (New York: Harry N. Abrams), 1984.

Danchev, Alex, *Cezanne: A Life*, (New York: Random House), 2012.

Degas, Edgar, *Degas by Himself*, (London: Macdonald Orbis), 1989.

Degas, Edgar and Jean Sutherland Boggs, *Degas* [Exposition] (Metropolitan Museum of Art), 1988.

De Jonge, Alex, *Baudelaire, Prince of Clouds: A Biography*, (New York: Paddington Press, 1976.

Denvir, Bernard, *Impressionists: The Painters and their Paintings*, (Ontario, Canada: NDE Publishing), 1999.

Düchting, Hajo, *Paul Cezanne, 1839-1906; Nature into Art*, (New York: Taschen), 2000.

Duret, Théodore, *Manet and The French Impressionists*, Trans. By J.E. Crawford Flitch, (Philadelphia: J.B. Lippincott & Company), 1912.

Feist, Peter H. *Auguste Renoir: 1841-1919: A Dream of Harmony*, (New York: Taschen, 1987.

Galignani A. and W., Galignani's *New Illustrated Paris* 1827,39,44) (Charleston, SC:

Nabu Press), 2010. Originally published 1827.

Goncourt, Edmond and Jules Goncourt, *The Goncourt Journals*, 1851-1870 (New York: Doubleday), 1958.

Gréard, Vallery C.O., *Meissonier His Life and His Art, with Extracts from His Notebooks and His Opinions and Impressions on Art and Artists Collected By His Wife,* (United Kingdom: William Heinemann), 1897.

Gruitrooy, Gerhard, *Degas: Impressions of a Great Master*, (New York: Todtri Productions, Limited), 1994.

_____, Auguste-Pierre, *Master of Impressionism*, (New York: New Line Books), 2006.

Haine, W. Scott, *The World of the Paris Café: Sociability Among the French Working Class, 1789-1914* (Baltimore: The Johns Hopkins University Press, 1996).

Harris, Nathaniel, *The Life and Works of Manet*, (New York: Shooting Star Press), 1994.

Hauptman, William, *Charles Gleyre, 1806-1876*, (Princeton, NJ: Princeton University Press), 1997,

Hause, Steven C., and William S. Maltby, *Western Civilization: A History of European Society*. (Singapore: Cengage Learning,) 2004.

Herbert, Robert L. *Impressionism: Art, Leisure, & Parisian Society,* (New Haven: Yale University Press, 1988.

Higonnet, Anne, *Berthe Morisot; Anne Higonnet*, (Berkeley, CA: University of California Press), 1995.

Hodge, Susie, *How To Paint Like The Impressionists*, (New York: Harper Design), 2004.

Horne, Alistair Sir, *Seven Ages of Paris*, (New York: Alfred A. Knopf), 2002.

King, Edward, *My Paris: French Character Sketches*, (University of Michigan Library), 1867.

King, Ross, *The Judgment of Paris: The Revolutionary Decade That Gave The

World Impressionism, (New York: Walker & Company), 2006.

Lanier, Doris, *Absinthe: The Cocaine of the Nineteenth Century* (Jefferson, North Carolina: McFarland & Company, Inc., Publishers), 1995.

Les Dames cited in Oberthur, Mariel, *Cafes and Cabarets of Montmartre*, (Salt Lake City. UT: Peregrine Smith Books), 1984.

Levine, Steven Z., and Claude Monet, *Monet, Naracissus, and Self-Reflection: The Modernist Myth*, (Chicago: University of Chicago Press). 1994.

Locke, Nancy, *Manet and the Family Romance*, (Princeton, NJ: Princeton University Press), 2001.

Loyrette, Henri, *Degas: The Man and His Art*, (New York: Harry N. Abrams, Inc, Publishers), 2001.

Matthews, Nancy Mowll, *Mary Cassatt*, (New Haven, CT: Yale University Press), 1994.

Mathey, FranCois, *The Impressionists*, (New York: Henry Holt), 1961.

Mauclair, Camille, *The French Impressionists* (1860-1900), (London: Duckworth & Co.), 1903.

Manet, Édouard, *Masters in Art: Manet,* (Boston, MA: Bates and Guild Company Publishers), vol. 9, 1909.

Manet, Édouard and Pierre Courthion, *Portrait of Manet by Himself and His Contemporaries*, (New York: Cassell), 1960.

Manet, Édouard, Françoise Cachin, Juliet Wilson Bareau, Galeries nationales du Grand Palais (France), Metropolitan Museum of Art (New York, NY), 1983.

Mathews, Mary, *Monet and His Muse: Camille Monet in the Artist's Life*, (Chicago: University of Chicago Press), 2010.

Maupassant, Guy de, *Contes et Nouvelles, 1875-1884* (Paris: Editions Robert Laffont), 1988.

McCullough, David, *The Greater Journey: Americans in Paris*, (New York: Simon &

Schuster), 2011.

McMullen, Roy, *Degas: His Life, Times, and Work*, (Boston, MA: Houghton), 1984.

Meyers, Jeffrey, *Impressionist Quartet: The Intimate Genius of Manet and Morisot, Degas and Cassatt*, (Orlando, FL: Harcourt), 2005.

_____, "Degas and Manet: a study in friendship: Jeffrey Meyers explores the intense, admiring, but often wary relationship between two great artists whose lives, as well as art, had many parallels." *Apollo*, February 1, 2005

Milner, Frank, *Monet*, (London: PRC Publishing Limited), 2001.

Mollett, John W., *Meissonier*, (New York: Scribner and Welford), 1882.

Monneret, Sophie, *Renoir: His Life and Complete Works*, (New York: Long Meadow Press), 1995.

Monet, Claude and Richard Kendall, *Monet by Himself: Paintings, Drawings, Pastels, Letters*, (Martinez, CA: Knickerbocker), 1999.

_____, and Charles F. Stuckey, *Monet: A Retrospective*. (Paris: Beaux Arts Editions), 1985.

Moore, George, *Confessions of a Young Man*, (New York: Brentano's), 1901.

Morisot, Berthe & Denis Rouart, *The correspondence of Berthe Morisot, with her Family and Friends: Manet, Puvis de Chavannes, Degas, Monet, Renoir and Mallarmé*, (Rochester, NY: Camden), 1986.

Oberthur, Mariel, *Cafes and Cabarets of Montmartre*, (Salt Lake City, UT: Peregrine Smith Books, 1984).

Proust, Antonin, *Salon, Vol. 1899* (Classic Reprint) (Hong Kong: Forgotten Books), 2012.

Reff, Theodore, *Notebooks of Edgar Degas: Catalogue of the Thirty-eight Notebooks in the Bibliotheque Nationale and Other Collections*, (Cambridge: Cambridge University Press), 1977.

Renoir, Jean Renoir, *My Father* (London: Collins, 1962, 1st published, 1958.

Rewald, John, *The History of Impressionism,* (New York: Harry N. Abrams), 1990.

Richardson, Joanna *La Vie Parisienne* (London; Hamish Hamilton Ltd.), 1971.

Richardson, John, *Edouard Manet; Paintings and Drawings*, (London: Phaidon), 1958.

Roe, Susan, *The Private Lives of the Impressionists*, (New York: HarperCollins Publishers), 2006.

Rouart, Denis, *Claude Monet*, (New York: Crown Publishers), 1972.

Sagner- Düchting, Karin, *Monet, 1840-1926: A feast for the Eyes*, (Amsterdam; Lowe & B. Hould), 1990.

Seigel, Jerrold, *Bohemian Paris: Culture, Politics, and the Boundaries of Bourgeois Life*, 1830-1930. (Baltimore: The Johns Hopkins University Press), 1986.

Shackelford, George, T. M., and Edgar Degas, *Degas, The Dancers*, vol. 1984, part 2, (National Gallery of Art), 1984.

Skeggs, Douglas, *River of Light: Monet's Impressions of the Seine*, (New York: Knopf), 1987.

Snow, Edward, *A Study of Vermeer,* (Berkeley, CA: University of California Press), 1994.

Song, Misook, *Art theories of Charles Blanc, 1813-1882*, (Studies in Fine Arts, (Ann Arbor, MI: UMI Research Press), 1984.

Spence, David, *The Impressionists*, (Chicago: *TickTock* Books Ltd.,) 2010.

_____, *Renoir: Color and Nature*, (Chicago: *TickTock* Books Ltd.,) 1998.

Stuckey, Charles & William Scott, *Berthe Morisot – Impressionist*, (New York: Hudson Hills, 1987).

Sutton, Denys, *Edgar Degas: Life and Work*, New York: Rizzoli), 1986.

Todd, Pamela, *The Impressionists at Leisure*, (London: Thames & Hudson,

Limited), 2007.

Tucker, Paul Hayes, *Claude Monet: Life and Art*, (New Haven, CT: Yale University Press), 1995.

Valéry, Paul, *Degas, danse, dessin* (Paris: Gallimard), 1938.

Vollard, Ambroise, *Renoir: An Intimate Record*, (New York: Dover Publications), 1925.

_____.*Degas: An Intimate Portrait*. Trans. Randolph Weaver. (New York: Dover), 1986.

_____, *Recollections of a Picture Dealer*, (Mineola, NY: Courier Dover Publications), 2011.

Washburne, E. B., *Recollections of a Minister to France, 1869-1877*, vol. 11662, (New York: Charles Scribner's Sons, 1889.

Wellington, Hubert, *Journal of Delacroix*, (London: Phaldon Press), 1995.

White, Barbara E., *Impressionists Side by Side: Their Relationships, Rivalrie And Artistic Exchanges*, (New York: Knopf Doubleday Publishing Group) 1996.

Zola, Émile, *The Masterpiece* (Gloucester: Alan Sutton Publishing Limited), 1986.

About The Author

Jean-Louis-Ernest Meissonier (1815-1891), French painter extraordinaire, once commented, "If I had not been a painter, I should have liked to be a historian. I don't think any other subject could be so interesting as history." Substituting professor for painter, summarizes my sentiments as well. My interest in history and biography began several decades ago and the last several years have been consolidating my researching and reading culminating in two recent works: *Franz Joseph and Empress Elisabeth: The Last Great Monarchs of Austria-Hungary, They Changed The World*. Prior to writing these books, as a professor of developmental psychology and visiting lecturer in England, my published works have included authoring college textbooks, *The World of The Child* and *Child and Adolescent Development*. My research interests in self-esteem and children's learning styles have resulted in two works, *Raising Your Child's Inner Self-Esteem* and *Critical Thinking*. My current writing project is of the High Renaissance in Italy and the fascinating lives of Leonardo da Vinci, Michelangelo and Raphael, whose work's fill us with a sense of awe; the book is aptly entitled The Age of Perfection.

Of course, my desire is that you have a response that is as favorable as was my passion in writing this book. As one who loves history and biography about legends of our past and present, I hope you'll share your valued opinion.

Karen Owens Ph.D. September 30, 2013

Printed in Great Britain
by Amazon